The Future of Natural Museums

Natural history museums are changing, both because of their own internal development and in response to changes in context. *The Future of Natural History Museums* considers these changes and the reasons behind them and begins to develop a cohesive discourse that balances the disparate issues that our institutions will face over the next decades.

Historically, the aim of collecting from nature was to develop encyclopaedic assemblages to satisfy human curiosity and build a basis for taxonomic study. Today, with global biodiversity in rapid decline, new reasons emerge to build and maintain collections, which also need to cater to audiences who are more diverse, numerous, and technically savvy. This book explores key elements of this topic and, through commentary and synthesis, develops a cohesive picture of the trajectory of the natural history museum sector in the next 20 to 50 years. Arguing that institutions must learn to embrace new technology, the book considers how they might retain the authenticity of their stories and the value placed on their objects in the process.

This book contributes to the study of collections, teaching and learning, ethics, and running non-profit businesses and will be of interest to museum and heritage professionals, academics and senior students in Biological Sciences and Museum Studies.

Eric Dorfman is Director of Pittsburgh's Carnegie Museum of Natural History and President of the International Council of Museums Committee for Museums and Collections of Natural History (ICOM NATHIST). He is Deputy Chair of the ICOM Ethics Committee (ETHCOM) and co-authored *ICOM Code of Ethics for Natural History Museums*. He is a board member of Visit Pittsburgh, an Adjunct Professor at University of Pittsburgh and on the editorial board of *Museum Worlds: Advances in Research*. Prior to his current position, he was Director of Whanganui Regional Museum in New Zealand and lectured in the Museums and Heritage Studies Department of Victoria University of Wellington.

ICOM Advances in Museum Research
Series Editor: ICOM

This research series, developed by the International Council of Museums (ICOM), draws on the expertise of ICOM's worldwide network of museum professionals, representing a range of museum- and heritage-related disciplines.

Bridging theory and practice, the series addresses diverse issues of broad interest to the museum field and is of relevance for institutions around the world, featuring contributions by representatives of a range of cultures. Focusing on different types of museums and diverse fields of activity within the museum, the titles in the series will provide useful and thought-provoking insights for today's museum professionals. Its multi-perspective approach ensures its relevancy for academics, researchers and students of museology. The behind-the-scenes glimpses offered into the state of the field will also appeal to the general museum-going public.

Recently published titles:

The Future of Natural History Museums
Eric Dorfman

https://www.routledge.com/museumandheritage/series/ICOMAMR

The Future of Natural History Museums

Edited by
Eric Dorfman

Routledge
Taylor & Francis Group

LONDON AND NEW YORK

First published 2018
by Routledge
2 Park Square, Milton Park, Abingdon, Oxon OX14 4RN

and by Routledge
711 Third Avenue, New York, NY 10017

Routledge is an imprint of the Taylor & Francis Group, an informa business

British Library Cataloguing-in-Publication Data
A catalogue record for this book is available from the British Library

Library of Congress Cataloguing-in-Publication Data
A catalog record has been requested for this book

ISBN: 978-1-138-69264-0 (hbk)
ISBN: 978-1-138-69263-3 (pbk)
ISBN: 978-1-315-53189-2 (ebk)

Typeset in Sabon
by codeMantra

Printed in Canada

Contents

Illustrations

Figures

Table

Contributors

George Amato is Director, Sackler Institute for Comparative Genomics, and Affiliated Professor, Richard Gilder Graduate School at the American Museum of Natural History. Dr. Amato's current research interests include genetic threats associated with habitat fragmentation in endangered species, molecular ecology, taxonomic and phylogenetic questions related to determining units of conservation, using molecular markers for assessing priority areas for biodiversity conservation, non-invasive sampling techniques for endangered species, and monitoring the trade in endangered species products using DNA-based forensic science. Dr. Amato has participated in research activities worldwide, including research in China, Cuba, Madagascar, Malaysia, Peru, Saint Vincent and the Grenadines, South Africa, and Tanzania. He has published and lectured extensively on conservation strategies for endangered species and especially on using molecular analyses to determine conservation priorities. Dr. Amato earned his PhD, MS, and MPhil degrees at Yale University, and his BS from the University of Connecticut.

Felicity Arengo is Associate Director of the Center for Biodiversity and Conservation at the American Museum of Natural History, where she helps oversee strategic planning, project development and administration, and fundraising efforts. She is a conservation biologist with twenty years of field research and project management experience in Latin America and is currently the Americas Coordinator of the IUCN Flamingo Specialist Group. In South America, she is working with partners monitoring flamingo populations, to develop and implement a long-term regional conservation strategy that will ensure conservation of wetland systems. Dr. Arengo earned her MS in 1994 and PhD in 1997 from the SUNY College of Environmental Science and Forestry. She is an Adjunct Research Scientist at the Earth Institute, Columbia University, where she is on the Steering Committee of the Consortium for Environmental Research and Conservation (CERC).

Mary E. Blair is the Assistant Director of Research and Strategic Planning at the Center for Biodiversity and Conservation at the American Museum of Natural History (AMNH). She studies the conservation biology of primates and has ten years of field research experience in Latin America and Asia, where she studies the evolutionary processes that generate primate diversity to inform the spatial prioritization of conservation actions. Most recently, she has been studying the diversity of slow lorises in Vietnam, and the patterns, scales, and drivers of illicit trade in these and other animals through an NSF Science, Engineering, and Education for Sustainability (SEES) Fellowship. In 2013, she coedited *Primate Ecology and Conservation: A Handbook of Techniques*, published by Oxford University Press, and her blogs for the *New York Times*'s *Scientist at Work* and AMNH's *From the Field* have reached a global audience. Dr. Blair is Affiliated Faculty at Columbia University and the Richard Gilder Graduate School at the AMNH and is President of the AMNH Chapter of the Association for Women in Science. She received her BA from Swarthmore College in 2005 and her MPhil and PhD in Evolutionary Primatology from Columbia University in 2011.

Kara Blond is the Director of Exhibitions at the Smithsonian's National Museum of Natural History (NMNH). A member of the NMNH executive team, Ms. Blond provides strategic direction for exhibitions as part of the museum's overall public engagement program. Her team oversees all aspects of exhibit development, design, and production for a broad suite of compelling, accessible, and progressive science exhibits. Previously, Kara served as Chief of Exhibition Development and Project Management at NMNH, managing experience planning and project coordination. From 2003 to 2010, Kara worked at the Smithsonian's National Zoological Park, where she was Manager of Exhibit Development. At the zoo, Kara received the Smithsonian's 2007 Achievement in Education accolade for her work on the award-winning Asia Trail exhibition. Kara was previously a newspaper reporter at *Newsday* in New York. She earned her bachelor's degree in English and Psychology from the University of Pennsylvania and a master's degree in Education: Learning, Design, and Technology from Stanford University.

Gerald Dick earned his PhD in Behavioral Ecology under the supervision of Hans Winkler and the late Konrad Lorenz. After working in applied nature conservation, he was responsible for international conservation projects in the Austrian Ministry of the Environment and was Lecturer for International Conservation at the University of Vienna. After working for environmental development cooperation projects in Thailand and Nicaragua, he joined the World Wide Fund for Nature (WWF) Austria in 1995 and later was responsible for WWF International's species program in Europe and the Middle East. He became executive director of World Association of Zoos and Aquariums (WAZA) in 2008. Under his leadership, the association grew substantially in membership; its international profile has been enhanced via working relationships with

other global conservation bodies such as International Union for Conservation of Nature (IUCN) or Committee on Biological Diversity (CBD)
and, most recently, International Council of Museums Committee for
Museums and Collections of Natural History (ICOM NATHIST). As
part of the conservation work of WAZA, he initiated and designed the
project Biodiversity Is Us.

Eric Dorfman is Director of Carnegie Museum of Natural History (CMNH).
Before joining CMNH, he was Director of Whanganui Regional
Museum in New Zealand and, prior to that, Senior Manager of Science
Development at the Museum of New Zealand Te Papa Tongarewa. He
is President of the ICOM Committee for Museums and Collections of
Natural History (ICOM NATHIST), a registered ICOM mediator, and a
member of the group's Ethics Committee. Dr. Dorfman obtained a bach-
elor's degree in Ecology, Behavior, and Evolution at the University of
California–San Diego, followed by an MS in Marine Sciences from San
José State University and a PhD on cormorant behavioral ecology from
the University of Sydney. He is an author of popular books on natural
history, including *Inside New Zealand's National Parks* (Penguin, 2010).
He has also published children's fiction and scholarly papers on museum
operations, public programming, and the ecology of wetland birds.
His most recent publication is *Intangible Natural Heritage* (Routledge,
2012), which he edited.

Colette Dufresne-Tassé is past President of the International Committee
of the International Council of Museums for Education and Cultural
Action (ICOM CECA) and remains a co-opted board member. At the
University of Montreal, her research interests include the experiences of
adult museum visitors and museum education adult learning, creativity
in adults, methods-applied research, as well as various issues related to
the museum exhibition, including its characteristics and how visitors treat
and profit from it. Professor Dufresne is the author of *Familles, écoliers
et personnes âgées au musée: Recherches et perspectives* (ICOM, 2006).

Christopher Filardi, in addition to his work as an evolutionary biologist, has
a long history of conservation practice across the tropical Pacific and western North America. Combining natural history, biodiversity research, and
partnership with indigenous or local peoples, Dr. Filardi's professional
focus emphasizes commitment to bridging research interests with public outreach and grassroots conservation. In keeping with the American
Museum of Natural History's century-old legacy of island ornithology,
and inspired in part by childhood days spent roaming the halls of the
museum, his research has centered on studying mechanisms driving the
genesis of new bird species across the tropical Pacific and on the natural
history and evolution of island birds more generally. Dr. Filardi's conservation efforts have similarly concentrated on Pacific land- and seascapes

long part of the museum's research and exploration legacy, including the vast temperate rain forests of western North America where coastal peoples carved the great canoe that adorns the 77th Street entrance to the building. His conservation work has resulted in the establishment of protected areas around the world, driven by partnerships between indigenous peoples, scientists, and public- and private-sector leadership. He currently directs Pacific Programs at the Museum's Center for Biodiversity and Conservation, integrating biodiversity research, mentorship, and direct conservation action to inspire large-landscape and marine conservation across the Pacific region. Dr. Filardi received his PhD in 2003 from the University of Washington, where he studied patterns of speciation and the biogeographic history of tropical Pacific flycatchers.

Christopher J. Garthe is Head of Concept and Content at the Berlin-based creative agency Studio KLV. He specializes in participatory approaches in museums as well as exhibitions devoted to topics concerning nature, the environment, and sustainable development, and has developed the concept and produced content for more than forty exhibitions and institutions. Dr. Garthe received a PhD in Environmental Planning from Leibniz University in Hannover, a degree in Geography and Nature Conservation from that same institution, and a degree in Journalism from the German Specialist Journalism School.

Frank Howarth trained as a geologist, completing a BSc in Geology at Macquarie University, followed by a Master of Science and Society from the University of New South Wales, focusing on Science and Biotechnology Policy. Frank joined the NSW government in 1981, holdings positions with the Department of Industrial Development and Decentralization, NSW Science and Technology Council, the Public Service Board, and the Roads and Traffic Authority. In 1996, he became Director and Chief Executive of the Royal Botanic Gardens and Domain Trust. In September 2003, he spent six months as Executive Director, Policy and Science, at the NSW Department of Environment and Conservation, before taking up the role of Director of the Australian Museum from February 2004 to 2014. He is currently President of Museums Australia.

Osamu Kamei is the Head of the Centre of the History of Japanese Industrial Technology within the National Museum of Nature and Science, Tokyo. He studies the history of industrial technology such as the importance of knowledge and skills necessary to the continued existence of all humankind, which contributes to understanding humanity's "past" and "future" with nature. His research focuses on local issues but in collaboration with global specialists from the perspective of the Anthropocene. He is a member of the Japan Museum Management Academy, and was the chief of secretariat for the International Council of Museums' Asia-Pacific Alliance (ICOM ASPAC) in 2009, a member of the Museum Rescue Committee for the Great East Japan Earthquake in 2011, and of the working group for Museum Principle and Museum Ethics by the Japan Museum Association in 2012.

Lynda Knowles is a United States attorney who has worked for the Denver Museum of Nature and Science since 2007. She is currently serving as Secretary for the ICOM Committee for Museums and Collections of Natural History. Ms. Knowles is a graduate of the University of North Carolina–Chapel Hill and the University of Denver Sturm College of Law, where she was Editor-In-Chief of the University of Denver *Journal of International Law and Policy*. She participates in the Sturm College of Law externship program as faculty and mentor and is a volunteer judge for cultural heritage and international law moot-court competitions at the University of Denver and DePaul University. She is a member of the U.S. Lawyers Committee for Cultural Heritage Property and the American Inns of Court-Intellectual Property, Colorado. She has written articles on fossil protection and the auction of Native American artifacts in Europe and has most recently served as a legal-review panelist for *Rights and Reproductions: The Handbook for Cultural Institutions*, co-published by the Indianapolis Museum of Art and American Alliance of Museums in 2015.

Emlyn Koster has a BSc from the University of Sheffield in England and a PhD from the University of Ottawa in Canada, both in Geology. His career began with faculty appointments at Montreal's Concordia University and the University of Saskatchewan. His interest in engaging the public in global sustainability issues grew while conducting fieldwork for the Alberta Geological Survey at a UNESCO World Heritage Site. Choosing the vehicle of major museums for their great potential, CEO appointments followed at Alberta's Royal Tyrrell Museum of Paleontology, the Ontario Science Centre in Toronto, Liberty Science Center in Jersey City, New Jersey, and, since 2013, at the North Carolina Museum of Natural Sciences. Founded in 1879 and becoming the largest institution of its kind in the Southeastern United States and among the nation's most innovative nature and science museums, the accredited North Carolina Museum of Natural Sciences is maximizing the dividends from its public and private sector investments with new collaborations to propel its mission to illuminate the interdependence of nature and humanity. In 2014, this institution was honored at the White House with a national medal for its outstanding community service. Dr. Koster is a past President of the Geological Association of Canada and currently also an Adjunct Professor in the Department of Marine, Earth, and Atmospheric Sciences at North Carolina State University.

Isabel Landim Isabel graduated in Biological Sciences from the Federal University of Rio de Janeiro, holds a master's in Biological Sciences (Zoology), Federal University of Rio de Janeiro, and a PhD in Biological

Sciences (Zoology), University of São Paulo. She is currently Professor of the Museum of Zoology of the University of São Paulo; Deputy Coordinator of the Nucleus of Research on Education, Dissemination, and Epistemology of Biological Evolution (EDEVO-Darwin); Deputy Coordinator of the Post-Graduate Program in Museology of University of São Paulo; and Investigator on Museology in Emerging Centers of FAPESP (São Paulo Research Foundation). She has experience in Zoology with an emphasis in Systematic Ichthyology and undertakes research on Evolutionary Narratives in Natural History Museums.

Conal McCarthy has degrees in English, Art History, Museum Studies, and Māori Language. He has strong links with museums, art galleries and heritage organizations throughout New Zealand, and has worked in a variety of professional roles, among them education and public programming, interpretation, governance, collections, and curatorial work. His academic research interests include museum history, theory and practice, exhibition history, Māori visual culture, and contemporary heritage issues. He is an Assessor for the Australian Research Council (ARC), and has completed an ARC-funded research project on museums, anthropology, and governmentality with an international team. The New Zealand component of this research focused on museum collecting, fieldwork ethnography and indigenous agency, and is the subject of several recent and forthcoming publications. His next research project, "Indigenous Museologies," will examine the relationships between museums and indigenous people in post-settler nations in collaboration with several overseas and local scholars.

Christopher A. Norris received his doctorate in Zoology from the University of Oxford in 1992 and has worked in natural history collections for more than twenty years at Oxford, the American Museum of Natural History, and Yale, respectively. He is a former President of the Society for the Preservation of Natural History Collections, a founding member of the Integrated Pest Management Working Group, and a member of the Advisory Council for the Biodiversity Collections Network. His current research focuses on the development of web-based tools for educational access to collections data and quantification of value and development of value-based advocacy strategies for natural history collections. He is one of the lead editors of the multi-author volume *Preventive Conservation: Collection Storage* (scheduled for publication), and has written and blogged extensively on issues related to natural history collections (see paleocoll.blogspot.com).

Terry Nyambe works for the Livingstone Museum in Zambia as the Assistant Keeper of Ichthyology in the Natural History Department. His work involves research, curation, and documentation of the fish collections, as well as mounting exhibitions and organizing museum public programs.

He holds a BS in Ecology from the University of Zambia, has studied Museology in Japan, and undertook a course in Fish Taxonomy at the Royal Belgian Institute of Natural Sciences. He also holds a diploma in Information Technology from the University of Zambia. Currently, Mr. Nyambe is studying for his MBA at Heriot-Watt University. Alongside his professional work, he has been an active member of the International Council of Museums (ICOM) since 2006. He is currently the Chairperson of the Zambia National Committee for ICOM (ICOM Zambia), a position he has held since 2009. He is a member of the ICOM Ethics Committee and the only African representative. He is also a board member of the International Council of African Museums (AFRICOM) and a member of the Commonwealth Association of Museums (CAM).

Anna Omedes received a PhD in Animal Behavior from University College of Wales in 1981. She was Director of the Zoology Museum of Barcelona between 1997 and 1999, and has been Director of the Natural Science Museum of Barcelona since 1999, where she is author of its museological study, project manager of the new site, the Museu Blau, and co-curator and coordinator of the three-thousand-square-meter permanent exhibition *Planet Life* (2011). Dr. Omedes is author or editor of articles and books on Museology and Bioacoustics as well as scientific advisor to biological and museological publications. She has lectured and delivered papers at conferences on Museology and Museography and been a consultant on projects devoted to those areas. She was a member of the Executive Council of ICOM Spain between 2004 and 2010. She is now the Vice President of the board of the European Network of Science Centers and Museums (Ecsite) Nature Group, a member of the board of directors of ICOM NATHIST, the President of the Association of Science and Technical Museums and Centres of Spain, and member of the board of the Catalan Committee of Scientific Communication.

Ernesto Páramo is Director of the Science Centre and Museum in Granada, and in 1990 was author of the *Museum Project*. He holds a master's in Forensic Genetics and Anthropology and a law degree from the University of Granada. In 1993, he completed the course of study in Museum Management from the Deutsches Museum, where he also served as a guest researcher in 2010–11. Mr. Páramo is currently performing doctoral research in Education and Museology. In 2011, he was elected to the Board of Ecsite. He is the author or co-author of several books and some fifty guides and training materials on Science and Environmental Education and has presented at more than three hundred conferences, national and international. He has organized nearly forty temporary exhibitions, some in collaboration with museums such as the Natural History Museum, London; City of Space, Toulouse, France; the American Museum of Natural History, New York; and the Natural History Museum of Barcelona. He recently oversaw the expansion of the (now more than seventy-thousand-square-meter) Science Centre and Museum, featuring exhibits such as *Science in Al-Andalus*, *The Culture of Prevention*, *Techno-Forum*, *Journey to the Human Body*, *The Loft of the Museum*, and *Darwin Workshop*. He is a consultant to various cultural undertakings and museums.

Pierre Pénicaud became Professor of Natural Sciences in France and in French lycées in Abidjan, London, and Vienna, after completing his studies in Biology, Population Genetics, and the History of the Theories of Evolution. Back in France, he became the Director of the Muséum Henri Lecoq in Clermont-Ferrand where he was responsible for over thirty temporary and permanent exhibitions alongside participating in a network of museums in Auvergne and in France. In 2009, he relocated to the Museum of Natural History in Paris, where he was put in charge of the permanent exhibitions and the development of the public galleries of the Jardin des Plantes, of which he later became the director. Most recently, he joined the team of the new Musée de l'Homme to realize the Balcon des Sciences in preparation for the museum's reopening in 2015. Dr. Pénicaud is a member of the Administrative Council of ICOM France.

Hanna Pennock studied Art History and Italian Language and Literature at the University of Utrecht. She then worked in several museums as a researcher, exhibition coordinator, and curator, after which she served as Inspector of the national collections in the country's privatized state museums. She spent one year as Acting Director General of the International Council of Museums in Paris. She went on to assume the role of manager of the *Safe Heritage* program at the Dutch Cultural Heritage Agency, the aim of which is to develop and divulge knowledge and information on safety and security in the area of cultural heritage. Ms. Pennock has also served as Acting Head of Research and Library at the Museum Catharijneconvent in Utrecht. She is currently Senior Advisor at the Cultural Heritage Agency, which is part of the Ministry of Education, Culture, and Science.

Ana Luz Porzecanski is the Director of the Center for Biodiversity and Conservation (CBC) at the American Museum of Natural History. As Director of the CBC, Dr. Porzecanski oversees strategic planning, project development, and fundraising, and manages a multidisciplinary staff undertaking over twenty leading conservation research and capacity development initiatives around the world. She is a conservation biologist with experience in scientific research, education, training, and capacity development on multiple levels. She has over a decade of experience coordinating, leading, and evaluating conservation capacity development projects, designing teaching materials for university professors and conservation professionals, and leading professional development and assessment with diverse educator audiences in Africa, Asia, Latin America, and the United States. She has led capacity development activities with academic and professional partners in Bolivia, Colombia, and Peru since 2003. Dr. Porzecanski, who spent her childhood in Mato Grosso do Sul, Brazil, earned her undergraduate degree in Biological Sciences from the University of the Republic, Uruguay, and her PhD from Columbia University, where she conducted research on the systematics and historical biogeography of South American arid-land birds, alongside international environmental policy issues. She is an adjunct faculty member at Columbia University and New York University.

Eleanor J. Sterling is Chief Conservation Scientist in the Center for Biodiversity and Conservation at the American Museum of Natural History (AMNH). A scientist with interdisciplinary training in biological and social sciences, Dr. Sterling was the director of AMNH's Center for Biodiversity and Conservation from 2000 to 2014 before becoming Chief Conservation Scientist. She has more than thirty years of fieldwork experience with direct application to conservation in Africa, Asia, and Latin America. Her current research focuses on the intersection of biodiversity, culture, and languages, and the factors influencing resilience in biocultural approaches to conservation. She has extensive expertise in strategic planning and in developing environmental education programs and professional development workshops. She has trained teachers, students, and US Peace Corps volunteers in various subjects related to biodiversity conservation. Currently an Adjunct Professor at Columbia University, where she served as Director of Graduate Studies for the Department of Ecology, Evolution, and Environmental Biology for ten years, Dr. Sterling earned the 2012 Faculty Mentoring Award from Columbia's Graduate School of Arts and Sciences. She is a board member of the Yale Institute for Biospheric Studies and was honored in 2013 by the Society for Conservation Biology (SCB) for her contributions to the conservation of biological diversity and for inspiring students of Conservation Biology. Dr. Sterling received her BA in Psychology and Biology from Yale University in 1983, and her MPhil and PhD in Anthropology and Forestry and Environmental Studies, respectively, from Yale University.

Foreword

Natural history museums are the children of the Enlightenment and represent the physical manifestation of our species' attempt to integrate rational thought with the understanding of the natural and cultural worlds. Curiosity about curious objects gave rise to the first collections, and these collections drew audiences. By the mid-nineteenth century, this curiosity had matured into natural history science, whose early practitioners took advantage of increasingly easy travel to begin to sample the entire world and to summarize its contents. Most museums will proudly point to their founding expeditions and their earliest curators.

The end of the nineteenth century saw a surge in transportation and communication technology, a dramatic increase in urbanization, and an emerging recognition that plants, animals, and cultures were endangered by the growth and expansion of the world population's, which had nearly doubled from 1 billion in 1800 to 1.9 billion in 1900. The "new museum men" of the 1870s realized that urban audiences craved knowledge of the natural world and were concerned about its conservation. To meet this need, they built large, cathedral-like museums in a host of cities between 1880 and 1920. These museums explicitly recognized three goals: new knowledge, preservation of heritage, and public education. In a world before television, these institutions brought the broad world to cities and presented it as a series of dioramas, taxidermy mounts, interesting objects, and lantern-slide lectures.

Fast forward to 1960 and the world had accelerated, adding another billion people and launching the space age. In the United States, the Sputnik surprise sent educators scrambling to retool their science game, and they responded with the creation of science centers that were designed to engage young audiences with technology. Many American cities soon had a shiny new science center to compete with their now elderly natural history museum. By the 1980s, many natural history museums had reached their nadir. Some closed their doors, others gave away their collections or decreased their curatorial staff, and still, others simply morphed into science centers.

Fortunately, interest in natural science is resilient, and something wonderful began to happen. Cities began to revitalize and to appreciate the strength of their cultural offerings and diverse audiences. People returned from the suburbs. Museums began to utilize new technologies to augment communication and to catalogue and analyze their collections. Emerging awareness of pollution, poaching, habitat loss, and global warming began to mobilize citizen-based action. Advances in digital technology and genetics rebirthed the relevance of natural history collections. *Indiana Jones*, *Jurassic Park*, *Planet Earth*, and *Dinosaur Train* fanned the flames. New expeditions to fossil fields yielded amazing new finds and reminded us that the best stuff still awaits discovery. Museums began to renovate their 1920s dinosaur halls with twentieth-century insights from Earth System science, biology, ecology, and astrophysics. Dioramas came to be recognized as much-loved time capsules of lost habitats. Repatriation laws fostered new and genuine collaborations between museums and native communities. The forces that disrupted many industries seemed to strengthen natural history museums.

Now, in the eighteenth year of the twenty-first century, natural history museums find themselves with a powerful mandate to understand the natural world and humanity's place in it. The human population now stands at 7.3 billion and is headed toward a peak of 10 billion by 2050. Curatorial careers are traditionally long, and curators hired today will likely still be at their posts when the world hits "peak human." Most kids born today will live to see the year 2100 and will be citizens of the twenty-second century. Natural history museums were invented to understand the world and now is their moment.

Against all odds, natural history museums are experiencing a revolutionary rebirth in the digital century. Their collections, when seen together, represent what our species has collected to understand the natural and cultural worlds. With a growing focus on the needs of a young and empowered global audience of digital natives, natural history museums have the potential to become a network of fact-based reality in a post-truth world. I have long used the double entendre "Natural history museums save the world." This aspiration will only be achieved if the natural history museum world is populated by visionary leaders.

It is in this light that Eric Dorfman, Director of the Carnegie Museum of Natural History, assembled a talented group of museum practitioners and scholars to assess the future of natural history museums and provide a road map of best practices.

Kirk Johnson
Sant Director
National Museum of Natural History,
Smithsonian Institution, Washington, DC

Acknowledgments

I would like to acknowledge the board members of ICOM NATHIST, past and present, for encouraging me to take on this venture. Without their collegiality and, in some cases, participation, this book would not have been realized. To all the authors, I owe an enormous debt of thanks. Your involvement in this work helps to set the stage for a future about which we can do little better than guess.

Aedín McDevitt, Head of Publishing at ICOM, was a wonderful sounding board for many aspects of the publication process. Both she and Matthew Gibbons of Routledge were instrumental in the inclusion of this book in their partnership arrangement on museology. It has been a privilege to work with them.

My colleagues at Carnegie Museum of Natural History and Carnegie Museums of Pittsburgh have been of great help, discussing ideas, and reviewing and challenging ideas where necessary. Jane Friedman was an enormous help pulling together the formatting and proofing, and did an outstanding job creating the index. Michael Forde gave me invaluable advice and support throughout the preparation of this manuscript. I am truly grateful.

This book was funded in part by a special-projects grant from the International Council of Museums.

Introduction

Eric Dorfman

This book is about natural history museums. Not the old-fashioned, infa-
mously dusty halls full of dreary objects (not that most of them have ever
really been either) but a new breed of institution, one that exists in the
future—responsible and responsive to its community, employing newly developed methods to unravel the mysteries of the world and weave them into
engaging stories for an eager and engaged public.

In her opening to the 2016 edition of *TrendsWatch*, an industry report
published by the American Alliance of Museums, author Elizabeth Merritt
muses on the big philosophical questions currently facing museums:

> How does society impose identity on me (or you), and who controls
> how that identity is portrayed? How do I experience the world and
> empathize what it's like for other people? What is the basic meaning of
> being human: How have we mischaracterized that in the past, and will
> it change in the future?
>
> (p. 4)

Clearly, the museum sector is beginning to ask itself some hard questions
about what it does, why, and for whom. For natural history institutions,
whose main business it is to study and interpret the diversity of life, the
state of the Earth must by necessity play an important role, at the minimum
contextualizing the collection and, at best, catalyzing people to explore
their identity and connection to one another through the lens of nature.
Thus, no book on the future of natural history museums would be complete
without at least touching on the future of the planet's environment, as well
as the ethics, science, and politics of its use.

What will be the environment that natural history museums study and
interpret? By most measures, conditions on the planet we bequeath to our
descendants are highly uncertain. Even if you remove from the picture the
inescapable reality of anthropogenic climate change, plenty of factors im-
pede our ability to predict the world that tomorrow's natural history museums, and their visitors, will inhabit. Will we run out of power? Meat? Will
plastic and mercury pollution render produce from the oceans inedible? Will

the Alzheimer's epidemic continue to grow before we find a cure (or even a cause)? Will at least some of the planet run out of water in the face of increasing desertification? The answer to at least some of these questions and a host of others is, undoubtedly "yes." But how many of them, which ones and in what time frame they will affect us are still in the realm of speculation. These are "wicked problems" (Churchman, 1967; Levin et al., 2012)—issues that have so many facets that we cannot know the answers, but for which at least some of the alternative outcomes are negative. Adding to this complexity is that so many of these issues are interrelated.

These effects have been recently amalgamated into the concept of the Anthropocene, a proposed geological era that reflects human impacts so pervasive as to influence the geological record. These effects will be detectable millions of years from now, by whoever might be looking, as an unprecedented band of plastics, fly ash, radionuclides, metals, pesticides, reactive nitrogen, and consequences of increasing greenhouse gas concentrations (Waters et al., 2016) and changed fossil composition, featuring an overwhelming preponderance of chickens. How will this "age of humanity" structure our visitors' perceptions and what role it will play in the questions they pose concerning their environment? How will it influence our research?

At the same time, the opportunities provided by new technologies have never been greater. Virtually all museums have websites, often leading the field in design aesthetics, accessibility, and usability. Many of them have associated smartphone apps and active social media sites. The best museums have at least some of their collections online, available to researchers and an increasingly interested public. There are new ways of engaging with the public, too, such as citizen science programs collecting real research data and exhibits from which one can take information home via in situ interactives.

Natural history museums have traditionally been known for telling stories that face the viewer toward the past. They have famous collections of fossils and minerals. Our collections often hold species that have become extinct since accession and are displayed in dioramas that show no influence of human impact in their intricately painted backdrops. In times past our invitation has been to come to the museum and escape into nature, albeit represented by specimens that have been shot and stuffed and constrained to a cabinet in a wood-paneled hall.

Much like the wildlife they represent, natural history museums have had to adapt or die. Since the 1960s and 1970s, they have been adapting to Jacques Cousteau and David Attenborough, whose television documentaries have brought wildlife to generations of living rooms. Since the late 1990s, they have been adapting to the world of the Internet, which today brings Wikipedia entries detailing the minutiae of animals' life habits. It brings YouTube on which (should you care to), you can see a python wrestling an alligator or a lion adopting a baby gazelle. Coming in to see the "dead zoo" is simply no longer enough.

Zoos of living animals are also competitors. They offer a significant improvement on their visitor experience as compared with the institutions of only a generation ago. They are conservation organizations (Barongi et al., 2015), the most effective of which represent actual habitat that blurs the boundaries between the visitor and animals and breed individuals for rerelease into flagging wild populations.

How do museums compete in this noisy world with a relevant offer that is uniquely theirs? Visitors want to engage (Black, 2005; Simon, 2010). Those visitors who care about wildlife, and there are many, want natural history museums to deepen and expand their understanding. Museums like to feel that they occupy a place of credibility in the hearts and minds of the public that other channels of information, for all their worth, do not (but see Museums Association, 2013). Whether or not we truly are more credible than other types of institutions, our self-perception provides a significant opportunity to strive for best practice.

Today, best practice includes changing attitudes surrounding ethics, especially with respect to museums' responsibility for partnering with indigenous peoples over their objects and histories. Natural history museums have a significant role to play in consideration of this issue. They are also ideally placed to explore an ethical mandate to provide stewardship for the wildlife populations from which their specimens derive. Many museums give life to this through actively protecting biodiversity, addressing wildlife trafficking, and providing data to other conservation agencies.

To some degree, natural history museums are working hard to find their niche in the world of today, making thinking about the future somewhat speculative. And yet, that conversation will prepare them for whichever future appears as the net result of those multifarious issues. If we do not decide our future, it will be decided for us; that is what this book is about.

The concept for the volume came from two annual conferences of the International Council of Museums' Committee for Museums and Collections of Natural History (ICOM NATHIST). The first, "The Future of Natural History Museums: Relevance, Balance, and Innovation," was hosted in 2014 by the Krapina Neanderthal Museum in Croatia. It focused on challenges faced by natural history museums and strategic initiatives being developed to meet them. The second, "Natural History Museums: Building Our Future," held in 2015, was hosted by the National Taiwan Museum in Taipei. The meeting took a more operational approach, taking the time to consider practical applications of strategic thinking that would allow institutions to achieve their long-term goals. Several of these chapters originated as talks at one of these conferences.

This book is divided into four sections. The first is devoted to the collecting and preserving of objects, as well as what we do with them—the research we conduct and the principles that guide our activities. This section begins with a chapter on the future of natural history collections, by Christopher A. Norris, Senior Collections Manager for Vertebrate Paleontology at Yale Peabody

Museum. The world's natural history collections are the fundamental currency of our field. Collectively, they represent a massively distributed facility for research and education. Norris writes about the ability of museum collections to revisit the biotic, cultural, and physical history of our planet, as well as the development of new analytical tools to enable them to be studied in new ways. Thinking about the future, he points out the fiscal constraints placed on many museums, especially with large and specialist collections, constraints that may endanger the long-term preservation of the physical specimens that form the basis of collections. Given the legion abiding challenges that face humanity, Norris suggests that there is an urgent need not just for renewed investment in collections and collection infrastructure, but also new, sustainable systems of preventive conservation.

How we deal with collections is also an ethical issue. The fact that the addition of almost every living specimen into a museum collection means a death of that organism has caused ICOM to publish a Code of Ethics for Natural History Museums (ICOM, 2013) that sets forth best practice guidelines parameters pertaining to collecting, documentation, and dissemination of information. In Chapter 2, Emlyn Koster, Director, North Carolina Museum of Natural Sciences; Eric Dorfman, Carnegie Museum of Natural History; and Terry Simioti Nyambe, Assistant Keeper of Ichthyology at Livingstone Museum in Zambia and a member of ICOM's Ethics Committee, write about the nuanced ethical issues that natural history museums face now, and considering how they may develop in the future. The writers point out that because many natural history museums house vast collections collected over the course of decades and even centuries, and because most specimens are housed in perpetuity, the majority of institutions experience some space issues, and large segments of collected material remain perpetually uncatalogued. Can taking a living creature from the wild be justified if it remains forevermore in a container of unsorted material in the back of a collection storehouse? Or if it has been studied, but the results never published? Adding to this complexity is the Taipei Declaration on Natural History Museums and Biodiversity Conservation, issued by ICOM NATHIST (2015), which calls upon natural history institutions to participate in protecting the wild populations from which their collections have arisen:

> Increased human activities have created catastrophic declines in biodiversity. Both ethics and logic point to a mandate to conserve vulnerable habitats and species. To achieve best practice, natural history museums take action to conserve natural habitats and populations.

If stewarding collections can be considered an ethical obligation, then managing the attendant risks to those collections can as well. In Chapter 3, Hanna Pennock, Senior Advisor at the Cultural Heritage Agency of the Netherlands; former Manager, Safe Heritage; and former Acting Director General of

ICOM, writes about managing the risks that natural history museums face at present, and speculates on how those risks will develop in the future. Many "basic" risks, such as fire, theft, and water, will always threaten museum collections, as well as the staff who work with them, and there are many good best practice guides to dealing with these risks (for example, Matassa, 2011). Unfortunately, there is a growing danger of black-market-related burglary of objects that are overlooked as valuable by curators. The ongoing trend of theft of rhinoceros horns and elephant tusks, mostly from Europe, underscores the fact that even material that would seem to be an obvious target can be left vulnerable. With the precipitous decline of so many wild species (see, for instance, Brook, Sodhi, and Bradshaw, 2008), the future of natural history museums and zoos must include an ever-increasing focus on security.

What we do with our collections, however, to some degree justifies the risks inherent in housing them and keeping them safe. By design, the fundamental use for our collections is research. Frank Howarth, former Director of the Australian Museum, writes in Chapter 4 about future trends in research in natural history museums. He argues that research in natural history museums, with the exception of an elite few, is under serious threat from loss of funding, loss of direction, and, more profoundly, loss of relevance, although he suggests this need not be the case.

The early to mid-twentieth century represented a boom period for natural history museum research, when governments and communities in the developed world paid willingly and unquestioningly to know more about the "natural" world: the world of plants and animals, rocks and minerals and "native" peoples, philosophically distinct from modern, urbanized Western culture. More recently, the inescapable seriousness of global environmental issues has begun to impinge on research at natural history museums, concomitant with ever-improving technologies that allow greater scales of exploration. At the same time, indigenous peoples are demanding a say in the dissemination of their arcane knowledge and sacred artifacts. Research surrounding repatriation of cultural property is an increasingly important subject of exploration. These and related topics are set to guide the future of research in natural history museums and, Howarth maintains, will breathe new life and relevance into our field.

In Chapter 5, Felicity Arengo, Ana Porzecanski, Eleanor J. Sterling, Christopher Filardi, Mary E. Blair, and George Amato from the American Museum of Natural History explore important trends in the direct stewardship of wild populations and their habitats. The chapter provides a brief history of natural history museums' role in this regard and illustrates the innovative ways in which museums contribute to conservation today, and how they may continue to do so into the future. Museums have led the way in biodiversity discovery through specimen collection, inventory, and taxonomic and systematic study, all of which continue to evolve through new technologies that enable us to uncover growing layers of information concerning each specimen or artifact.

Museum collections house a detailed record of the planet's biota as it has changed over time, and in the face of accelerating environmental change. The rich geographic and biological data contained within collections is increasingly used for spatial conservation planning and priority setting, and to guide management under climate change. In addition to traditional specimen collections, newly frozen tissue repositories provide extraordinarily valuable specimens amenable to genomic research and other areas of conservation research. These repositories can hold population-level samples collected less invasively—with critical examples represented by vouchered specimens. Natural history museums leverage this capacity in part through long-term partnerships that connect local and global communities and stakeholders and draw from multiple sources of knowledge for conservation action on the ground. Arengo and her colleagues offer examples of how museums use partnerships to take on important conservation projects as well as raise awareness and engagement in conservation among their visitors through powerful experiences and public programming.

Section 2 has several chapters that look more outwardly, at our external stakeholders. In the first of these, Chapter 6, Kara Blond of the Smithsonian Institution explores the future of natural history exhibitions. The prevalence of multimedia, social media, and crowdsourcing, for instance, affords not only different opportunities for natural history museums (for example, to augment classic dioramas), but also differences in the way we engage with, and are evaluated by, our visitors. Topics such as the Anthropocene and climate change also comprise new challenges for museum content to meet visitors' expectations and concerns. They present a need for interdisciplinary approaches that embrace participatory techniques, rapid responses, and multilingual dialogues. To address these topics, Blond uses examples and ideas from a diverse set of museum exhibition thinkers based around the world.

Interacting with the public is, however, far more than engaging people who walk through the door on a casual basis. Leveraging the content on display through education programs is a key area of activity that is also undergoing significant development. In Chapter 7, Colette Dufresne-Tassé of the University of Montreal, and Pierre Pénicaud of the National Museum of Natural History, Paris, propose various tracks for learning and the adaptation of museum activities in light of changes in the needs of our public. By using examples from natural history museums, they explore the notion of "making meaning" in a visitor's experience and attempt to define this experience through its various components of cognition, imagination, and emotion. They also observe that teaching museology to university students should be rethought to incorporate the advantages of a holistic vision of the visitor's experience into the syllabus.

Participation and interactivity are recurring themes in this section of the book. For Christopher J. Garthe, of Studio KLV, Berlin, they are so vital that they underpin his proposal, in Chapter 8, for a reconceptualization of the natural history museum, which he terms the "natural futures museum." Garthe envisions this as a future-oriented institution that is the place to address global

challenges and the future of the planet, and in which interaction and participation will be the main instruments to implement this change. He suggests
that using digital data will open new possibilities for participatory practices
inside and outside the institution and that, by utilizing these opportunities,
natural history museums can evolve into a forum for public-facing research,
discussion, and action. He challenges institutions to embrace their role as the
facilitator of the collaboration of scientists and laypeople, along with their responsibility to contribute toward solutions to global problems.

The third section of the book, "Interfaces," examines the future of
partnerships between natural history museums and other types of institutions, as well as legislation and organization in this vein. In the first of
these, Chapter 9, Gerald Dick, former Executive Director of the World
Association of Zoos and Aquariums, explores the shared field of study and
advocacy among natural history museums, zoos, and aquariums, especially
in the areas of biodiversity, research, awareness raising, and conservation.
He argues that the time is right for more interaction and collaborative activities, and advocates for moving past the traditional borders separating
our "tribes," to overcome the boundaries that define our fields in the name
of developing synergies that will increase impact while saving resources.

Natural history museums also overlap to some degree with science
centers, especially in their mandate to offer programming around science,
technology, engineering, and mathematics (STEM) and to inspire the next
generation of young people to tackle real-world problems. In Chapter 10,
Anna Omedes, Director of the Natural Science Museum of Barcelona, and
Ernesto Páramo, Director of the Parque de las Ciencias, Granada, explore
the emergence of science centers during the last decades of the twentieth
century, simultaneous with a renewed effort on the part of natural history
museums to embrace greater interactivity. The differences and similarities
between these two types of institutions, they contend, mark their coevolu-
tion and a convergence toward a common point, allowing them to imagine
the role that both will play at the end of the twenty-first century as agents
of social change.

Everything discussed in the book up to this point, as indeed everything
not covered, happens in the context of legislation. It impacts the way we
interact with our visitors, serve our food, conduct human resource activities, loan objects to other institutions, and spend the money we receive in
donations. In some cases, our institutions were founded by a specific act
of government. Our legislative context is always changing, whether in response to newly arriving political parties or evolving perspectives on ethics
and social justice. While a complete treatment of this subject is deserving of
a book on its own, international legislation, something we can sometimes
have the luxury of overlooking, is changing in some important ways. In
Chapter 11, Lynda Knowles, Legal Counsel at the Denver Museum of Nature
and Science, addresses significant international developments in legal areas
affecting natural history museums. She summarizes developments surrounding the 1954 Hague Convention for the Protection of Cultural Property and

the 1970 UNESCO Convention on the Means of Prohibiting and Preventing the Illicit Import, Export, and Transfer of Ownership of Cultural Property, particularly as those developments affect natural history museums.

Knowles also discusses the connection between natural history museums and the 1972 Convention on International Trade in Endangered Species of Wild Fauna and the 1992 Convention on Biological Diversity, as well as customary international law, which is not codified into treaties, that is, created by consistent practice and relative uniformity among state actors. She explores selected cases where natural history museums have entered into novel collaborations with other global institutions that enhance the understanding of natural history and suggests that, over time, and with the advent of technology, the ability to create fruitful engagements with other global partners will become more common, and the opportunities for worldwide change and consensus all the greater.

It is necessary to run the museum as an effective business to achieve forward momentum on any of these fronts while maintaining the balance of its various mandates and stakeholders. In Chapter 12, I consider what allows natural history museums to function as response-ready, effective businesses, bringing in best practices from other fields to elucidate issues and opportunities for natural history museums. Aspects of this could feature in a chapter devoted to any professional sector, but in ours, the variety of our activities make having robust systems for efficient operations even more imperative.

This chapter is about grappling with these challenges and opportunities in the decades ahead. I consider institutions' ability to cope with change, especially unplanned events, and examine trends within the areas of development and accountability. I explore opportunities for monetizing collections, catalyzed in part by disruptive innovations from other industries, especially the Internet and the maker movement. These factors come together to encourage us to rethink the ways museums do business, especially the way we achieve— and maintain—strategic clarity through prioritization of our activities and advancing systems that provide the space to focus on innovation.

In the final section of the book, "Commentary and Synthesis," Conal McCarthy from Victoria University of Wellington adds and elaborates on the perspectives of the other contributors, drawing from a global set of experiences.

While no book can comprehensively address every issue facing natural history museums in the future, several important patterns do emerge. In the final discussion, Chapter 17, I collaborate with Isabel Landim (Brazil) and Osamu Kamei (Japan) to ponder these patterns and discover synergies that will contribute to subsequent thinking in the sector.

This conversation is one we must have. Most of us who work in natural history museums do so because we feel that we are doing something valuable both for the planet and for human societies. It follows, then, that preparing for the future, managing risk, and utilizing opportunities that are presented, protects not only our future as institutions but also the futures of the collections we steward, the children we inspire, and the wild populations our research enables us to protect.

References

Barongi, R., Fisken, F., Parker, M., and Gusset, M., eds. (2015). *Committing to Conservation: The World Zoo and Aquarium Strategy*. Gland: World Association of Zoos and Aquariums.

Black, G. (2005). *The Engaging Museum*. New York: Routledge.

Brook, B. W., Sodhi, N., and Bradshaw, C. (2008). Synergies among extinction drivers under global change. *Trends in Ecology and Evolution* 23(8), pp. 453–460.

Churchman, C. W. (1967). Wicked problems. *Management Science* 14(4), pp. B141–142.

ICOM NATHIST (2015). *Taipei Declaration*. [online] Available at: https://icomnathist. wordpress.com/taipei-declaration-on-nhms-and-biodiversity-conservation/ [Accessed 1 Jan. 2017].

Levin, K., Cashore, B., Bernstein, S. and Auld, G. (2012). Overcoming the tragedy of super wicked problems: Constraining our future selves to ameliorate global climate change. *Policy Sciences* 45(2), pp. 123–152.

Matassa, F. (2011). *Museum Collections Management: A Manual. London*: Facet Publishing.

Merritt, E. (2016). *TrendsWatch 2016*. Washington, DC: American Alliance of Museums.

Museums Association (2013). *Public Perceptions of—and Attitudes to—the Purposes of Museums in Society: A Report Prepared by BritainThinks for Museums Association. Museums Association, London.* [online] Available: at www.museumsassociation.org/download?id=954916 [Accessed 19 Dec. 2016].

Simon, N. (2010). *The Participatory Museum*. Santa Cruz: Museum 2.0.

Waters, C. N., et al. (2016). The Anthropocene is functionally and stratigraphically distinct from the Holocene. *Science* 351(6269), p. 137.

Part 1

Collecting and preserving in a changing world

1 The future of natural history collections

Christopher A. Norris

Introduction

In 2016, the Yale Peabody Museum of Natural History celebrated its 150th anniversary. It was an occasion to look back on an illustrious history of scientific collecting, through the publication of two books (Conniff, 2016; Skelly and Near, 2016), a program of talks, and a temporary exhibit entitled *Treasures of the Peabody Museum: 150 Years of Exploration and Discovery*. In a darkened exhibit hall a handpicked selection of objects was presented, drawn from the nearly 13 million specimens that make up the Peabody's collection: an eclectic physical précis of the museum's holdings that encompassed a rifle belonging to Buffalo Bill; a type specimen of a Tahitian fern collected on the US Exploring Expedition of 1838–42; a pickled tentacle of a giant squid captured in Newfoundland in 1873; the first microscope ever used at Yale, from 1735; and a dog-drool collector belonging to Ivan Pavlov.

Natural history museums and their collections are often thought of in terms of the past, which is not surprising. We are probably the only type of scientific research facility that can claim the ability to time travel, albeit in a patchy and far from perfect way. Our business is intimately connected with the past, both recent and deep time, and much of what humans know about the natural world of a hundred, a hundred thousand, or a hundred million years ago arises directly or indirectly from the specimens held in our collections. When your child states with certainty that *Tyrannosaurus rex* lived in the Cretaceous period they are, knowingly or unknowingly, drawing on the results of research done using museum collections.

There is, however, a considerable difference between studying the past and belonging in the past. A cursory glance at the cavalcade of sepia-toned images, polished brass instruments, and handwritten jar labels in the Peabody's anniversary exhibition might give the impression that the Museum's glory days are behind it. Nothing could be further from the truth. Closer inspection of the exhibition revealed specimens that were collected only a few years ago, research performed with cutting-edge technology, and collection-based science projects that address some of the most pressing issues facing us today; fundamental questions about the future of the planet and our species.

Natural history collections face four main challenges: acquiring material, preserving that material, making it available for use, and making the case that the first three activities are worthy of support. These challenges are eternal ones, which have faced museums since their inception and are likely to persist for as long as museums exist. But natural history collections have undergone a quiet revolution in the last thirty years, which has the potential to create an exciting future in which collections play an even greater role in society.

To say that natural history collections are facing a dynamic future that is both exciting and alarming may surprise many people. But in some ways, that future is already here, and the extent of the surprise being expressed is one of the challenges we face in responding to it.

The challenge of collecting

In 1921, a caravan of heavily loaded Dodge automobiles passed through the Great Wall of China at Kalgan and headed west, into the deserts of Mongolia. Led by Roy Chapman Andrews (frequently cited as the inspiration for George Lucas's Indiana Jones, despite repeated denials from Lucas), the American Museum of Natural History's (AMNH) Central Asiatic Expeditions have shaped the public perception of natural history collecting. Between 1921 and 1928, Andrews and his colleagues shipped thousands of paleontological, zoological, and botanical specimens back to New York. The tales and images of weather-beaten explorers, gun-toting bandits, camel trains, and dinosaur bones being hacked from the rocks of the Gobi Desert in books and periodicals made Andrews very much the media star of his time (Gallenkamp, 2001).

But the expeditions were also a product of their time, as was Andrews. Frequently forgotten amid the triumphalism of their finds was the underpinning purpose of the trip: to find evidence of early humans that would support the theory of American Museum of Natural History (AMNH) President Henry Fairfield Osborn that Central Asia was the cradle of human evolution. In Osborn's worldview, people of color occupied the far-flung edges of the planet, having been displaced by the more "advanced Nordics" situated in Eurasia. Absurd though this idea may seem today, in the 1920s such racially based theories were not considered outside the scientific mainstream. They reflected prevailing attitudes of the time, which could also be seen in the conduct of the expedition. Neither Osborn nor Andrews showed much respect for their Chinese hosts, who they variously described as corrupt, callous, effeminate, self-indulgent, and lazy. Team photographs show the expedition personnel to be almost entirely white and male. The few Mongolians present are relegated to the role of cooks, camel drivers, and porters (Regal, 2002).

The Central Asiatic Expeditions reflected a belief that American knowledge exceeded that of the Chinese and Mongolians, and that this justified taking possession of specimens and data from their territories (Rainger, 1991, p. 104). The great natural history collections of the world were born in the heyday of Western colonialism when the right of their scientists to collect specimens from around the world was unquestioned. Today we work in a world that is very different, and our assumptions about our role and that of others are, we hope, also very different from those that underpinned the building of the museum collections in which many of us work. For natural history museums, one of the key elements of this is the Convention on Biological Diversity (CBD), which was launched at the 1992 Earth Summit in Rio de Janeiro and has been in force since 1993. The principles behind the CBD were that biodiversity should be conserved for the benefit of humanity, that the benefits should be derived from sustainable usage, and that those benefits should be shared fairly and equitably (United Nations, 1992).

Traditionally, natural history museums saw their role as supplying the science on which our understanding of biodiversity was based, but there were cases where more directly commercial benefits could accrue. For example, alkaloids extracted from specimens of poison dart frogs collected in Ecuador by the AMNH form the basis of a number of promising analgesic drugs under commercial investigation (Angerer, 2011). But the implementation of the 2010 Nagoya Protocol to the Committee on Biological Diversity (CBD), which sets out the legal framework for access and benefit sharing of genetic resources came as an unpleasant surprise to many museums. With the implementation of the protocol in 2014, biological collections of the sort that museums have been making for decades are regarded as valuable resources and treated accordingly (Neumann et al., 2014).

This has implications not just for collecting, but also for routine operations such as processing of specimens, sampling, or loans of specimens from one museum to another. All these operations require Prior Informed Consent (PIC) for the procedure from the country of origin beforehand and Mutually Agreed Terms (MAT) for how any resulting benefits will be handled. The country of origin for the material is entitled to place limitations on the purposes for which specimens are used, and to specify conditions that ensure a reciprocity of benefits. Those benefits can be monetary or non-monetary, which means that arguing that the results of museum-based research are rarely commercialized makes no difference—in principle, any benefits obtained from the possession or study of the genetic material in the specimens, be they commercial, scientific, educational, or promotional—should be shared with the country of origin (Neumann et al., 2014).

To some extent, museums are already addressing these issues, and have been for some time. Modern collecting expeditions are usually partnerships between the host country and the museum, encompassing multiple stakeholders, and with an emphasis on training staff, and building collection capacity in the host country. They are governed by a raft of documentation, including collaborative agreements, collecting permits, export permits, and import permits. In most cases, the collecting agreement will also specify the disposition of any specimens collected, limiting the number and type of specimens that can be exported, and for certain categories of rare material, such as vertebrate fossils, it is not unusual for the overseas institution to retain none of the material; instead, permission is granted to make casts of the fossils, with the originals and molds returning to the host country.

Nonetheless, it is likely that Nagoya will bring more challenges, as host countries seek both to capitalize on their biodiversity and build local capacity. As museums, we should embrace this; greater stakeholder engagement, transfer of skills, and the creation of new collaborating partners are all good things for our long-term future. But it also raises the question of whether, as local capacity grows, Western institutions can continue to grow their collections globally. The countries in question are often the regions of greatest biodiversity—not only are they the places where everyone wants to collect, but they are also the areas in which collecting efforts should be concentrated, as they are often regions where the potential for biodiversity loss is most sizable. Previously, museums in the Western world took a rather asymmetric view of the collaborations necessary to achieve this.

One example of this is the concept of the "parataxonomist," attributed to the ecologist Daniel Janzen (1991) and embraced with enthusiasm by the taxonomic community during the 1990s. The parataxonomist was a local worker who had been given basic training in species identification. The idea was that this individual would carry out the initial bulk sorting of specimens, but as soon as something interesting emerged, an expert (usually not local, and often from an overseas institution) would be called in to describe it. The work of the parataxonomist thus saves the more valuable time of the taxonomist. It was a well-intentioned idea, which sought to cope with the very real resource challenges associated with describing massive numbers of species in a finite period, but it is questionable whether it could be described as truly collaborative.

In the twenty-first century, the only way this massive species description effort will work sustainably is with at least some of the leadership coming from the countries that actually "own" the biodiversity. As many of them are struggling to lift their people out of the trap of poverty, this will be a big hurdle to overcome. More recent efforts to address the biodiversity crisis, such as the "call to arms" by Wheeler et al. (2012), have placed a strong emphasis on providing resources to develop collections and in-country expertise in areas of high biodiversity; this is at least as important as developing expertise and building collections in the developed world. It was telling that of the thirty-nine authors and twenty-five institutions represented in the Wheeler et al. paper, thirty-four authors and twenty-one of the institutions were US based, and only one author was from a country with an emerging economy (in this case, Brazil), even though most of the world's undescribed biodiversity resides outside the United States and Europe. There is a considerable (and perhaps understandable) resentment in many parts of the world toward the mining of biodiversity by "first world" institutions, and any large-scale program of species description needs to address this imbalance.

The process of collecting itself is receiving increasing scrutiny. The emergence of social media and the ability of scientists to share their work with the public have resulted in valuable exposure for museums' biodiversity conservation activities, while raising uncomfortable questions concerning long-established work practices. One example of this was the first-ever collection of a male specimen of the moustached kingfisher (*Actenoides bougainvillea*), an endemic species from the Solomon Islands, by a team from the American Museum of Natural History. The discovery, in October 2015, was announced on the expedition blog by the ornithologist who captured the kingfisher (Filardi, 2015a). When it emerged that the animal had been euthanized there was a storm of protest, communicated via comments on the Audubon Society article that reported the discovery (Silber, 2015), a subsequent article by the collector explaining the basis of the decision to collect the bird (Filardi, 2015b), and negative coverage in mainstream media (for a typical example, see Klausner, 2015).

This is not a new issue, especially in ornithology (see Remsen, 1995; Donegan, 2000; Winker et al., 2010), but it has been given new urgency by the increasing use of technology in collecting. If a biologist can take digital images, sound recordings, deoxyribonucleic acid (DNA), and other tissue samples sufficient to produce a species description (see, for example, Sangster and Rozendaal, 2004; Athreya, 2006), is it still necessary to kill the individual in order to obtain a voucher specimen? Many members of the public would say "no," as do some academics. In 2014, a paper in *Science* by Minteer et al. (2014) argued that given the precipitous decline in abundance for many species, it was unethical for museums to kill additional members of these species when nonlethal alternatives exist. There are, of course, strong counterarguments in favor of physical vouchers. Any species whose long-term viability can be significantly affected by the removal of one or two individuals is already effectively extinct: without aggressive human intervention (through, for example, capture and captive breeding), natural mortality will far exceed this. The process of capturing, anesthetizing, and sampling a small animal will significantly compromise its fitness, increasing mortality rates. Finally, a blood sample and a photograph can provide only a very limited amount of information about a species—a fraction of what could be obtained from a full body voucher specimen. It is not possible to re-examine the type specimen to validate the original description, and any new questions not answered by the type description will require the collection of another specimen, compromising the fitness of yet another individual.

The Minteer paper triggered an immediate response from the taxonomic community (Rocha et al., 2014), and the resulting debate was extensively reported in the media, supplying a valuable opportunity to expose the public and opinion formers to the underlying issues in a way that was not possible in the specific case of the kingfisher. But it does raise the question of whether, as we seek to engage a wider range of stakeholders in the work of the museum, we need to modify our long-held work practices to address the concerns of the public. We can no longer rely on distance, be it physical or intellectual, to protect us from criticism.

Another question is whether we should be putting resources into field collection. It is widely recognized in the museum community that thousands of new species are already sitting, undescribed, in museum collections (Bebber et al., 2010). Because of the steady erosion of curatorial support, the "shelf life" of these species (the time between collection and description) is getting longer, and continued field collection is only increasing the size of the backlog. Also increasing is the space required to store the collections and the energy costs of conserving them. Technology may offer a way to "mine" existing collections for new species (see below), but that will still require the significant investment of resources. It could be argued that a more sustainable and cost-effective approach would be to pump resources into the training of staff and building of collections in areas of high biodiversity while focusing the efforts of the first world museums on curation and care of their existing collections.

The challenge of preserving

The question of whether museums can continue to grow their collections hinges on sustainability. Given our responsibility of stewardship, is it ethical to continue collecting new material when we cannot properly care for the material we already have?

The preservation challenges facing natural history collections in the twenty-first century are, at least in part, a result of the collections community's significant improvement in the standards of collections care. Past practices, particularly during the middle of the twentieth century, when many collections were undergoing rapid growth, amounted to nothing more than benign neglect. Physical care and curation of collections were prioritized according to curatorial research interests, environmental controls were largely absent, and pest management involved the application of large quantities of toxic chemicals whose adverse effects were not limited to pest species.

In the last four decades, however, we have seen a revolution in our understanding of how to care for natural history materials. This change is rooted in conservation science and stresses a layered approach to the preservation of specimens, which starts with control of variables within the building environment, including light, temperature, and relative humidity; encompasses specialized sealed cabinetry that excludes gaseous and particulate pollutants; and, finally, applies archival standard materials to enclose and support specimens within the cabinets (Rose and Hawks, 1995). Specialized environments, such as low-oxygen enclosures, are used to deal with specific problem materials (Collins, 1995), while application of pesticides has largely been replaced by integrated pest management systems that emphasize preventive measures, mitigation strategies, and the use of barriers to separate pests from specimens (Strang et al., forthcoming).

Because of these changes, many natural history collections are in better shape now than in previous decades and more likely to survive into the future, which is not to say, however, that the problem of preservation has been solved. These new practices come at a cost that not all institutions can meet. Even when the direct costs are met, the improvements in preservation have rarely led to an expansion of staffing; as a result, preservation now competes with curation for staff resources. Institutions are required to balance improvements in the physical housing of specimens with basic collections activities such as identification of specimens, cataloging, and taxonomic description. This balancing act raises fundamental questions pertaining to the role of museums as it relates to collections. Is it our primary responsibility to preserve collections, or to study them, and to what extent do these two activities feed off one another?

Another effect of improved collection care has been dramatically increased energy costs. Per square foot, the Yale Peabody Museum's Class of 1954 Environmental Science Center, which houses the collections of six of the museum's divisions, is one of the most expensive of the university's buildings to run, and is less energy efficient than the original 1926 Peabody building (Bratasz et al., 2016). This is because of the energy cost of maintaining temperature and relative humidity in the relatively narrow range specified by community standards for collection environments. Yet it is debatable whether the high costs of running modern collection storage facilities are justified. The building envelope, combined with the well-sealed collection cabinetry, is capable of buffering most of the environmental fluctuations that could lead to collection damage, while the rapid cycling between high and low relative humidity (RH) necessary to keep the average within the limits set may actually prove more damaging to objects in the long term than a slow, seasonal progression from high RH to low and back again.

These issues are pressing enough when they are addressed by relatively affluent institutions like Yale, but they become urgent as we look to encourage and support the building and maintenance of collections in the emerging economies that are the home of much of the world's undescribed biodiversity. In these countries, tight environmental controls and elaborate engineering solutions are neither feasible nor sustainable. There is a real need for more research on achievable standards and the use of passive controls. These topics comprise the subject of ongoing research and discussion within the International Council of Museums collections community (ICOM-CC, 2014), but what is clear is that if museums are to take a leading role in tackling the environmental challenges facing the planet, they may need to start close to home (AAM, 2013).

When considering future challenges, it is also important for museums to embrace the reality of a changing climate. For many areas, this may involve new risks or changes in the frequency of risk. More frequent storms, a higher probability of wind damage, or flooding from rain or coastal storm surge needs to be factored into planning. This will require not only robust plans for business continuity, emergency response, and salvage in collections, but also the use of objective measures of risk assessment in planning new collection storage, or renovating of existing facilities. Given the limited resources available, a risk assessment will play a key role in ensuring that appropriate funds are directing toward mitigating potential risks to a collection in the light of a changing environment (AAM, 2015).

The challenge of access

Preservation of collections is only one part of the totality of museum operations; providing access to collections is another. It is a much-quoted, but nevertheless, core maxim of collection care that collections not used are useless collections.

The dramatic expansion of the World Wide Web over the last twenty years has fundamentally changed how the public accesses information and other material. To their credit, museums have been quick to recognize and respond to this change. Within the natural history collections community, this has resulted in the formulation of national and international strategies to digitize specimens and data from collections and to create tools and infrastructure to make these available to users (NIBA, 2010). The potential, in terms of both increased access and availability of novel forms of use, is enormous (Beaman and Cellinese, 2012).

However, this should not blind us to the enormous task that faces the natural history collections community in terms of converting our analog resources to digital ones. The funding made available from public bodies thus far falls well short of what will be required for mass mobilization of collections data. Novel approaches, such as the Notes from Nature project (Hill et al., 2012), which engages members of the public in a crowdsourced effort to transcribe field notes from museum collections, reveal the imagination and creativity needed to overcome some of the shortfalls in funding, but ultimately mass digitization will require fundamental realignments of museum resources to put digital assets and infrastructure, and the capture of data to populate this, on an equal footing with other core programmatic areas. At the level of collections, it will also require adjustment of workflows to incorporate digitization as a routine activity and changes in staff training and recruitment to support this effort (Wheeler et al., 2012).

Some museums have already embraced these changes; others have been slower to do so. Given finite resources, there are understandable concerns that museums might be tempted to follow the model of libraries, where the growth in digitized books and journals has enabled them to move physical volumes to cheaper, but much-less-accessible high-density storage. This is not a model that natural history collections can adopt: digital access to specimens complements physical access, but does not replace the ability to examine the specimen directly; not all information from the specimen can be captured or transmitted digitally.

Unfortunately, specimens do not have to be moved off-site to become inaccessible. The inevitable competition for resources between physical and digital curation may have the same effect, by diverting funds away from preservation and provision of physical access. There *are* ways in which increased digital accessibility could be leveraged to address shortfalls in other areas. For example, interactive online interfaces for specimen databases would enable specialists to curate collections remotely, providing identifications and flagging potential new species or other interesting material for examination or loan. But as with all the potential benefits of digitization, this will require institutions to invest in the underpinning infrastructure and technical support required.

One of the oft-cited benefits of digitization is the increased accessibility of collections. By making specimens and data available online, we are broadening the public's access to the collections that we hold in trust for them. But in doing so we negate our traditional role as gatekeepers for the collections, deciding who accesses them and how. Previously, these decisions could be justified based on the limited resources available to support physical access, but with digital assets, there is no good resource-based reason why, having made the assets available online, you would need to restrict their accessibility. This is certainly more in keeping with the increasingly connected, participatory world in which we live, but it raises some interesting dilemmas.

Some of these are already becoming apparent. The data and tools already exist to enable specimen localities to be mapped and displayed online, including those of rare and potentially valuable resources such as fossils or endangered plant species. Concerned about the prospect of illegal collecting, many in the museum community believe that locality data online should automatically be redacted, either to an arbitrary level such as the county where a specimen was found or by deliberate "fuzzing" of coordinate data. Anyone with a "legitimate" reason to access the complete data would be able to request these from the museum, thus returning the institution to its prior role as gatekeeper. This would also have the coincidental but desirable effect of preserving a potential revenue stream from companies carrying out environmental impact surveys for construction projects, which also need access to locality data. But it raises ethical issues about whether museums who have received public funds to make their data available online are then justified in restricting access to those data (Norris and Butts, 2014). Similar arguments could be made for restricting access to high-resolution specimen images or scan data (to control potential commercialization of public assets), or field notes and correspondence (because of privacy concerns).

Questions of access extend beyond digitization to challenge some of the fundamental assumptions that we make regarding our stewardship of collections. As collection professionals, we tend to assume that the collections exist for the purpose for which they were created: as research and education resources underpinning the missions of our institutions. As we look to broaden access to collections and to make the public more aware of their contents, we will inevitably be challenged to look at the material in new ways (Balachandran and McHugh, forthcoming). There are areas of natural history, notably anthropology and ethnology, where this has long been the case, and the involvement of the wider community, including in areas such as questions pertaining to access and ownership, in some cases carries the force of law (Fine-Dare, 2002). Museums now frequently accommodate access to, and interaction with, certain artifacts for purposes of worship.

But all specimens, regardless of discipline, are to some extent items of material culture. People may place different values on them than we do; in the case of collecting, as has already been discussed, they may question our long-established collecting practices, based on their view of the natural world. They may wish to use our data as evidence of past malpractice on the part of a museum, such as illegal collecting. They may want to download specimen images and data to support theories that we regard as scientifically untenable, such as creationism or intelligent design. If our aim is genuine and is to increase accessibility, how comfortable are we with accommodating usage with which we are unfamiliar, or with which we disagree?

Perhaps the ultimate expression of this is the question of whether we should be holding some of this material at all. If, as discussed earlier, we accept that our collections were obtained under circumstances and reflecting attitudes that we now reject, what responsibility do we have to make them accessible through loan or repatriation? How do we weigh the "global museum" model of increased accessibility against challenges to access for those in the country of origin? These issues have already challenged many museums, including Yale Peabody (Donadio, 2014), and it is almost inevitable that more cases will arise as the natural history collections community looks to support and build collections capacity worldwide.

The challenge of image

The developed world is already facing the economic and demographic reality of an aging population. Put simply, people are living longer and require more health care, and more expensive treatments, to maintain life in their final years. This presents public funders with a considerable challenge (International Monetary Fund, 2010). The cost of public health care and benefits continues to rise, putting increased pressure on discretionary funding, including funds for museum collections. If these funds are to be secured for the future, we need to do a better job of arguing for our indispensability. Surveys undertaken by organizations in the museum field have shown that natural history museums are both liked by the public and trusted as a source of information (Lake Snell Perry and Associates, 2001; Griffiths and King, 2008). Unfortunately, being liked is not the same as needed, just as interest by the public is not the same as being in the public interest. A variety of factors including declining public engagement with nature (Balmford et al., 2009), and a shifting focus in undergraduate and graduate education from organismal biology to more lab-based molecular and theoretical approaches (Gropp, 2003; Tewksbury et al., 2014) are eroding some of the traditional support for collections even though their fundamental importance endures.

Natural history collections are widely recognized as part of the national and international research infrastructure for science and humanities (Interagency Working Group on Scientific Collections [IWGSC], 2009; Johnson et al., 2011; Hanken, 2013). Recent advances in digitization and networking of collections, as described above, as well as network biocollections, lend weight to the argument that collections comprise a macroscale research facility (Baker, 2011; Johnson et al., 2011), analogous to other scientific infrastructures such as large telescopes, particle accelerators, or supercomputing clusters, which can be used to support research across a wide range of disciplines. Paradoxically, at least in the United States, most of the operating costs of these national systems are borne by private and public non-governmental entities, which in many cases struggle with affordability (Gropp, 2003; Menninger, 2007; Mares, 2009).

Advocates for collections-based research cite benefits across a wide range of areas of public interest, including human health, education, agriculture, land management, conservation, and national security (Suarez and Tsutsui, 2004; Winker, 2004; Wandler et al., 2007; IWGSC, 2009; Mares, 2009; Johnson et al., 2010; Cook et al., 2014). Evidence for these benefits is almost invariably provided in the form of exemplar projects, such as the frequently cited contribution of museum data to elucidating the source of the 1993 Sin Nombre virus outbreak (Yates et al., 2002). There is a critical need to develop quantitative metrics that complement and reinforce this evidence.

Beyond this, there is a pressing need to change the wider public perception of natural history collections from something that is nice to something that is essential. One of the strengths and weaknesses of natural history collections is the accessibility of the research they support. Many large research facilities are expensive to run, but in the absence of easily understandable research, they are obliged to work hard to improve their ability to explain long-term societal benefits. By contrast, when natural history museums speak to the public about collections, they tend to focus on novelty or quirkiness. This undoubtedly catches the public's attention, but does it do so in a helpful way? Arguably, we should have more gravitas.

As public funding declines, museums will be competing in a shrinking pool of discretionary funds with highly valued programs such as defense, public health, and education. The potential for museums to compete directly with these for funding is negligible. Instead, we need to show how the building, preserving, and using of natural history collections helps contribute to these programs. Museums need to develop value-based arguments for what they do, moving away from catchy anecdotes towards quantitative measurements of impact in science, education, and public health. We also need to talk less about the past and more about the future. As discussed earlier, the fact that we work with the past does not mean that we belong in the past. The pervasive use of the adjective "dusty" in press articles relating to even the most technologically advanced collections-based research is perhaps an inevitable consequence of our own obsession with history.

A vision of the future

The preceding and only partial list of challenges may have given the impression of a grim future for natural history collections in the twenty-first century and beyond. Quite the contrary. While the challenges are real, the opportunities for the museums holding these collections are considerable.

First, it is difficult to overemphasize how transformative the effect of large-scale digitization of collections could be. Natural history collections are, in principle, a massive, distributed facility that can support research in a multitude of fields. In the past, the scope of that research has been limited by the extent to which researchers could visit collections or obtain material on loan. As more and more data become available online, this will change profoundly. Researchers will be able to combine digitized collections data from large numbers of museums to produce massive, aggregated data sets that can be mined using big data techniques to reveal patterns in the natural world that might otherwise be missed (Mayer-Schönberger and Cukier, 2013). These could include modeling changing patterns in disease vectors or using digitized data on species distribution to target areas of high biodiversity for conservation activities. Such activities are already taking place; they will only become easier as more data become available.

The same technologies will increase the efficiency of our own curation efforts. Just as we can map biodiversity hot spots from museum data, we will be able to use these data to predict areas of high biodiversity and compare these models against museum records to help focus collecting activity. By developing interactive technologies to interface with digitized collections, we will have the potential to leverage specialist expertise to identify and curate material in our collections, even if the specialist and the collection are on opposite sides of the planet. By scanning specimens and making scan data available online, researchers will be able to download and print specimens for use without having to travel to the collections in person, a critical issue for museums in emerging economies where travel funds may be limited.

Digital networking will improve our ability to collaborate internationally. Rather than moving people and material between field sites in areas of high biodiversity and museums in the first world, we will be able to shift our focus to building capacity locally, using networking technologies to support training and to access the specimens and data collected. We will combine conservation science with work on building sustainability to develop energy-efficient systems and methods of passive climate control that not only make existing developed-world facilities more energy efficient, but that can be applied to preserving collections in emerging economies where funding for complex engineering solutions is not available. By finally recognizing that collecting without curation jeopardizes our mission of collections accessibility, we may be able to refocus resources on mining our existing collections for undescribed biodiversity.

These activities will be far more visible to the public, as the collections themselves become more accessible. The same networking technologies that support professional collaboration will allow a degree of public participation in crowdsourced projects that has not been seen before. With this exposure, there will undoubtedly be uncomfortable conversations: about our collection practices, past and present, the moral authority under which we hold and display certain categories of material, and the extent to which we share or withhold information. The conversations may be uncomfortable, but they should not be unwelcome either. Just as collections have come a long way from the days of Andrews and Osborn, we should expect them to continue to evolve for the remainder of this century and beyond.

References

AAM (2013). *Museums, Environmental Sustainability, and Our Future*. Washington, DC: American Alliance of Museums.

AAM (2015). A rising tide: The changing landscape of risk. In: *TrendsWatch*. Washington DC: American Alliance of Museums.

Angerer, K. (2011). Frog tales: On poison dart frogs, epibatidine, and the sharing of biodiversity. *Innovation: The European Journal of Social Science Research* 24(3), pp. 353–369.

Athreya, R. (2006). A new species of *Liocichla* (Aves: Timaliidae) from Eaglenest Wildlife Sanctuary, Arunachal Pradesh, India. *Indian Birds* 2, pp. 82–94.

Baker, B. (2011). New push to bring U.S. biological collections to the world's online community. *BioScience* 61, pp. 657–662.

Balachandran, S., and McHugh, K. (forthcoming). Respecting our collections. In L. Elkin and C. A. Norris, eds., *Preventive Conservation: Collection Storage*. Washington, DC: American Institute for Conservation, George Washington University, the Smithsonian Institution, and Society for the Preservation of Natural History Collections.

Balmford, A., et al. (2009). A global perspective on trends in nature-based tourism. *PLOS Biology* 7, (art.e 1000414).

Beaman, R. S., and Cellinese, N. (2012). Mass digitization of scientific collections: new opportunities to transform the use of biological specimens and underwrite biodiversity science. In: V. Blagoderov and V. S. Smith, eds., No Specimen Left Behind: Mass Digitization of Natural History Collections. *ZooKeys* 209.

Bebber, D. P., et al. (2010). Herbaria are a major frontier for species discovery. *Proceedings of the National Academy of Sciences USA* 107, pp. 22169–22171.

Bratasz, L., et al. (2016). Evaluation of climate control in Yale Peabody Museum of Natural History—energy consumption and risk assessment. *SPNHC*.

Collins, C. (1995). *Care and Conservation of Palaeontological Material*. London: Butterworth-Heinemann.

Conniff, R. (2016). *House of Lost Worlds: Dinosaurs, Dynasties, and the Story of Life on Earth*. New Haven, CT: Yale University Press.

Cook, J. A., et al. (2014). Natural history collections as emerging resources for education. *BioScience* 64, pp. 725–734.

Donadio, R. (2014). Repatriated works back in their countries of origin. *New York Times*, 17 Apr. Available at: https://www.nytimes.com/2014/04/20/arts/design/repatriated-works-back-in-their-countries-of-origin.html [Accessed 30 Sept. 2016].

Donegan, T. M. (2000). Is specimen taking of birds in the Neotropics really "essential?" Ethical and practical objections to further collecting. *Ornitologia Neotropica* 11, pp. 263–267.

Filardi, C. (2015a). *Field Journal: Finding Ghosts*. Available at: www.amnh.org/explore/news-blogs/from-the-field-posts/field-journal-finding-ghosts [Accessed 29 Sept. 2016].

Filardi, C. (2015b). *Why I Collected a Moustached Kingfisher*. Available at: www.audubon.org/news/why-i-collected-a-moustached-kingfisher [Accessed 29 Sept. 2016].

Fine-Dare, K. S. (2002). *Grave Injustice: The American Indian Repatriation Movement and NAGPRA.* Lincoln, NE: University of Nebraska Press.

Gallenkamp, C. (2001). *Dragon Hunter: Roy Chapman Andrews and the Central Asiatic Expeditions.* New York: Viking.

Griffiths, J.-M., and King, D. W. (2008). *InterConnections: The IMLS National Study on the Use of Libraries, Museums, and the Internet.* Washington, DC: Institute of Museum and Library Services.

Gropp, R. E. (2003). Are university natural history collections going extinct? *BioScience* 53, p. 550.

Hill, A., et al. (2012). The notes from nature tool for unlocking biodiversity records from museum records through citizen science. In: V. Blagoderov and V. S. Smith, eds., No Specimen Left Behind: Mass Digitization of Natural History Collections. *ZooKeys* 209.

ICOM-CC (2014). *Declaration on Environmental Guidelines.* Available at: www.icom-cc.org/332/-icom-cc-documents/declaration-on-environmental-guidelines/#.V-58sKuvEUU [Accessed 30 Sept. 2016].

International Monetary Fund (2010). *From Stimulus to Consolidation: Revenue and Expenditure Policies in Advanced and Emerging Economies.* Washington, DC: Fiscal Affairs Department, International Monetary Fund.

IWGSC (2009). *Scientific Collections: Mission-Critical Infrastructure for Federal Science Agencies.* Washington, DC: National Science and Technology Council, Committee on Science, Interagency Working Group on Scientific Collections.

Janzen, D. (1991). How to save tropical biodiversity. *American Entomologist* 37, pp. 159–171.

Johnson, K. G., et al. (2011). Climate change and biosphere response: Unlocking the collections vault. *BioScience* 61, pp. 47–153.

Klausner, A. (2015). American scientist tracks down one of the rarest birds in the world and then kills it for "research." *Daily Mail*, 10 Oct. 2015. Available at: www.dailymail.co.uk [Accessed 29 Sept. 2016].

Lake Snell Perry and Associates (2001). *The Engaging Museum: Developing Museums for Visitor Involvement.* Washington, DC: American Association of Museums.

Mares, M. (2009). Natural science collections: America's irreplaceable resource. *BioScience* 59, pp. 544–545.

Mayer-Schönberger, V., and Cukier, K. (2013). *Big Data: A Revolution That Will Transform How We Live, Work, and Think.* New York: Houghton Mifflin Harcourt.

Menninger, H. 2007. Government looks into health of federal science collections. *BioScience* 57, p. 736.

Minteer, D., Collins, J. P., Love, K. E., and Puschendorf, R. (2014). Avoiding (re)extinction. *Science* 344, pp. 260–261.

Neumann, D., et al. (2014). Access and benefit sharing—global implications for biodiversity research, collections, and collection management arising from the Nagoya Protocol. *SPNHC Connection* 28 (2), pp. 40–42.

NIBA (2010). *A Strategic Plan for Establishing a Network Integrated Biocollections Alliance.* Available at: https://digbiocol.files.wordpress.com/2010/08/ niba_brochure.pdf [Accessed 30 Sept. 2016].

Norris, C. A., and Butts, S. (2014). Let your data run free? The challenge of data redaction in paleontological collections. *Collection Forum* 28(1–2), pp. 114–119.

Rainger, R. (1991). *An Agenda for Antiquity: Henry Fairfield Osborn and Vertebrate Paleontology at the American Museum of Natural History, 1890–1935*. Tuscaloosa, AL: University of Alabama Press.

Regal, B. (2002). *Henry Fairfield Osborn: Race and the Search for the Origins of Man*. Burlington, NJ: Ashgate.

Remsen, J. V. (1995). The importance of continued collecting of bird specimens to ornithology and bird conservation. *Bird Conservation International* 5, pp. 145–180.

Rocha, L. A., et al. (2014). Specimen collection: An essential tool. *Science* 344, pp. 844–845.

Rose, C. L., and Hawks, C. A. (1995). A preventive conservation approach to the storage of collections. In C. L. Rose, C. A. Hawks, and H. H. Genoways, eds., *Storage of Natural History Collections: A Preventive Conservation Approach*. Washington, DC: Society for the Preservation of Natural History Collections.

Sangster, G., and Rozendaal, F. G. (2004). Systematic notes on Asian birds. 41: Territorial songs and species-level taxonomy of nightjars of the *Caprimulgus macrurus* complex with the description of a new species. *Zoologische Verhandelingen* 350, pp. 7–45.

Silber, E. (2015). *Moustached Kingfisher Photographed for the First Time*. Available at: www.audubon.org/news/moustached-kingfisher-photographed-first-time [Accessed 29 Sept. 2016].

Skelly, D. K., and Near, T. J. (2016). *Exploration and Discovery: Treasures of the Yale Peabody Museum of Natural History*. New Haven, CT: Yale University Press.

Strang, T., Jacobs, J. J., and Kigawa, R. (forthcoming). Integrated pest management. In: L. Elkin and C. A. Norris, eds., *Preventive Conservation: Collection Storage*. Washington, DC: American Institute for Conservation, George Washington University/Smithsonian Institution/Society for the Preservation of Natural History Collections.

Suarez, A. V., and Tsutsui, N. D. (2004). The value of museum collections for research and society. *BioScience* 54, pp. 66–74.

Tewksbury, et al. (2014). Natural history's place in science and society. *BioScience* 64, pp. 300–310.

United Nations (1992). *Convention on Biological Diversity, Rio 1992*. File No. CH_27_8, Vol. 2, Chapter 27.

Wandler, P., Hoeck, P. E. A., and Keller, L. F. (2007). Back to the future: Museum specimens in population genetics. *Trends in Ecology and Evolution* 22, pp. 634–642.

Wheeler, Q. D., et al. (2012). Mapping the biosphere: Exploring species to understand the origin, organization, and sustainability of biodiversity. *Systematics and Biodiversity* 10(1), pp. 1–20.

Winker, K. (2004). Natural history collections in a postbiodiversity era. *BioScience* 54, pp. 455–459.

Winker, K., et al. (2010). The importance, effects, and ethics of bird collecting. *The Auk* 127(3), pp. 690–695.

Yates, T. L., et al. (2002). The ecology and evolutionary history of an emergent disease: Hantavirus pulmonary syndrome. *BioScience* 52, pp. 989–998.

2 A holistic ethos for nature-focused museums in the Anthropocene

Emlyn Koster, Eric Dorfman, and Terry Simioti Nyambe

It seems evident that the natural history museum has reached a stage in the evolution of its relationship to society where the generally prevailing opportunistic vagueness of intentions is becoming a liability which must be replaced by a well-considered, well-integrated, and well-defined philosophy concerning the museum's place in the general research and educational system.

(Parr, 1959, p. 21)

The Anthropocene represents a new phase in both humankind and of the Earth, when natural forces and human forces became intertwined, so that the fate of one determines the fate of the other.

(Zalasiewicz et al., 2010, p. 2231)

An institution such as a museum has a responsibility to empower the electorate to make informed, scientifically literate decisions about their lives. If in 2050 we were delivering the same messages, either we've failed at affecting change in society and still needed to give those messages, or we just got left behind and we were no longer on the frontier of what mattered in society.

(American Alliance of Museums [AAM], 2011, pp. 50–51).

Museums, in the twenty-first century, loom larger than they ever have before. They are more socially and economically vital, they seek to offer their publics more, and they arguably succeed in doing so in those countries in which they have long been established.

(Thomas, 2016, p. 7)

Relevance

At the start of this century, the Smithsonian Institution's scholar emeritus Stephen Weil coined the phrase "making museums matter" as the title of his much-quoted book (Weil, 2002). This quickly became popular because it resonated with a growing awareness of the challenges and opportunities facing societies and environments, both locally and globally. Yet "the awkward fact remains," he would lament, "that, for a variety of reasons, the museum field has never agreed—and until recently, has scarcely even sought to agree—on some standard by which the relative worthiness of its constituent member institutions might be measured" (Weil, 2006, p. 4). The museum sector had, however, begun to differentiate between those institutions still at ease with internally focused traditions, those striving for a new relevancy-driven approach, and those increasingly immersed in external value contexts (Koster and Falk, 2007). Chronicling the reinvention of philosophies and practices across the museum sector toward more externally valuable paradigms was the two-step selection of influential papers for publication by Anderson (2004, 2012).

For a museum to aspire to its most externally valuable state requires clarity on what being relevant entails in exact terms. Often used, but seldom defined, "relevant" means relating to the matters at hand: clearly, contextual matters require specification. In the twenty-first century, what makes a natural history museum and its kindred institutions (museums of anthropology, nature, nature and science, and the natural sciences—in this chapter, all referred to as "nature-focused museums") maximally relevant is surely their most pivotal undertaking.

Whether the Anthropocene, which was introduced in 2000 (Crutzen, 2002), becomes formalized by the geological profession, it has become a widespread term in many other disciplines and in news editorials and headlines referring to humanity's impacts on natural systems (Robin and Steffen, 2007; *Economist*, 2011; *New York Times*, 2011; *New York Times*, 2012; Carrington, 2016; Yang, 2017). As a pressing matter of accountability, our response in this chapter to the relevancy question is that nature-focused museums should wholeheartedly become resources to illuminate the meaning and implications of the Anthropocene.

The resources that nature-focused museums should arguably be in modern biodiversity and related contexts are analogous to museums in regions with a high-magnitude earthquake or volcanic risk acquainting their communities concerning hazardous phenomena and safety measures. For their part, nature-focused museums have unique expertise and resources to responsibly inform a brighter journey for humanity and nature together (Koster, 2012). Indeed, not to mobilize these attributes would be to marginalize them on the sidelines of the challenges and opportunities that surround life, both human and non-human. Cameron and Kelly (2010) recognized that museums' progress on the societal and environmental fronts is inevitably punctuated by challenging moments that Koster (2010) discussed in his review of the evolution of purpose in science centers and science museums. Encouragement to pursue this direction comes with new book and article titles such as "The Endangered Dead" (Kemp, 2015), "What Museums Are Good for in the 21st Century" (Thomas, 2016), and "Museums as Catalysts for Change" (Rees, 2017).

This chapter reviews the evolving paradigms that surround collections; discusses the contributing factors to our sector's past inertia; explores the

Anthropocene as an encompassing framework for the future; touches on several other related and timely opportunities for the sector; and profiles what a holistic ethos entails in order to advance an institution in the most efficient and effective manner, "to do things right" and "to do the right things," respectively.[1] Several concepts from the business realm are infused into our approach, including generative thinking:

> The most important work that takes place in an organization is when people first begin to identify and discern what the important challenges, problems, opportunities, and questions are... It's the way in which the intellectual agenda of the organization is constructed... The question should be: do we have the problem right?... Generative thinking is getting to the question before the question... It's not about narrow technical expertise.[2]

Evolving collection paradigms

The impetus of collections as the primary raison d'être of museums has been predominant. In a provocative paper entitled "From Being about Something to Being for Somebody...," we learned that "the overwhelming majority of American museums and museum training programs continue to operate as if... collections were still at the center of the museum's concerns" (Anderson, 2012, p. 181). Today, numerous museum collections total in the many millions and, collectively, natural history museums worldwide store about three billion specimens (Wheeler et al., 2012). In this regard, it is noteworthy that science centers that may function without collections have been a source of innovation for the wider museum field (Koster, 1999); specifically fit within the museum definition of, for example, the American Alliance of Museums;[3] and engage with collections-based museums through, for example, the US-based Association of Science Museum Directors.[4]

"Collection" was the keyword in six of the eight sections comprising the worldwide code of ethics for the museum profession (International Council of Museums [ICOM], 2006). The codes for the American Alliance of Museums and the United Kingdom's Museums Association, like other examples, present a similar picture with these statements:

- Museums make their unique contribution to the public by collecting, preserving and interpreting the things of this world. Historically, they have owned and used natural objects, living and nonliving, and all manner of human artifacts to advance knowledge and nourish the human spirit. Today, the range of their special interests reflects the scope of human vision. Their missions include collecting and preserving, as well as exhibiting and educating with materials not only owned but also borrowed and fabricated for these ends.[5]

- Museums enable people to explore collections for inspiration, learning, and enjoyment. They are institutions that collect, safeguard and make accessible artifacts and specimens, which they hold in trust for society.[6]

Declarations of the natural history museum sector from over the last decade are instructive windows into its evolving consciousness and the contextual purpose of its collections:

- 2007, Paris: Representatives from natural history museums and research institutes issued the Buffon Declaration:[7] "Given that science is critical for sustainable management of biodiversity and ecosystems and, through it, survival of human populations on this planet, the vital contributions of these institutions are fourfold: a) They are the primary repositories of the scientific samples on which understanding of the variety of life is ultimately based; b) Through leading-edge research they extend knowledge of the structure and dynamics of biodiversity in the present and the past; c) Through partnerships, and through programs of training and capacity-building, they strengthen the global capability to address current and future environmental challenges; and d) They are a forum for direct engagement with civil society, which is indispensable for helping bring about the changes of behaviour on which our common future and the future of nature depend."
- 2012, Washington, DC: Learning-focused representatives from mainly US natural history organizations issued the following declaration: "Humanity is embedded within nature and we are at a critical moment in the continuity of time. Our collections are the direct scientific evidence for evolution and the ecological interdependence of all living things. The human species is actively altering the Earth's natural processes and reducing its biodiversity. As the sentient cause of these impacts, we have the urgent responsibility to give voice to the Earth's immense story and to secure its sustainable future" (Koster et al., 2012, pp. 22–23).
- 2015, Taipei: The ethical focus of this Declaration on Natural History Museums and Biodiversity Conservation, as noted by Dorfman (2016, p. 56), was to "give back... to the wild populations that have provided their collection objects... A major role of natural history museums is to collect and steward natural history objects, generating knowledge regarding these objects and disseminating this knowledge to the community. Natural history museums also engage the public to form deep bonds with the natural world and commit to its preservation. Increased human activities have caused catastrophic declines in biodiversity. Both ethics and logic point to a mandate to conserve vulnerable habitats and species. To achieve best practices, natural history museums take action to conserve natural habitats and populations" (ibid.).

The concluding sentences of the Taipei declaration approach the baseline concept in this chapter's purpose—namely, that nature-focused museums illuminate the meaning and implications of the Anthropocene. With respect to the checklist of questions to achieve progress with conservation efforts posed by Miller and colleagues (2004), Dorfman (2016, pp. 56–57) noted:

> the natural history museums sector has not yet made great strides towards adopting conservation action as an industry standard, despite the exceptional work undertaken by some institutions.

In her assessment of conservation, museums, and codes of ethics, de Roemer (2016, p. 249) opened with this statement: "Less a matter of differences rather than of interconnectivity, the lines of what defines the museum, what is the role of conservation and the nature and extent of their relationship, are blurred." In concluding, she observed, "conservation and museums are interlinked; questions of which came first are, however, of less significance than the recognition of their shared purpose and values" (ibid., p. 263).

Illegal wildlife trade, itself a massive and harrowing global issue, has been poignantly reviewed by the United Nations (2014), and is a developing focus of ICOM's Committee for Museums and Collections of Natural History (ICOM NATHIST Wildlife Trafficking Working Group, 2016). How collections are most appropriately integrated into exhibitions also demands diligent consideration. This applies most acutely to human remains, around which intercultural respect with multilingual presentations is imperative, as is the need to construct narratives surrounding identity, partnering authentically with indigenous peoples on the conservation, interpretation, and display of their heritage (Alberti et al., 2008; Torsen and Anderson, 2010; Dorfman, 2016). For instance, the National Taiwan Museum collaborated with the island's indigenous Atayal and Paiwan tribes to revitalize and celebrate traditional weaving and glass techniques, both re-creating traditional motifs and carrying the art forward with modern interpretations (Li, 2014). In New Zealand, the Whanganui Regional Museum worked closely with local Māori communities to research, restore, and interpret the region's treasures in a groundbreaking exploration of material culture and intangible heritage (Horwood and Wilson, 2008).

Overcoming inertia

The persistent traditional separation in museums between a collections and research priority and a secondary educational function began to be tackled a quarter century ago in a widely-circulated benchmark publication (AAM, 1992). While the dichotomy has diminished, differential funding often continues to be an issue in terms of connections with academia, salary scales, and operating funds.

Another fundamental, but clearly related question, is why museums have been hesitant to shift the time frame of their missions from a virtually sole focus on the past. We contend that adding the present-into-the-future time frame to the familiar past-until-the-present time frame reflects new influences on the community-building potential of museums (AAM, 2001) and escalating anxieties over humanity's environmental impacts (Koster, 2010). With contexts of social responsibility more common than environmental responsibility, this trend had some early prescient moments but has accelerated since the 1990s as the following highlights make clear:

- Quoting John Dana from the early 1900s, "Learn what aid the community needs [and] fit the museum to those needs" (Peniston, 1999, p. 16). As Koster (2016, p. 235) noted, the use of needs rather than wants was a visionary new kind of calling on the museum's sense of its external responsibilities.
- The "introverted focus has engendered the belief that artifactual collections are the 'reason for being' for museums, rather than a tool through which we gain and disseminate knowledge" (Duckworth, 1993, p. 15).
- "Almost all of the great natural history museums emerged in late 19th-century cities under the lengthening shadow of the Victorian paradigm of ascending progress... The urgency of the vulnerability of natural and cultural systems have transformed the nature of our interests in them... What is the outcome and use of our research and interpretative programs?... Most visitors have little or no tangible contact or comprehension of the ecosystem they live in and depend on" (Sullivan, 1992, pp. 41–43).
- Quoting Harold Skramstad, "Increasingly, the mission statement of a museum, its essential statement of value-added, is going to have to contain not only a concise and clear statement of what the museum does, but a sense of the value that this outcome has in the larger work of the community in which it serves. If there is nothing unique and special about its work and the value of this work in solving a problem in peoples' lives, then so what? What's the point?" (Weil, 1997, pp. 13–14).
- "Now is the time for the next great agenda of museum development. This agenda needs to take as its mission nothing less than to engage actively in the design and delivery of experiences that have the power to inspire and change the way people see the world and the possibility of their own lives... This will not be an easy task. It will require change in focus, organization, staffing, and funding for museums" (Skramstad, 1999, p. 125).
- "To be sure, museums remain showcases for collections and repositories for scholarship, but they have also become pits of popular debate... They are no longer places where people look on in awe but where they learn and argue."[8]
- "In an era where budgets are tight... Museums provide a necessary service to scientists and the public by housing specimens in a long-term

stable environment, providing specimens and data for research, education and public outreach, and working to develop new technologies to track speciation, biodiversity, and environmental change, just to name a few" (Watters and Siler, 2014, p. 21).

- In reviewing Rader and Cain (2014), Johnson writes: "the book ends in 2005, with both natural history museums and science centers seen as trusted, articulate voices grappling with new and evolving challenges. Science literacy has been vastly complicated by a growing antiscience movement. The urgent issues of preserving biodiversity, mitigating climate change, and promoting cultural diversity are driving some museums to take on additional roles such as conservation, advocacy, and inclusion" (2015, p. 618).

The evolution of conscience in nature-focused museums has helped set the stage for their agenda of relevance in the Anthropocene. However, since the future cannot be collected per se, the question arises as to how nature-focused museums can meaningfully illuminate the Anthropocene in a future-oriented time frame. A starting point is a rigorous reflection on museum practice with a view to engaging audiences in current scientific debates, an example being the research partnership between the Carnegie Museum of Natural History and the University of Pittsburgh (Steiner and Crowley, 2013). The recent *Welcome to the Anthropocene* temporary exhibition at the Deutsches Museum used this approach: "in keeping with [our] tradition... displays of historic and contemporary objects from the fields of science and industry bring the topic to life, while installations encourage active participation from the visitors' (Möllers et al., 2015, p. 6). At the Smithsonian's National Museum of Natural History, a discussion series entitled "Anthropocene: Life in the Age of Humans," including topics such as "Imagining the Human Future: Ethics for the Anthropocene" and "Evolution and the Anthropocene: Science, Religion, and the Human Future,"[9] is en route to becoming a planned new exhibition. "This provocative exhibit will focus on the Anthropocene, the slice of Earth's history during which people have become a major geological force... Alongside the typical displays of *Tyrannosaurus rex* and *Triceratops*, there will be a new section that forces visitors to consider the species that is currently dominating the planet... We want to help people imagine their role in the world, which is maybe more important than many of them realize."[10]

Into the Anthropocene

While the geological debate continues surrounding the pros and cons of different dates for the Anthropocene, with some expressing the view that "the formalization should not be rushed" (Ellis et al., 2016), its value as a catalyzing force for new approaches at nature-focused museums and across society has emerged in the form of ominous alarms (Janes, 2009; Purdy, 2015).

The Anthropocene represents the best available frame of reference for engaging society in planet Earth's best possible future (Koster, 2016). It prompts us to illuminate the past, present, and future of the human journey in an ecological framework with natural systems. Especially welcome, therefore, is the 2017 conference theme of ICOM's Committee for Museums and Collections of Natural History, which is "The Anthropocene: Natural History Museums in the Age of Humanity."[11]

The Anthropocene draws attention to the array of human-caused, generally intensifying, changes in each of the outer concentric shells of the Earth System: all are also affected by pollution. Here are their recent key dimensions:

- Atmosphere—decreasing ozone, increasing carbon dioxide, climate warming, and weather extremes
- Hydrosphere—ocean current changes, summertime Arctic Sea ice loss, snow cover and glacier ice reduction, sea level rise, coral bleaching, and river flow regime changes
- Biosphere—ecosystem disruptions, reduced biodiversity, invasive species, extirpations, extinctions, and trafficking
- Pedosphere—paving over of soil, deforestation, farmland loss, and tundra melting
- Lithosphere—nuclear waste disposal, hydraulic fracturing, dewatering, and geological hazards in increasingly populous areas

Due to the high news volume regarding average weather trends, climate implications, and coastal inundation, the evidently changing dynamics between the atmosphere and the hydrosphere tend to dominate public attention, but the others are no less important to grasp, try to mitigate, and present to museum audiences. Here's an example: ahead of Elizabeth Kolbert's (2014) book *The Sixth Extinction: An Unnatural History*, the *New York Times* (2012, p. 5) published a pictorial tally of life under threat based on an evaluation by the International Union for Conservation of Nature on the ability of 52,025 species to survive. The most confident data was for birds, with 99 percent of known species assessed and 13 percent, or 1,253, threatened; for mammals, with 85 percent assessed and 25 percent, or 1,138, threatened; and amphibians, with 70 percent assessed, and 41 percent, or 1,017, threatened. For reptiles with 29 percent of species assessed, 772 were listed as threatened, and for fishes, 2,028, or 23 percent, were listed as threatened. An accompanying article by Pearson (2012, p. 5) emphasized that vibrant ecosystems are essential for human survival. Although the above data are distressing, the overall picture worsens considerably when the analysis of Tedesco et al. (2014) is included: they estimated the proportions of species in several understudied taxonomic groups that went extinct before they were described as between 15 and 59 percent. In his keynote address to an ICOM congress almost three decades ago, cultural critic Neil Postman[12] opined that "a good museum will always direct attention to what is difficult and painful to contemplate" (Postman, 1989, p. 40).

The interdependence of virtually all the Earth's shells is behind the additional, and instructively encompassing, terms "ecosphere," which refers to all areas occupied by life, and "technosphere," which denotes the realm of human technological activity. In their overview of the history of life, Williams et al. (2015) summarized several "fundamental stages": a microbial stage starting 3.5 billion years ago, a metazoan phase beginning 650 million years ago, and a modern biosphere dominated by Homo sapiens, including human-directed evolution of other species and increasing interaction between the biosphere and the technosphere. Summing up, they remarked that in:

> an intertwined biosphere and technosphere... [the] anthropogenic influence would be responsible for a lasting change in the Earth System, initiating a new trajectory for the biosphere that could last over geological timescales.
>
> (Williams et al., 2015, p. 18)

On an uplifting note, the Anthropocene also provides a transdisciplinary framework for science literacy at all ages and stages of learning. The drawback of so-called Science, Technology, Engineering and Mathematics (STEM)—that surged in popularity over the last decade is that it emphasizes separate traditional disciplines while excluding others that are also fundamental (for example, art, the humanities, medicine), rather than innovative pedagogies toward realizing an encompassing purpose. This acronym would, therefore, be more powerfully used in the manner of the North Carolina Science, Technology, and Mathematics Education Center, which is "Strategies That Engage Minds."[13] In a similar vein, David Skorton, secretary of the Smithsonian, recently remarked:

> The traditional scientific method has been wonderfully successful. Modern life is indebted to it. However, the method has proven less successful on its own in solving some of society's more complex and seemingly intractable problems, such as poverty, hunger, lack of education, social justice, access to health care and in economic equality—all problems that require close listening, emotional distancing, weighing of arguments and counter arguments—and direct participation of those affected by the issues... one of the most effective ways is to do so through the arts and humanities... It has been said that science helps us understand what we can do; the arts and humanities—our culture and values—help us decide what to do. Studying the arts and humanities develops critical-thinking skills and nimble habits of mind, provides historical and cultural perspectives and fosters the ability to analyze, synthesize and communicate... In my new role as secretary of

the Smithsonian, I am learning quickly the leading role museums and other cultural institutions can play in our communities, the country and the world, and how they can affect and stimulate discourse and action.

(AAM, 2016, pp. 40–42)

On the matter of the natural and human sciences, Van Praët (2015, pp. 8–9) observed that these two fields "should now come together again to address the current societal issues of humankind's relationship with nature and our complex relationship with the living world." As much as the Anthropocene concept helps museums to integrate prehistorical, historical, contemporary, and forward-oriented contexts, the Big History concept creates a long view— actually, a very long view all the way back to the Big Bang—of natural and human history as one continuous story.[14] This approach has been advanced by historian David Christian[15] and promoted by philanthropist Bill Gates.[16] It deserves inclusion in nature-focused museums because society has great conceptual difficulty with the expanses of geological and astronomical time frames. Big History also fosters society's grasp of anthropology's increasingly detailed apprehension of the prehuman to human evolutionary transition,[17] and of the transformative overview experience of planet Earth by astronauts (Beaver, 2016).

Condensing the almost 14 billion years since the Big Bang into one calendar year has the Solar System forming in early September, and condensing the 4.6 billion years of Earth's history has all human history squeezed into the last minute before midnight on December 31. The Big History approach helps greatly to link the more familiar—human history and very recent prehistory—with the widely unfamiliar, and in many quarters the unbelieved or rejected, course of Earth and pre-Earth history. From the standpoint of nature-focused museums, Big History helps to bring all of nature and humanity into one holistic perspective: clearly, all feasible progress in this regard is vital.

There are several other big-picture concepts that arguably need to infuse thinking and action in nature-focused museums:

- The Sustainable Development Goals of the United Nations[18] represent a bold cooperative approach to realizing progress with regard to the world's largest societal and environmental challenges. Each goal, as agreed upon in 2015, has aspirational targets to be achieved by 2030. Entitled "Transforming Our World: The 2030 Agenda for Sustainable Development,"[19] the noble intentions of cooperating countries are focused on five areas: people, planet, prosperity, peace, and partnership. The second summary statement reads: "We are determined to protect the planet from degradation, including through sustainable consumption and production, sustainably managing its natural resources and taking urgent action on climate change, so that it can support the needs of the present and future generations." UNESCO's 2016 World Science Day for Peace and Development[20] called upon science museums and science centers to align their efforts with the United Nation's Sustainable Development Goals (UN SDGS), while the 2017 Science Centre World Summit to be hosted by Japan's National Museum of Emerging Science and Innovation has a "Connecting the World for a Sustainable Future" theme.[21]

- The Triple Bottom Line approach[22] was introduced in 1994 by the founder of a British consultancy firm called SustainAbility. Advocating that sustainable decisions need balanced attention to three bottom lines—people (referring to social responsibility), planet (referring to environmental responsibility), and profit (referring to feasibility and growth)—the concept has proven difficult to quantify. It does, however, offer an important reminder that organizations should take a long-term perspective to consider the future consequences of decisions. Nature-focused museums could decide to seek support from corporations that subscribe to this approach preferentially.

- *Blue Ocean Strategy* (Kim and Mauborgne, 2015) describes an approach contrary to conventional profit motives. It advances the notion of "uncontested market space," of which the Cirque de Soleil[23] is often cited as a prime example. Formed in 1984 in Quebec, the group innovatively reinvented the traditional attributes of a circus, with artistic performers replacing trained animals. Its success, along with this year's news that two circuses are ending their 146-year run[24] and that a marine park is ending its orca performances,[25] comports with the belief "in a better future for all living things" by the Association of Zoos and Aquariums,[26] and which envisions "a world where all people respect, value, and conserve wildlife and wild places." How nature-focused museums can best leverage the refreshing principles of a blue ocean strategy is an evocative question for our field.

- Concerned that "civilization is revving itself into a pathological short attention span," the Long Now Foundation[27] was established in 1996 "to become the seed of a very long-term cultural institution; [it] hopes to provide a counterpoint to today's accelerating culture and help make long-term thinking more common... in the framework of the next 10,000 years."

Related opportunities

Koster (1999) discussed several emerging facets of science and natural history museums, including new approaches to engaging audiences in the research process and collections, through exhibitions and dialogues, and through applications of child development psychology. Almost twenty years later, the following statement seems more pertinent than ever to both science and nature museums: "There is a growing recognition that [they] do not need to have all the answers on a given subject in order to present an illuminating experience to the public... It seems eminently preferable to open minds by offering partial insights than it is to fill minds with an authoritative account—or to fail entirely to address a subject' (ibid., 289). He concluded: "The challenge facing the museum field, both in science centers and elsewhere, is to create compelling experiences on subjects of importance in ways that increasingly attract society to view museums as engaging resources for lifelong learning" (ibid., 294).

In the second decade of the twenty-first century, there are new areas such as the four introduced below that beckon the attention of nature-focused museums:

- More than ever, children must be our audience focus in prekindergarten, school, and family settings—onsite, offsite, outdoors, and online. That the traits of scientific inquiry are baked into our mental DNA from evolutionary survival needs was emphasized by Gopnik et al. (1999). Today there are annual conferences of the Children and Nature Network[28] and the Natural Learning Initiative,[29] and the focus of Sampson (2015), a science communication specialist, is the art and science of falling in love with nature.
- Connecting adults to nature, outside, is another worthy focus of our institutions and a movement spurred by several new books. A journalist has explored how nature makes us happier, healthier, and more creative (Williams, 2017) and, striking a similar note, Selhub and Logan (2012) are naturopathic doctors who reviewed the science of nature's influence on our health, happiness, and vitality.
- Citizen science is a surging movement that is likely the best route for society at large to directly engage in the challenges and opportunities of the Anthropocene. In 1990, a Canadian physicist envisioned: "The task of the future is to build knowledge and understanding among and between citizens and scientists, so that the distinction between the two groups vanishes—so that both become citizen scientists, potentially able to solve our problems together" (Franklin, 1990, p. 268). Today, the movement is professionally supported by numerous websites,[30] television documentaries,[31] and several associations that hold annual or biannual conferences; the newest book on the subject (Cooper, 2016) was reviewed by the *Washington Post*.[32]
- Evolutionary medicine raises the specter of a new, more informed, type of doctor-patient relationship to elucidate the personal relevance of human evolution. "Evolutionary medicine poses a fundamentally new kind of question about disease. Instead of only asking how bodies work and why some people get sick, evolutionary medicine also asks why natural selection has left all of us with traits that make us vulnerable to disease. Why do we have wisdom teeth, narrow coronary arteries, a narrow birth canal, and a food passage that crosses the windpipe?

Evolution explains why we have traits that leave us vulnerable to disease, as well as why so many other aspects of the body work so well. For instance, the usual question about back pain is why it afflicts some individuals. Evolutionary medicine also asks why back problems have been a problem for all hominid species since they first walked on two legs."[33] Furthermore, it sheds light on interdisciplinary collaborations across all aspects of health care for humans, animals, and the environment.[34]

Toward a holistic ethos

Building upon Korn's (2013) advocacy for holistic intentionality, the core conclusion of this chapter is that the maximized relevance of a nature-focused museum is enabled by its holistic ethos. That is, the museum's traditional collections-based code of ethics is insufficient as the needed compass for nature-focused museums in the Anthropocene. Going forward, not only is the salience of collections undiminished but in fact, they are of ascending significance given the substantial loss of prehuman biodiversity and the substantial ongoing human interference with natural systems. In the nature-focused museum of the future, all parts of the institution need their contributing voice to be heard in a completely integrated and holistic manner.

In mainline dictionaries, ethos is defined as the characteristic spirit of a culture or community as manifested in its beliefs and aspirations, the underlying sentiment that informs the beliefs, customs, or practices of a group or society. Ethics is defined as a branch of philosophy dealing with what is morally right or wrong, a system of moral principles, and an area of study that explores ideas concerning good and bad behavior. A code of ethics for museums—as set forth by the American Alliance of Museums and the International Council of Museums, with added emphasis by the North Carolina Museum of Natural Sciences on the needed duality of environmental and societal contexts—would be a single document describing museums' commitment to putting the interests of society and the environment ahead of the interests of the institution or any individual; as a cornerstone document, it sets forth standards for professional practice and accountability.

Along these lines, the approach to an encompassing code of ethics taken by the North Carolina Museum of Natural Sciences[35] (the institution for which the first author is the director) is offered as an example. Its outlook is rooted in the State's motto from 1893—*Esse quam videri*, "To be, rather than to seem": in modern parlance and from an ethical perspective, these words match the idiom of "walking the walk." This stance is reinforced by North Carolina itself as an instructive crossroads of nature (Earnhardt, 2013). Stretching from Cape Hatteras, where the Gulf Stream swings northeastward toward Europe, to the almost seven-thousand-foot-high Mount Mitchell along the Appalachian drainage divide, North Carolina ranges from subtropical to subalpine with habitats including many unique features in global biodiversity terms. Although a state museum, the North Carolina Museum of Natural Sciences' research, collections, and education horizons are necessarily national and global in scope. In 2014, post-expansion, the institution adopted "To illuminate the interdependence of nature and humanity" as its mission statement and "What do we know?" "How do we know?" "What is happening now?" and 'How can the public participate?" as its propelling questions. Spurred by a sense that a museum's mission statement should feel like the institution's beating heart, the museum's approach to its 2016 Code of Ethics was mindful of the above-noted 2007 and 2012 nature-focused museum declarations in Paris and Washington, DC, as well as emerging trends in the museum field captured by such conversational phrases as "Safe places for difficult ideas," "From nice to necessary," and "From indifference to indispensability." This institution views the geological past as the key to the present and the future; regards whole Earth thinking as a mindset to help narrow the gap between humanity and nature in the reality of one biosphere; and embraces the Anthropocene as its best conceptual framework for long-range approaches. The museum expresses its public value as advancing the forefront of knowledge regarding the dynamic world of nature in statements addressing, among others: the need to make data collection and scientific research accessible to schools and the public; the goal of providing experiences for all ages and backgrounds to be immersed in nature; the objective of enabling quality family time in engaging and meaningful ways; the desire to eliminate accessibility barriers to those with disabilities; and the wish to engage the public in global sustainability issues. The Code of Ethics then lays out the contributing responsibilities of each governing body and each organizational section with these statements:

- Through the Director's Office, the institution's entire team, functioning holistically and attentive to local, regional, national and global needs, exemplifies the greater potential of nature and science museums by expanding resources for the institution, demonstrating its unique public value, and helping to advance the field as a whole through sharing of best practices.
- The Resource Administration team oversees the resource needs of the institution, staff, and visitors by managing its portfolio of business services, including human resources, budgets and grants, information technology, and facility and security services in close cooperation with state government, universities, and other partners.
- The Research and Collections team increases knowledge and insight into the natural world by collecting, preserving, and documenting specimens and objects, conducting original research, making data and results available and accessible to the broader scientific community and the public, and inviting society's participation in collections and research opportunities.

- The Living Collections team enhances awareness and understanding of the animal world by maintaining, displaying, and interpreting a healthy living collection; promoting conservation; enhancing the visitor experience through integrated approaches to exhibitions, onsite, and offsite programs; and advancing the fields of animal husbandry and wildlife veterinary medicine.
- The Exhibits and Digital Media team propels the institution's collections, research, and programs to the forefront of public knowledge and enjoyment by developing and maintaining an engaging array of interpretive experiences and media that address the learning styles of a diverse public and the changing knowledge regarding natural and cultural environments.
- The School and Lifelong Education team engages all ages and backgrounds by creating and delivering a menu of engaging and inspirational learning experiences onsite, offsite, online, and outdoors to assist with the understanding and appreciation among students, teachers, and the public of the natural sciences, the natural world, and humanity's relationship to it.
- The Community Engagement team maximizes the institution's positive external impacts by understanding, attracting, welcoming, involving, engaging, and re-engaging traditional and nontraditional audiences via a scheduled menu of topical programs and events, excellent and inclusive visitor service, and effective marketing and communications strategies.
- The Regional Network team connects communities statewide with the natural world by developing and maintaining programs, services, partnerships, and learning areas geared to the needs of each region and providing administrative oversight and program optimization for the state's science museums grant program.
- The Development team, integrating the institution and its supporting Friends organization, manages and grows contributed revenues by linking the internal array of supportable activities with external sources of government, corporate, foundation, and individual support, in turn, building member and donor loyalty and the institution's capacity to advance its mission.

The North Carolina Museum of Natural Sciences, since 2015 a division of the state's Department of Natural and Cultural Resources,[36] has recently completed its decadal reaccreditation by the American Alliance of Museums. A gratifying outcome is that the alliance's report concludes: "the museum has forthrightly evolved its interpretative philosophy and strategy to address bigger stories about humans as an inseparable element in the ecosystem of all life, and therefore to be concerned about matters of conservation and sustainability."

Conclusions

As Koster (2016, p. 237) pointed out:

> In hindsight, the first mission of Apollo and introduction of the Anthropocene should have bracketed a period of profound introspection, reflection and inspiration across the nature and science museum sector. This was a powerful opportunity to manifest the founding *raison d'être* of the museum from The Muses in Greek mythology... For nature and science museums, the odyssey of their evolution since Apollo's transformative photographs of Planet Earth to today's serious calling to be resources for societal and environmental needs in the Anthropocene has become a journey in which the 'right conduct' [as in the core definition of ethics] has become unequivocally clear.

Having advocated in 2007 that "the search for greater relevance should never cease" (Koster and Schubel, p. 119), Koster in 2010 (p. 90) emphasized that three facets of institutional culture should be in place:

> The first concerns mission and vision—is there a clear and firm commitment to be of value to the societal and environmental problems we face? The second concerns leadership—is there a preparedness to be an activist? The third concerns strategy—is there a relentless pursuit to be more externally useful and to nurture new perspectives in funding stakeholders.

In the Anthropocene, nature-focused museums should not only aspire toward our sector's most valuable contributions to date in direct response to the intertwined needs of societies and environments but also become an exemplar of what relevance means to the entire museum profession.

Acknowledgments

The authors gratefully acknowledge their respective, and in many cases overlapping, networks of international colleagues with whom their ideas have germinated and who have cumulatively informed elements in many of the background concepts in this chapter. We are also grateful for the editorial comments on a draft of this chapter by Joanne DiCosimo, former Director of the Canadian Museum of Nature; Lucy Laffitte, a board member of the International Big History Association; and Jason Cryan and LuAnne Pendergraft of the North Carolina Museum of Natural Sciences, respectively, its chiefs of Research and Collections and of Community Engagement.

Notes

1 https://johnfrederickabueva.wordpress.com/2012/10/11/doing-the-right-things-vs-doing-things-right-ethics-blog-3/.
2 http://hbswk.hbs.edu/archive/4735.html.

3 www.aam-us.org/about-museums.
4 www.asmd.org/Home/SitePage/3#.
5 www.aam-us.org/resources/ethics-standards-and-best-practices/code-of-ethics.
6 www.museumsassociation.org/ethics/code-of-ethics.
7 www.bfn.de/fileadmin/ABS/documents/BuffonDeclarationFinal%5B1%5D.pdf.
8 www.economist.com/news/special-report/21591707-museums-world-over-
   are-doing-amazingly-well-says-fiammetta-rocco-can-they-keep.
9 www.smithsonianmag.com/science-nature/your-guide-all-things-anthropocene-
   180960599/.
10 www.nature.com/news/anthropocene-the-human-age-1.17085.
11 https://icomnathist.wordpress.com/conference-2017/.
12 https://en.wikipedia.org/wiki/Neil_Postman.
13 www.ncsmt.org/about/smt-center/.
14 https://en.wikipedia.org/wiki/Big_History.
15 https://en.wikipedia.org/wiki/David_Christian_(historian); www.ted.com/talks/
   david_christian_big_history.
16 https://www.nytimes.com/2014/09/07/magazine/so-bill-gates-has-this-idea-
   for-a-history-class.html?_r=0; https://www.bighistoryproject.com/home.
17 https://www.nytimes.com/2017/01/11/magazine/neanderthals-were-people-
   too.html?_r=0.
18 http://www.un.org/sustainabledevelopment/sustainable-development-goals/.
19 https://sustainabledevelopment.un.org/post2015/transformingourworld.
20 http://www.un.org/en/events/scienceday/.
21 https://scws2017.org/.
22 http://www.economist.com/node/14301663.
23 https://en.wikipedia.org/wiki/Cirque_du_Soleil.
24 https://www.nytimes.com/2017/01/14/us/ringling-bros-and-barnum-bailey-
   circus-closing-may.html?_r=0.
25 http://www.dailymail.co.uk/news/article-4098292/SeaWorld-San-Diego-ending-
   killer-whale-show.html.
26 https://www.aza.org/.
27 http://longnow.org/about/.
28 https://www.childrenandnature.org/about/nature-deficit-disorder/.
29 https://naturalearning.org/about-us.
30 https://scistarter.com/.
31 https://www.youtube.com/watch?v=qvjDp93eiSo.
32 https://www.washingtonpost.com/opinions/have-a-scientific-passion-become-
   a-citizen-scientist/2017/01/27/647e8a22-dcc9-11e6-918c-99ede3c8cafa_story.
   html?utm_term=.50581f068e40.
33 http://www.randolphnesse.com/whatisevolutionarymedicine.
34 http://www.onehealthinitiative.com/about.php.
35 http://naturalsciences.or.
36 https://www.ncdcr.gov/.

References

AAM (1992). *Excellence and Equity: Education and the Public Dimension of Museums.* Washington, DC: American Association of Museums.
AAM (2001). *Mastering Civic Engagement: A Challenge to Museums.* Washington, DC: American Association of Museums.
AAM (2011). The future is in the stars: An interview with Neil deGrasse Tyson. *Museum*, pp. 47–51.
AAM (2016). What do we value? *Museum*, pp. 38–43.

Anderson, G., ed. (2004). *Reinventing the Museum: Historical and Contemporary Perspectives on the Paradigm Shift*. Lanham, MD: AltaMira Press.

Anderson, G., ed. (2012). *Reinventing the Museum: The Evolving Conversation on the Paradigm Shift*. Lanham, MD: AltaMira Press.

Beaver, D. (2016). The case for planetary awareness: How the new space age will profoundly change our worldview. *Space Times* 2(55), pp. 4–11.

Cameron, F., and Kelly, L., eds. (2010). *Hot Topics, Public Cultures: Museums*. Newcastle-upon Tyne: Cambridge Scholars.

Carrington, D. (2016). The Anthropocene epoch: Scientists declare dawn of human-influenced age. *Guardian*, 29 Aug.

Cooper, C. (2016). *How Ordinary People Are Changing the Face of Discovery*. New York: Overlook Press.

Crutzen, P. (2002). The geology of mankind. *Nature* 425, p. 23.

de Roemer, S. (2016). Conservation: How ethics work in practice. In: B. Murphy, *Museums, Ethics, and Cultural Heritage*. New York: Routledge.

Dorfman, E. (2016). Ethical issues and standards for natural history museums. In: B. Murphy, *Museums, Ethics, and Cultural Heritage*. New York: Routledge.

Duckworth, D. (1993). Museum-based science for a new century. In: *Research within the Museum: Aspirations and Realities*. Taichung: National Museum of Natural Sciences.

Earnhardt, T. (2013). *Crossroads of the Natural World: Exploring North Carolina*. Chapel Hill, NC: University of North Carolina Press.

Economist (2011). Welcome to the Anthropocene, 26 May.

Ellis, E., Maslin, M., Boivin, N., and Bauer, A. (2016). Involve social scientists in defining the Anthropocene. *Nature* 540, pp. 192–193.

Franklin, U. (1990). *Planet under Stress: The Challenge of Global Change*. Royal Society of Canada. Toronto: Oxford University Press.

Gopnik, A., Meltzoff, A., and Kuhl, P. (1999). *The Scientist in the Crib*. New York: HarperCollins.

Horwood, M., and Wilson, C. (2008). *Te Ara Tapu: Sacred Journeys*. London: Random House.

ICOM (2006). *ICOM Code of Ethics for Museums*. Washington, DC: International Council of Museums.

ICOM NATHIST Wildlife Trafficking Working Group (2016). *Natural History Museums and Wildlife Trafficking: A Framework for Global Action; A White Paper*. Washington, DC: International Council of Museums, Committee for Museums and Collections of Natural History / Denver Museum of Nature and Science.

Janes, R. (2009). *Museums in a Troubled World: Renewal, Irrelevance or Collapse?* New York: Routledge.

Johnson, K. (2015). Surrounded by science. *Science* 347(6222), p. 618.

Kemp, C. (2015). The endangered dead. *Nature* 518, pp. 292–293.

Kim, W. C., and Mauborgne, R. (2015). *Blue Ocean Strategy*. Cambridge: Harvard Business Review Press.

Kolbert, E. (2014). *The Sixth Extinction*. New York: Henry Holt.

Korn, R. (2013). Creating public value through intentional practice. In: C. Scott, ed., *Museums and Public Value: Creating Sustainable Futures*. Burlington: Ashgate, pp. 31–43.

Koster, E. (1999). In search of relevance: Science centers as innovators in the evolution of museums. *Daedalus* 128, pp. 277–296.

Koster, E. (2010). Evolution of purpose in science museums and science centers. In: F. Cameron and L. Kelly, eds. *Hot Topics, Public Culture: Museums*. Newcastle-upon-Tyne: Cambridge Scholars, pp. 76–94.

Koster, E. (2012). The relevant museum: A reflection on sustainability. In: G. Anderson, ed., *Reinventing the Museum: The Evolving Conversation on the Paradigm Shift*. Lanham, MD: AltaMira Press.

Koster, E. (2016). From Apollo into the Anthropocene: The odyssey of nature and science museums in an external responsibility context. In: B. Murphy, ed., *Museums, Ethics, and Cultural Heritage*. New York: Routledge.

Koster, E., and Falk, J. (2007). Maximizing the usefulness of museums. *Curator: The Museum Journal* 50(2), pp. 191–196.

Koster, E., and Schubel, J. (2007). Raising the relevancy bar in aquariums and science centers. In: J. Falk, L. Dierking, and S. Foutz, eds., *In Principle, In Practice*. Lanham, MD: AltaMira Press.

Koster, E., Watson, B., and Yalowitz, S. (2012). Natural history: Past, present, future. *Informal Learning Review*, pp. 22–24.

Li, T.-N., ed. (2014). *Rainbow and Dragonfly: Where the Atayal Clothing Meet the Paiwan Multi-Colored Glass*. Taipei: National Taiwan Museum.

Miller, B., et al. (2004). Evaluating the conservation mission of zoos, aquariums, botanical gardens, and natural history museums. *Conservation Biology* 18, pp. 86–93.

Möllers, N., Schwägerl, C., and Trischler, H. (2015). *Welcome to the Anthropocene: The Earth in Our Hands*. Munich: Deutsches Museum / Rachel Carson Center.

New York Times (2011). The Anthropocene, 7 Feb., p. A22.

New York Times (2012). Are we in the midst of a sixth mass extinction? 3 June, p. 5.

Parr, A. (1959). *Mostly about Museums*. New York: American Museum of Natural History.

Pearson, R. (2012). Are we in the midst of a sixth mass extinction? Opinion. *New York Times*.

Peniston, W. (1999). *The New Museum: Selected Writings of John Cotton Dana*. Washington, DC: Newark Museum Association/American Association of Museums.

Postman, N. (1989). Extension of the museum concept. In: *Museums: Generators of Culture*, Washington, DC: International Council of Museums.

Purdy, J. (2015). *After Nature*. Cambridge, MA: Harvard University Press.

Rader, K. A., and Cain, V. E. M. (2014). *Life on Display*. Chicago: University of Chicago Press.

Rees, M. (2017). Museums as catalysts for change. *Nature Climate Change* 7, pp. 166–167.

Robin, L., and Steffan, W. (2007). History of the Anthropocene. *History Compass* 5, pp. 1694–1719.

Sampson, S. (2015). *How to Raise a Wild Child*. Boston: First Mariner.

Selhub, E., and Logan, A. (2012). *Your Brain on Nature*. Toronto: HarperCollins.

Skramstad, H. (1999). An agenda for America's museums in the twenty-first century. *Daedalus* 128, pp. 109–128.

Steiner, M. A, and Crowley, K. (2013). The natural history museum: Taking on a learning agenda. *Curator: The Museum Journal* 56(2), pp. 267–272.

Sullivan, R. (1992). Trouble in paradigms. *Museum News*, pp. 41–44.

Tedesco, P. A., Bigorne, R., Bogan, A. E., Glam, X., Jézéquel, C., and Hugueny, B. (2014). Estimating how many undescribed species have gone extinct. *Conservation Biology* 28(5), pp. 1360–1370.

Thomas, N. (2016). *The Return of Curiosity*. London: Reaktion.

Torsen, M., and Anderson, J. (2010). *Intellectual Property and the Safeguarding of Traditional Cultures: Legal Issues and Practical Options for Museums, Libraries, and Archives*. Geneva: World Intellectual Property Organization.

United Nations (2014). *Illegal Wildlife Trade*. Geneva: UN Chronicle, Outreach Division, Department of Public Information, vol. 11, p. 2.

Van Praët (2015). Museums sounding the alarm. *ICOM News*, pp. 3–4.

Weil, S. (1997). Introduction. In: *Museums for the New Millennium*. Washington, DC: Smithsonian Institution / American Association of Museums.

Weil, S. (2002). *Making Museums Matter*. Washington, DC: Smithsonian Institution Press.

Weil, S. (2006). Beyond management: Making museums matter. *ICOM Study Series 12: International Committee on Management*, pp. 4–8.

Watters, J., and Siler, C. (2014). Preliminary quantification of curator success in life science natural history collections. *University of Oklahoma Journal of Museum Studies* 8(1), pp. 21–33.

Wheeler, Q. D., et al. (2012). Mapping the biosphere: Exploring species to understand the origin, organization, and sustainability of biodiversity. *Systematic Biodiversity* 10, pp. 1–20.

Williams, F. (2017). *The Nature Fix*. New York: Norton.

Williams, M., et al. (2015). The Anthropocene biosphere. *Anthropocene Review* 2(3), pp. 1–24.

Yang, W. (2017). Is the "Anthropocene" epoch a condemnation of human interference— or a call for more? *New York Times*, 14 Feb.

Zalasiewicz, J., Williams, M., Steffen, W., and Crutzen, P. (2010). The new world of the Anthropocene. *Environmental Science and Technology* 44, pp. 2228–2231.

3   Natural history museum security

Hanna Pennock

Many of the risks that natural history museum collections currently face, and will face in the future—fire, water, theft, vandalism, natural disasters, and war—have always been present. It is the professional staff, the architects, and the designers of exhibitions that must ensure the safety and security of the museum, including its collections, the inventory of the collections, the visitors, staff, and buildings. When a museum decides on a new acquisition, the costs for its safety and security should be considered as a matter of course. Protection is neither an easy nor a glamorous task: it requires awareness, a good organization as well as discipline. And it requires funding for constructional and electronic preventative measures. The results are not visible in everyday museum life, and therefore an often heard complaint of heads of security is that their directors are not willing to spend on prevention. Yet the costs of a disaster are much higher than the expenses for prevention. Safety and security should be an essential and logical part of museum management.

An early example that refers to the safety and security of a museum can be found in the Netherlands, where, in the late nineteenth century, the Department of Arts and Sciences of the Ministry of Internal Affairs required that the state museums put on paper their fire regulations. The response of the director of the Museum Meermanno-Westreenianum, the oldest museum of books in The Hague, is kept in the National Archives of the Netherlands. In a risk analysis avant la lettre, he argued that there was no need to do so since the museum held no combustibles and was connected to the fire brigade. Besides, he had so few staff that separate instructions were not deemed necessary. Around the same time, Lindor Serrurier, director of the National Museum of Ethnology in Leiden, wrote a pamphlet that bore the telling title, *Museum or Midden?*, showing that in 1895 care for collections was as much of an issue as it is today.

The two world wars made abundantly clear that collections can be heavily damaged. For instance, in 1914 a fire caused by German soldiers destroyed the University Library of Leuven, Belgium. During air raids in the Second World War, the London Natural History Museum was hit several times. Although large parts of the collection had been evacuated, specimens and books in the

Botany Department were harmed or destroyed. In the Netherlands, Rembrandt's large painting *The Night Watch* in the Rijksmuseum was rolled up and evacuated from the museum to a bunker in the dunes on the North Sea coast. To protect cultural heritage, both movable and immovable, in times of war and occupation, United Nations Educational, Scientific and Cultural Organization (UNESCO) States Parties in 1954 in The Hague signed the Convention for the Protection of Cultural Property in the Event of Armed Conflict. Two protocols were added later that year and in 1999. By protecting cultural heritage, history is protected—the history of people and the history of mankind.

Nowadays, The Hague Convention is not universally adhered to in, for example, countries like Syria, where cultural heritage sites or even World Heritage sites such as Palmyra have been severely damaged. In 2016, the International Criminal Court condemned a jihadi leader to nine years in prison for the destruction of ancient mausoleums in Timbuktu, Mali (Bowcott, 2016; UNESCO, 2016). This was the first time that a person was sentenced for a crime against cultural heritage under the jurisdiction of The Hague Convention.

The many disasters that have affected museums and their collections make clear that disaster planning is not a luxury. Wars and bombs are not the only causes of a fire. In 2014, the Museum of Natural History in New York was evacuated when a maintenance worker with a blowtorch caused an air conditioning unit to catch fire. Fire can represent a devastating risk for museums, as happened in 2016 when the entire collection of the National Museum of Natural History in New Delhi was lost in a fire, the cause of which was an aging built infrastructure. Even a small blaze can have enormous consequences for a collection when it is extinguished with water, especially when compounded by a layer of soot with all its aggressive chemical components that have settled on objects and the walls and interior of the (historical) building.

Many other forms of damage to or loss of museum collections exist. The International Council of Museums (ICOM) Code of Ethics is clear: museums should take care of the health and safety of personnel and visitors; they should protect the public, personnel, collections, and other resources against natural and human-made disasters; and should ensure appropriate security to protect the collections (ICOM, 2013a). In the 1970s, especially in the context of ICOM and its International Committee on Security (ICMS), the first extensive books on museum security were published (for example, Tillotson, 1977). With the professionalization of museum management, preservation, and conservation, many further handbooks, guidelines, best practices, and publications on risk assessment and risk analysis have been published in print and online. In the last decades, the level of professionalization in disaster preparedness has developed, not only for the safety of staff and visitors but also for museum buildings and collections. Almost twenty years ago, only three out of twenty privatized state museums in the Netherlands had some measures concerning the safety and security of their collections (Pennock, 2000). Nowadays, that is 100 percent, and Naturalis in Leiden, the Netherlands' largest natural history museum, is one of them.

In many ways, natural history museums face the same risks for their collections as, say, art museums. In daily practice, objects can be damaged by handling or during transport. Visitors can bump into an object or remove a piece of it—a tooth, a feather, part of an installation—as a souvenir. Almost all museums keep valuable objects that can be attractive to thieves, and their collections are vulnerable to water damage, fire, vandalism, alongside sector-specific concerns, like the materials that make up the specimen, conservation methods that were used in the past, or the inflammable liquids in which specimens are prepared.

Security is all about awareness, both now and in the future. Museums must think about threats, do regular assessments to identify risks, work out scenarios, and draw up a policy and plans for risk preparedness and mitigation. A fully integrated risk management plan is focused on the organizational, constructional, and electronic measures, as well as on people, buildings, and collections. It is not a separate, isolated branch of the organization, but entirely a part of museum management. The level of preventive measures differs from museum to museum around the world, regardless of the composition of their collections. When ICMS undertakes risk assessments for museums, they are often found to be up to standard with their protection measures. However, it is not uncommon to find fire escape doors that are blocked or even locked, glass break detectors that have fallen into the display case, dangerous electrical installations, key boxes accessible by the public, or display cases with valuable objects that are not locked at all. Despite the large availability of informative publications on risk management, a considerable number of museums lag behind. Their organizational structure may be weak, or they must contend with old buildings, inadequate storage spaces, or malfunctioning electronic systems.

Old-fashioned organizations

In 1996, the National Museum of Ethnology in Leiden came out with the breaking news that 50,000 objects were missing, comprising fully one-quarter of the collection. This had partly to do with the registration of incoming collections. The museum, founded in 1837, had collections in its inventory that were inscribed in the nineteenth century but had never arrived, going instead to the Rijksmuseum in Amsterdam. Other items had been thrown away, being so deteriorated that they were considered a total loss. Deaccessioning procedures had not at that time been instituted.

The main cause of the loss, however, was the easy access to storage rooms that were open to staff and researchers. Of the 1,000-strong collection of netsuke (carved button-like ornaments, typically of ivory or wood, worn in Imperial Japan to suspend articles from the sash of a kimono), 124 were gone. These precious Japanese miniature sculptures represented an enormous sum. Being small, they were easy to abscond with—ironically, such a grouping is sometimes referred to as a "pocket collection": objects that are small enough to be hidden in one's pocket and removed unseen. Thanks to a massive subvention program, the Delta Plan for the Preservation of Cultural Heritage, the Museum of Ethnology and the other state museums in the Netherlands have been able to review their collections and registration, as well as improve the conditions of their collection stores, storage practices, preservation, and safety measures.

The importance of good record keeping cannot be overstated. Like other types of institutions, natural history museums provide physical access to the collection to a variety of researchers both from within and outside the facility (for example, from universities). Objects are, at times, even allowed to be taken to a researcher's home for study. Naturalis in Leiden has received bequests from researchers or former employees many years after retirement. They donate or leave their research collections to the museum—and, not uncommonly, museum staff recognizes items that come from the museum itself.

Natural history museums that still work in this way, giving easy access to the collections without keeping proper documentation, are at risk if they do not bring their collection management up to a minimum standard, starting with organizational measures. Achieving best practice requires instituting procedures for strictly limited access to the storage rooms. When objects must leave the museum for study purposes, they should be loaned out using a formal process, following accepted guidelines. In many cases, this will require a change of culture within the organization and toward its internal and external stakeholders.

The trend of showing more of the collections by means of open or visible storage can only be welcomed with open arms. Since only a very small proportion of a collection is typically on display, museums welcome opportunities to present more to the public. Open storage does not necessarily mean, however, that the museum opens the doors of the storage spaces to receive the public. In cases where this does occur, it must be as part of a guided tour for a restricted number of people. Otherwise, as is often the case, museums can install an exhibit to look like a storage room, giving it the same level of security as other types of exhibitions. The presentation of the items must always be done with care—a sloppy display with dusty objects gives the impression that security will not be in order, either (Figure 3.1).

Making collections accessible also means digitization, augmenting objects with high-quality imagery as documentation. With the enormous quantities of specimens that most natural history museums keep, often numbering in the many millions, this is a decades-long procedure for museums just beginning the process. If a museum is operating on public funds, it is only logical that its collections become available to the public and specialists

Figure 3.1 A sloppy display gives the impression that security will not be in order, either. Photo by Hanna Pennock.

online, as open and complete as necessary. The ICOM Code of Ethics for Natural History Museums states: "All natural heritage materials held within our institutions, and the related information about them, should be considered to be in global custodianship rather than the sole property of the institution in which such material resides" (ICOM, 2013b, p. 6).

Open access to collection data can, however, be considered a risk. To withhold information for reasons of safety of the collection does not seem necessary nor ethical. As a safety measure, data on a storage location, as well as other sensitive information, do not need to be included online. Detailed information in the inventory must also be protected against hacking and misuse, and a regular backup should be stored outside the museum in a safe place.

Theft

Theft is one of the main risk areas for natural history museums. The specimens they preserve can be appealing to collectors or souvenir hunters, or have an (unexpected) economic value outside the museum walls. Do natural history museums prize their collections as they should? Are they sufficiently aware of the risks that they face now, and, as the black market grows, in the future? Past prices fetched for a rare species, such as the Indo-Pacific predatory marine snail, the wentletrap (*Epitonium scalare*), are examples of the way the market can change quickly. In the seventeenth and eighteenth centuries, the wentletrap was rare in Europe and considered of considerable value for its beautiful, elegant spiral form and porcelain-like appearance.

In the early seventeenth century only three specimens were known, from the collections of Cosimo III de' Medici in Italy, of Johan de la Faille in the Netherlands, and of an unknown British collector. Throughout this period, they were a coveted specimen for curiosity cabinets, and enormous prices were paid to obtain one (Dance, 1969; Grout, 2016). In a way, this history can be compared to the tulip mania in the Dutch Golden Age, when the value of bulbs of the then recently introduced tulip went sky-high and even became the subject of economic speculation (Dash, 1999).

Many specimens of high financial worth are commonly found in natural history museums: commodities such as pearls, precious stones and minerals, fossils, meteors, precious metals, horns, and ivory, as well as specimens from species that have now become extinct, and artifacts once owned by a famous person. In housing specimens that are valuable on the black market, natural history museums are no different from other types of museums, and these objects will always be attractive to thieves.

Specific value may also come with technological developments. Cloning a bull from a carcass from the slaughterhouse, as occurred for the first time in 2012 in the West Texas A&M University's Department of Agricultural Sciences (Robertson, 2015), raises questions concerning the future value— to both mainstream and black markets—of specimens, and associated genetic material, in natural history collections. Will cloning become possible using dead genetic material and bring extinct species back to life, like the dodo, the passenger pigeon, or even the dinosaur? The utility of natural history specimens from natural history collections for medicine, or even biological warfare, also offers potential and risk. It behooves natural history museums to follow closely the developments in scientific research that might be linked to their collections and be aware of the risks they may bring, attendant with the possibilities.

As the world population continues to grow and control of seed production is in the hands of a relative few, seeds in natural history collections could become increasingly valuable as a means of creating new types of food that are easily produced. Other genetic sources held in natural history collections could be of great value for the production of food, medicines, cosmetics, clothing, or industrial applications. If they are difficult or impossible to find in nature, as natural habitats are increasingly destroyed, or the use or transportation is restricted by national legislation or international regulations, such as the 1992 Convention on Biological Diversity or the 2010 Nagoya Protocol, collection material could become important for illegal use with commercial or criminal purposes.

In its pursuit of health and happiness, humanity resorts to sources it thinks will cure disease or improve the quality of life. In the 1640s, the Dutchman Adriaen van der Donck, living in New Amsterdam (now Manhattan), calculated that every year eighty thousand beaver pelts were shipped to the fur market in Europe. Not only their fur was used; since ancient times, it was believed that beaver testes had miraculous medicinal qualities (Shorto, 2004).

When species become unavailable in the wild, or when poaching becomes more difficult because of armed protection, thieves turn to natural history museums as an easy place to steal. In recent years, at least twenty rhinoceros horns have been pilfered from natural history museums, most of them linked to a group of Irish Travellers, the Rathkeale Rovers. One kilo of horn is estimated to fetch about $50,000 on the black market (Big Life Foundation, 2012). In some Asian countries, the material, the same keratin as found in horses' hooves or human fingernails, is thought to cure cancer and all sorts of other diseases.

Since 2009, rhino horns have been stolen from museums in South Africa, Ireland, Germany, Portugal, Spain, Italy, England, Belgium, Austria, France, Sweden, and the Netherlands—in January 2014 alone, sixty-seven rhino horn thefts had taken place across fifteen European nations (Higginbotham, 2014). It is quite a surprise, then, that after all these dramatic burglaries, again in 2015 rhino horns were stolen from several Italian museums. Between January and September of that year, five museums, mostly university collections, were broken into for their rhino horn, all but one of which were successful. Among the loot were horns with long histories, dating back to the seventeenth and eighteenth centuries.

Pangolins, snakes, sea turtles, the gallbladder of a bear, the bones of tigers or lions, the ivory tusks of elephants—along with many other species and parts of animals—are said to have healing properties in the traditional medicines of a number of regions. Once these species are nearing extinction and forbidden to hunt, thieves will very likely turn to museums. The belief in the magical powers will not easily be erased, even if, for example, research indicated that the qualities of the horns of the still-common saiga antelope, water buffalo, and cattle are comparable to those of rhino horn as an antipyretic remedy (Pui-Hay But et al., 1990). Other species will be added to the list of medicinal qualities. In the future, museums will need to be increasingly aware of the (illegal) market and the attractiveness of certain parts of animals. An active information network for early warning and detection will strengthen the natural history museum community's ability to stay ahead of perpetrators.

As repeatedly happens in museums, libraries, and archives, internal theft seems to be an eternal problem. Commodities such as those mentioned above, in addition to historical archives and plates in books—items with a great financial value outside the museum or on the black market—can also be stolen by staff, or by researchers who are considered internal, and therefore trusted (Phys. Org, 2016). Internal theft seems to be a difficult subject to tackle, but must be addressed. When a colleague is found to have been stealing over a long period, it comes as a shock to the staff. They feel utterly betrayed and may even need counseling. Only strict measures and clear procedures can prevent internal theft, as well as an open culture in which staff feels free to address possible problems regarding the management of the museum and its collections. When it comes to problems in their personal situation, in particular, financial debts, the head of the department or the human resources department should be made aware of such situations in the lives of employees and seek solutions.

A curious risk, related specifically to staff, also exists surrounding research on collection items. Many scientists, whose life work has been in and around the collections they have stewarded, continue to undertake research into retirement. In many cases, they must continue to handle collection items, possibly reaching them via a stepladder or by taking other risks to access them. For the safety of both the objects and the researchers themselves, only people who are physically and mentally able should handle collections. Despite a natural reluctance to be disrespectful, institutions should provide proactive assistance where a risk is evident.

Large-scale disasters

With climate change destabilizing global weather patterns, the possibility of large-scale disasters befalling museums becomes an increasing reality. In certain parts of the world, hurricanes, tornadoes, or tsunamis bring enormous damage; in other parts, it can be earthquakes, floods, or heavy rain showers that threaten museum collections. The complete destruction in 2011 of Japan's Rikuzentakata City Museum serves as a stark reminder of the reality of these dangers.

Museums should take these threats into account in their disaster plans, checking the specific risks of the area in which they are situated. Museums should connect with their local fire department, water board, and/or conservancy and other rescue and information services appropriate to their region and circumstances. Those responsible for collection security should also prepare in advance a list of priorities for the collection that must be evacuated if there is time. In the case of flooding, it can often be enough to vacate items to a higher floor within the building, or to a higher neighboring building.

The necessity of a proper registration of the collection, and use of appropriate storage materials can be acute when it comes to water damage, be it from flooding, a leak, or fire extinguishing. For instance, an archaeological museum that was flooded had the inventory numbers on stickers glued upon the objects or their container. All the stickers were soaked off by the water; the loss of information meant that the archaeological objects had completely lost their value (pers. obs.). The loss of original information in ink on natural history specimens or the paper on which they are written could also contribute to a similar dissociation of objects from their data.

Business continuity is as much a necessity for museums as it is for commercial organizations. Fires and floods, earthquakes and tsunamis, conflicts and wars are serious threats not only to the collection but also to the continuity of the museum. An economic crisis, lack of funding, or lack of political or public interest could force a museum to close its doors or to change its policy drastically as a more public-oriented institution. Research could be put on hold, curators could be let go, and the collection put on standby, all in favor of outreach to the public, with the goal of generating income. For scientists, countering this risk requires an understanding of how to communicate the value of what they do in readily understandable language. While this is not always the easiest to accomplish, relevance is frequently insurance against neglect.

Another aspect of this issue is that, to enlarge their income, museums are increasingly prone to organizing exhibitions that attract large numbers of visitors. Blockbusters with an enormous influx of visitors bring their own risks and ask for crowd control (Keller and Associates, Inc., 1993, 1994). Several strategies can be employed to manage the largest visitor densities. These include selling tickets in time slots in advance and extending opening hours. The design of the exhibit also plays an important role, with a smooth and clear routing, a large enough space to move and to see the exhibits, clear indications of escape routes, and avoidance of congestion all desirable aspects. Starting an exhibition with an introductory text on the wall, for example, can cause an obstruction right away in the first room. Visitors' behavior typically involves looking closely, and for a longer time at the beginning of an exhibit, so more space and larger items are needed in the first galleries. Good training of the security staff—uniformed and visible—is, as always, a sine qua non. If there are queues outside the museum, indications must be clear. Visitors can be welcomed with information and the possibility of asking questions to staff that manage the lines. The visit and the experience of an exhibit start at home, though, with a well-informed website or messages through social media.

The continuity or at least the reputation of a museum can also be threatened by matters of ownership and claims. A fierce debate emerged in relation to the Cesare Lombroso Museum of Criminal Anthropology in Turin, Italy, more than one hundred years after Lombroso presented his nineteenth-century positivist criminological theories. It started around the remnants of a *brigante* (brigand), Giuseppe Villella from Calabria, in Southern Italy. In 1871, when race theories were developed, and the supposed superiority of one race over the other was being "proven," Lombroso published the findings of his research on a skull said to be Villella's. He stated that deviances in the latter's skull constituted the proof of criminal "primitive" behavior. Such eugenic theories are long past, and the museum's collection of human skulls and prototypes of "criminals" should be seen in the historical light of nineteenth-century positivist science.

Although the Lombroso Museum is careful not to espouse Lombroso's conclusions, in 2010 a movement arose against this promulgation of racism against Villella and Southern Italy in general. The website www.NoLombroso.org was created, claiming that Lombroso was, in fact, the criminal. A case was subsequently mounted and won, and the remains of Villella are, at the time of writing, to be returned to his native village, where they will be buried. The no-Lombroso campaigners' claim that the museum should be closed has, thus far, been to no avail. Whatever the outcome, this activist story shows that human remains in a museum collection, or specimens with a contested history, can evoke strong reactions that put the museum in a bad light or even on the brink of forced closure.

It is not only humans who invoke public scrutiny. The beloved figure of the teddy bear is related to the famous 1902 story of President Theodore Roosevelt who, at a bear hunt, is said to have refused to shoot a bear that was tied to a tree especially for him. Five years later, though, he did shoot a Louisiana black bear (a species now protected, at least for the time being). Roosevelt, who had a passion for nature, collected animals that he killed himself and had them prepared, to be donated to the American Museum of Natural History (AMNH, 2017).

Collection items with such a specific history, connected to a famous figure like Roosevelt or a scientist like Lombroso, can arouse fury in later periods, when attitudes toward nature, science, social justice, or history are completely different. While a century ago shooting was perceived as a heroic act of man mastering wild animals and nature, today wildlife is perceived by many as something to cherish and protect.

Another contested history related to Roosevelt and the AMNH concerns indigenous peoples, as seen when a demonstration was organized around his equestrian statue at the west entrance of the museum. The statue shows the president on horseback with a Native American and an African American beside him. The sculpture and the museum itself were the focus of the "Decolonize This Place Tour" on Columbus Day in October 2016. Over two hundred people demonstrated and called for the removal of the statue, after which a tour brought the demonstrators into the museum, through galleries that were also perceived as problematic (Vartanian, 2016). This is an example of how public outrage can be turned directly against an institution that is perceived to be acting unethically. Although in many cases, the stories and perspectives promulgated by a museum have been inherited by the current staff and leadership, it behooves natural history museums to be cognizant of the public's tenor and the zeitgeist. An in-house ethics committee, with broad community representation, also helps in understanding community needs and expectations.

Negative publicity can be a risk with severe consequences for museums. The Internet and social media can very quickly transform the stories surrounding even a small provincial museum into international news. When something happens in a museum during opening hours, the information can be disseminated through Twitter or other media by a visitor, even before the staff is aware. Especially when the news is accompanied by a photo or video, it can be shared and viewed by many in a short time. In such cases, the museum is no longer ahead of the story and is forced to do damage control. A press release comes too late; the museum must be prepared and use the same communication channels to maintain control of the image that is set.

A damaging story has the power to compound a difficult situation by reducing visitation, making it difficult to lend objects or receive loans, affect accreditation in countries where it exists, and even affect a museum's ability to obtain funding. Being response ready for media stories should be part of a museum's standard operations. Strict standards and procedures pertaining to the media are needed, particularly in challenging times: every message that goes out should be controlled, a single spokesperson should be appointed, and staff should not talk with the press nor send tweets, posts on Facebook, or messages through other means. Only factual information should be shared when responding to the media concerning a disaster or other negative story if necessary tailored in cooperation with the appropriate authorities.

Technology

Security technology will only improve in the decades to come. Advanced early warning systems will buy museums time to put in place their safety measures. Smart cameras, smart digital systems, digital key systems, and robotics will be refined and increase in precision. Surveillance in larger areas can already be achieved with drones equipped with cameras, linked to cameras and sensors. They can intercept communication signals and recognize faces (European Drone Convention, 2016). They can also be a threat, however, when they enter the airspace unauthorized and the operator is not known (Florjanowicz, 2016).

Developments in psychology and in recognizing human behavior will facilitate predictive profiling, a method of threat assessment that stems from airplane protection. Techniques of identifying indicators of intent are improving quickly with the help of experience and camera imagery of attacks. In addition, a burglar's preparatory visits to reconnoiter a situation, for example, studying the location of an object intended for later theft, can be recognized through predictive profiling. Staff must be trained to be alert to such unusual behavior, and learn how to address this preventively by making contact with this visitor. By simply having a casual chat, the visitor knows he or she has been seen and will be discouraged to continue with the plan.

Whatever the level of sophistication surveillance instruments will attain, the following will always ring true: they are useless if there is no adequate follow-up. Even if we have robots, behind them will always be the need for staff members or outsourced services to monitor the systems and ensure the right interventions. Yet a caveat is in order here: the newest technologies can create a false sense of security. A risk assessment must always lie at the basis of decisions, and often simple, organizational, and pragmatic measures prove to be the best solution.

Technology for presenting collections will develop as well, using new digital techniques such as three-dimensional scans, virtual reality, and augmented reality to enhance the experience of the visitor. As these techniques diminish the need to put originals on show, they can be a way to spare collection items at risk of theft or damage by exposure. At the same time, with the advancement of digital realities, the need for authenticity, for seeing the real objects and specimens, will only grow; the museum of the future will surely continue to exhibit original specimens.

With the refinement of the technology, new ways of creating replicas will arise—as will new ways of creating forgeries. For example, fossils can already be reproduced near to real using three-dimensional scanning and printing. New techniques also allow clever combinations of different "new species" to be fabricated out of unrelated specimens and presented to science (for example, the infamous story of "Archaeoraptor" (Rowe et al., 2001). Certainly, the technology of creating three-dimensional objects from two-dimensional photographs is improving all the time. In the future, natural history museums will have to rethink their policies surrounding photographs, or go the way of the Smithsonian Institution and others and publish three-dimensional scans of their objects free of charge and copyrighted on the web.

Developments in technology also bring better opportunities to retrieve stolen objects. Systems for tracking and tracing objects become smaller and lighter, and could be useful for high-value objects in the museum. The quality of analyzing Deoxyribonucleic acid (DNA) traces continues to improve, increasing the possibility to determine the identity of perpetrators. Museum staff at a crime scene must therefore always be alert to avoid erasing potentially helpful traces (Hekman, 2010).

Legislation and ethics

International laws and regulations such as the 1992 Convention on Biological Diversity, the 2010 Nagoya Protocol, import and export regulations, and the 1973 Convention on International Trade in Endangered Species of Wild Fauna and Flora have a direct and binding impact on natural history museums. These regulations can complicate the administration of loans of specimens and other collection items, requiring considerable paperwork when specimens are transferred from one institution to another, especially across borders. In the future, many nations can be expected to strengthen protection of their rights to specimens found within their territories, not only on ethical grounds of cultural patrimony character but for the very real economic potential of new discoveries. The movement of specimens to become part of an overseas museum collection may become the subject of increased regulation and potentially limit research and specimen exchange. When these regulations are not adhered to or incompletely understood, a further risk is that collection items may be seized, confiscated, or even destroyed by customs officials.

Conversely, natural history museums are often asked to provide research and advice when customs confiscate material of dubious origin. Because court cases can be lengthy, host museums often spend sizable resources housing them in appropriate conditions for what can be long periods. If in the end, the objects are earmarked for permanent confiscation or destruction, an ethical question arises as to whether the museum, which has invested resources in housing the object, should be allowed to keep it. While ethical guidelines exist, questions like these highlight the intersection between ethics and risks to business continuity and reputation.

Risks within the collection

The specimens themselves can sometimes present risks to those working in collections. Some plants and amphibians can be harmful if touched. Fossils and other geological objects can release harmful particulates as they are being worked on. Of greater concern are allergens or pathogens that cannot be seen, and might not be anticipated. These include fungal spores present in soils, including commercially available potting mix, remnants of pesticides in samples of wood and other plant material, as well as minerals that can emanate radioactive radiation or are composed of heavy metals.

Now, as in the past, chemicals are used in the preparation of biological specimens (Havermans, 2012, 2015). Currently outdated, some former conservation methods are highly poisonous, and specimens prepared with these techniques will remain toxic forever, polluting the air and posing a hazard when inhaled or swallowed. A prime example is a use of arsenic in taxidermy, widely popular from the eighteenth until the late twentieth century to preserve the material and prevent pest attacks (Marte et al., 2006). A century or more after preparation, arsenic dust can still be released from a taxidermy specimen in the form of minute crystals. No less poisonous than when the specimen was originally mounted, these crystals pose a serious hazard if ingested or inhaled.

In several countries, mercuric chloride is still used in the paper to preserve botany specimens and protect them from pests and molds. This chemical, which causes kidney damage and is a possible human carcinogen, can be found in the specimens, in the paper, in the collection boxes, and in the air around a herbarium collection. Formaldehyde and naphthalene are used to prepare insects and protect them from pest damage. Storage rooms are sprayed against pests, a practice that is now forbidden in most countries because of potential risks to human health.

In large natural history collections, these issues are not incidental. The collections are kept in enormous quantities, and so the risks for the people working with them are commensurate. Good ventilation, clear procedures, and strict discipline are the only healthy way of dealing with them. Naturalis in Leiden has written a list of Occupational Health and Safety Regulations for the staff, dividing the collections into "no risk," "low risk," and "high risk." Special attention, for example, is paid to young women working with the collection who might be pregnant and need to be excluded from working in some storage areas that pose specific risks. Research into conservation technologies to minimize these risks is ongoing, and solutions are underway that will assist future generations of museum workers (Havermans, 2012, 2015). Until then, museum management and staff must take precautions in working with the collections that include sound systems and good training.

Conclusions

The world is changing. As it does, risks that natural history museums face will grow and, in some cases, change along with it. Museums that are nimble enough to improve and adapt to changing conditions will be well-placed to continue their missions. For the most part, the fundamental character of the risks that natural history museums face now will not change in the future. Large-scale natural disasters such as floods, heavy rain, earthquakes, tsunamis, hurricanes, and tornadoes will probably occur with more frequency than before, as a consequence of anthropogenic climate change. However, the incidence of extreme weather and climate events has increased in recent decades, and good preparation will increasingly mean readiness for multiple weather events. While these pressures are similar to those experienced by other organizations inhabiting large buildings, the responsibility of collection stewardship means that additional measures are needed.

As pressures in the world at large increase and technology drives new opportunities for biospeculation, the risk of theft of collection items or parts of specimens will increase, whether internal, from the outside or a combination of both. Natural history museums must be aware of developments outside its walls, knowing the market value of specimens that they have in their collection and taking action to secure especially sensitive material.

Perhaps, in this changing world that spreads before us, the biggest risk to natural history museums is the loss of the perception of relevance in the eyes of the public. Although natural history museums have the capacity to contribute to developing answers for many of the world's most pressing sociocultural and environmental problems—spread of disease, loss of ecosystem goods and services, declining biodiversity, issues of social diversity, and inclusion, literacy, wildlife crime—museums' voices must be heard if they are to have a seat at the table and maintain sufficient resources to keep them functioning. Attaining recognition for their relevance goes beyond simply good marketing and promotion (although these are important). It also means being purposeful about speaking the authentic language of their varied stakeholders, understanding that one size does not fit all and ensuring that knowledge is always accompanied by humility. The risks in the future of natural history museums will always be easier to manage when accompanied by a strong bond with the community.

Acknowledgments

I thank René Dekker and Christel Schollaardt from Naturalis, Leiden, and Wouter Hijnberg, Helicon Conservation Support, Alphen aan de Rijn, for their highly valuable information. Many thanks go as well to Eric Dorfman for his critical eye and support.

References

Big Life Foundation (2012). *The Animals of Amboseli: Market Value*. Available at: https://biglife.org/on-the-ground/the-animals-of-amboseli-market-value [Accessed 4 Jan. 2017].

Bowcott, O. (2016). ICC's first cultural destruction trial to open in The Hague. *Guardian*. Available at: www.theguardian.com/law/2016/feb/28/iccs-first-cultural-destruction-trial-to-open-in-the-hague [Accessed 30 Nov. 2016].

Dance, S. P. (1969). *Rare Shells*. Berkeley and Los Angeles, CA: University of California Press.

Dash, M. (1999). *Tulipomania: The Story of the World's Most Coveted Flower and the Extraordinary Passions It Aroused*. New York: Three Rivers Press.

European Drone Convention (2016). *Security and Surveillance*. Available at: www.droneconvention.eu/security-and-surveillance.html [Accessed 7 Jan. 2017].

Florjanowicz, P. (2016). *Some Aspects of Protecting the Martyrdom Museums in Poland: Abstract*. ICMS Annual Conference, Milan 2016. Available at: http://network.icom.museum/fileadmin/user_upload/minisites/icms/pdfs/2016_Abstracts_of_presentations.pdf [Accessed 7 Jan. 2017].

Grout, J. (2016). Epitonium scalare Linnaeus 1758. *Encyclopaedia Romana*. Available at: http://penelope.uchicago.edu/~grout/encyclopaedia_romana/aconite/wentletrap.html. [Accessed 3 Jan. 2017].

Havermans, J. B. G. A. (2012). *Mercury and Other Contaminants in Natural History Collections*. Lecture for Centre for Environment and Sustainability, GMV Chalmers / Göteborgs Universitet. See also online presentation (2015). Available at: www.arbeidshygiene.nl/-uploads/files/insite/havermans-18maart.pdf [Accessed 4 Jan. 2017].

Hekman, W., ed. (2010). *ICMS Handbook on Emergency Procedures*. Available at: http://icom.museum/uploads/tx_hpoindexbdd/ICMS_Handbook_eng.pdf [Accessed: 27 Nov. 2016].

Higginbotham, A. (2014). The Irish Clan behind Europe's Rhino-Horn Theft Epidemic. *BloombergsBusinessweek*. Available at: www.bloomberg.com/news/articles/2014-01-02/the-irish-clan-behind-europes-rhino-horn-theft-epidemic [Accessed 7 Jan. 2017].

ICOM (2013a). *ICOM Code of Ethics for Museums*. Available at: http://icom.museum/the-vision/code-of-ethics/ [Accessed 27 Nov. 2016].

ICOM (2013b). *ICOM Code of Ethics for Natural History Museums*. Available at: http://icom.museum/the-vision/code-of-ethics/code-of-ethics-for-natural-history-museums/ [Accessed 27 Nov. 2016].

Keller, S. R., and Associates, Inc. (1993, 1994). *Museum Crowd Control*. Available at: www.architectssecuritygroup.com/Consulting/Articles_and_Downloads_files/CrowdControl.PDF [Accessed 4 Jan. 2017].

Liston, D. (1993). *Museum Security and Protection: A Handbook for Cultural Heritage Institutions.* London: Routledge. Available at: http://icom.museum/fileadmin/user_upload/pdf/Guidelines/guidelinesdisasters_eng.pdf [Accessed 4 Jan. 2017].

Marte, F., Pequignot, A., and Von Endt, D. W. (2006). *Arsenic in Taxidermy Collections: History, Detection, and Management.* Available at: https://repository.si.edu/bitstream/handle/10088/8134/mci_Collections_Forum_2,_2006.pdf?sequence=1&isAllowed=y [Accessed 4 Jan. 2017].

Pennock, H. (2000). *Het risicobeheer in 20 verzelfstandigde rijksmusea: Een inventarisatie.* The Hague: Cultural Heritage Inspectorate. Available at: www.erfgoedinspectie.nl/publicaties/rapport/2000/03/01/het-risicobeheer-in-twintig-verzelfstandigde-rijksmusea [Accessed 27 Nov. 2016].

Phys.org (2016). *French Museum Employee Sold Stolen Fossils Online.* Available at: http://phys.org/news/2016-12-french-museum-employee-sold-stolen.html [Accessed 4 Jan. 2017].

Pui-Hay But, P., Lai-Ching, L., and Yan-Kit, T. (1990). *Ethopharmacology of Rhinoceros Horn. I: Antipuretic Effects of Rhinoceros Horn and Other Animal Horns.* Department of Biology and Chinese Medicinal Material Research Centre, The Chinese University of Hong Kong. Available at: www.sciencedirect.com/science/article/pii/037887419090005E [Accessed 4 Jan. 2017].

Robertson, T. (2015). *Calves Mark Second Phase of WTAMU Cloning Project.* West Texas A&M University, WTAMU News. Available at: http://wtamu.edu/news/calves-mark-second-phase-of-wtamu-cloning-project.aspx [Accessed 7 Jan. 2017].

Rowe, T., et al. (2001). Forensic palaeontology: The Archaeoraptor forgery. *Nature* 410, pp. 539–540.

Shorto, R. (2004). *The Island at the Centre of the World: The Untold Story of Dutch Manhattan and the Founding of New York.* London: Doubleday.

Tillotson, R. G. (1977). *Museum Security/La Sécurité dans les Musées.* ICMS, London/Wisbech (Balding + Mansell). See also International Council of Museums. *Guidelines for Disaster Preparedness in Museums,* pp. 13–14. Available at: http://icom.museum/fileadmin/user_upload/pdf/Guidelines/guidelinesdisasters_eng.pdf [Accessed 4 Jan. 2017].

UNESCO (2016). *Timbuktu Trial: "A Major Step towards Peace and Reconciliation in Mali."* Available at: www.unesco.org/new/en/media-services/single-view/news/timbuktu_trial_a_major_step_towards_peace_and_reconciliati/ [Accessed 30 Nov. 2016].

United States National Park Service. *NPS Museum Handbook, Part I: Museum Collections.* Available from: www.nps.gov/museum/publications/MHI/mushbkI.html [Accessed 27 Nov. 2016].

Vartanian, H. (2016). *Hyperallergic: "DecolonizeThisPlace Demands Removal of Natural History Museum's Roosevelt Statue."* Available at: http://hyperallergic.com/329225/decolonizethisplace-demands-removal-natural-history-museums-roosevelt-statue/ [Accessed 3 Jan. 2017].

4 The future of research in natural history museums

Frank Howarth

Introduction

It continues to surprise me how many times people say to me that they don't know that natural history museums actually do research. As recently as 3 April 2016 Richard Conniff wrote in the *New York Times*:

> visitors may go there (to natural history museums) to be entertained, or even awestruck, but they are often completely unaware that curators behind the scenes are conducting research into climate change, species extinction and other pressing concerns of our day. That lack of awareness is one reason these museums are now routinely being pushed to the brink.
>
> (Conniff, 2016)

In this chapter I will look at the overarching trends that shaped the development of natural history museums with a focus on the impact of those trends on research carried out in those museums. I will then examine in more detail each research field and its influences. There are many factors at play that influence natural history museum research. My aim here is to introduce those factors and enable interested readers to delve further into particular areas.

What comprises "research" in natural history museums? The traditional Western natural history museum was born of the Age of Enlightenment. Such museums were created to define and classify an otherwise unruly world, initially the "Old" World, but particularly the New World colonized by Europeans during the age of empires. The natural world encompassed by those museums included plants, animals, rocks, minerals, and "native" peoples. So, for the purposes of this chapter I will define research at natural history museums as encompassing plant and animal biology; geosciences, including rocks, minerals, and paleontology; and anthropology, particularly the study of indigenous peoples.

It is my desire to ensure that all the information and commentary I use in this chapter is as up-to-date as possible. So, while I do quote print and digital sources, I also include insights gained from the many conversations with museum professionals that I have had while researching this chapter.

Big issues and overarching trends

The early years of natural history museums coincided with the Industrial Revolution, and that revolution, along with parallel scientific discoveries, shaped the science carried out in those original museums. Microscopes became much better, preservation techniques for specimens improved, and the availability of the printed word including science-based publications expanded rapidly. However, significant changes followed during the twentieth and early twenty-first centuries that informed all aspects of research in natural history museums.

The most significant of those changes was undoubtedly the Digital Revolution, including computers, the Web, mobile phones, social media, and miniaturized analytical devices. In natural history museum research, specific impacts included sophisticated genetic techniques, the growth of bioinformatics, remote sensing in earth sciences, and high resolution two- and three-dimensional imaging. Analytical techniques changed radically with the development of noninvasive imaging and analytical tools. The Digital Revolution shaped and enabled many changes in natural history museums and I will write more about impacts on research areas later in the chapter.

The internal cultures of natural history museums have also changed greatly during their long history. Initially, such museums were primarily research and collecting organizations with, in many cases, a secondary public and educational face. Curators and scientists in natural history museums related to their peers in their own scientific communities and subject areas, and their contact with the public was minimal, highly didactic, and unidirectional. Natural history museums were observers, collectors, and classifiers of the natural world, sitting apart from day-to-day debates among the general populace. In the latter part of the twentieth century, this all began to change.

Perhaps as a by-product of better education systems and the digital information revolution, individuals and communities began to openly question key aspects of science and to demand a greater say in its conduct and application. (See, for example, Achenbach, 2015.) The high-profile areas in this regard were genetic engineering and genetically modified foods, climate science, evolution science, and applications of nanotechnology, but they also included increasing demands by indigenous peoples for an increased role in how they were studied and how their material was collected and used. Cumulatively, a more assertive community began to transform natural history museums from ivory towers of knowledge to places of two-way conversation. This in part enabled the boom in citizen science of the late twentieth and early twenty-first centuries and much stronger dialogues between indigenous peoples and museums.

In parallel with this and alongside a host of other developments, most natural history museums achieved a new, if at times uneasy internal balance based on what I characterize as a tripartite structure: research, collections, and public engagement. The renewed significance of collections, of which I will say more below, combined with the growing partnership with the wider community, present both challenges and opportunities for research.

Natural history museums were born at the beginning of the understanding of evolution and a concomitant decline in creationist influence. But in the latter part of the twentieth century, prevailing political and religious norms began to exert greater impact on natural history museums, with some politicians and religious leaders challenging the scientifically based views of natural history museum displays and programs in areas such as evolution and climate change. In the United States, the National Center for Science Education has drawn attention to this issue in an article titled "Climate Change Denial Is Affecting Education" (National Center for Science Education, 2016). The situation is more complex in parts of the Islamic world where science and religion are apparently inextricably combined. Edis (2009) writes:

> Familiar Western debates about religion, science, and science education have parallels in the Islamic world. There are difficulties reconciling conservative, traditional versions of Islam with modern science, particularly theories such as evolution... both intellectually and institutionally, the Islamic world harbors many tensions between science and religion.

One of the most significant recent influences on natural history museums, and one dogged by sometimes hostile interest groups, is climate change and the resultant global warming. While climate change has fostered new areas of biological research, it has involved geosciences through study of ancient climate fluctuation, as well as the impact on indigenous peoples threatened by sea level rise. The American Museum of Natural History's website *Museums and Climate Change Network* (American Museum of Natural History, 2016b) is a good example of a contemporary museum response to climate change.

A parallel and sometimes related trend in the latter part of the twentieth century and certainly in the early years of the twenty-first is the overall decline in government funding of museums in general, and of research in particular. This has largely been the result of economic downturns and increasing competition from sectors such as health, education, and defense. The impact on natural history museum research is varied. Available government funds are increasingly tied to areas of perceived need rather than based simply on excellence. In some countries, philanthropy, sponsorship, and commercial income have grown to fill the gap to some degree, but in many parts of Europe where there is a tradition of all funding coming from the government, the consequences of cuts have been dire (for example, see Network of European Museum Organisations, 2016). But those new funding sources also come with their own strings and priorities. Segments of the general public are more likely to question relationships between major museums and philanthropic-or sponsorship-based funding from sources perceived by some as problematic, for example, mining companies.

The reduction in traditional funding has also fostered the trend for museum researchers to be more collaborative, particularly with universities. This is manifested in a growing number of joint research appointments with universities and the location of externally funded research within natural history museums. Universities have increasingly shifted from being rivals to partners and collaborators. As universities have moved away from traditional areas of museum science, for example, taxonomy, they have begun to realize that if they are to attract students, then relationships with museums are useful. These changes have also seen a move away from the "career for life" museum researchers to greater mobility.

Another significant area of change has been in the use of collections. Initially natural history museum collections served as reference collections for researchers, with the more spectacular objects, whether biological, geological, or anthropological, displayed for the public. However, changes in scientific and analytical techniques are increasingly enabling new ways to utilize biological and geological specimens, from detecting pesticide residues in eggshells to identifying isotope ratios in geological core samples.

In the nineteenth and early twentieth centuries, collecting specimens and observing peoples were comparatively easy. Much of the lands and waters visited "belonged" to a colonial power, and professional and amateur scientists essentially took what they wanted. Biological and geological specimens were usually collected from the wild; human-created materials were traded, purchased, or simply taken, with or without the informed consent of the creator communities.

In the second half of the twentieth century, many countries enacted laws designed to control or prevent collection and export of antiquities, fossils, minerals, and meteorites. On the biological front, new genetic techniques helped create a boom in bioprospecting, and in parallel concern rose concerning the endangering of species, increasing rates of extinction, and exploitation of the developing world by the developed world. In response, international conventions such as the Convention on International Trade in Endangered Species (CITES) and the Convention on Biological Diversity (CBD) came into force. Both seek to regulate the movement of biological material, with the CBD in particular also allowing for the sharing of benefits arising from bioprospecting and exploitation of the knowledge of indigenous peoples.

If we look back over the life of natural history museums, the number of human-like species, or "hominins" (the group consisting of modern humans, extinct human species, and all our immediate ancestors), has fluctuated widely as skeletons were found, which tended to increase species numbers, and genetics went to work, which has also tended to reduce these numbers (Curnoe and Thorne, 2003). The dilemma for natural history museums, from a research and public engagement perspective, is that the science is moving rapidly, with disputes among scientists not uncommon. This is seen, for example, in the debate surrounding the question of whether *Homo floresiensis* is a new hominin species; the debate remains vigorous, with the majority siding with it being a separate species (for example, Castro, 2016).

Human evolution is also the area of biology most impacted by religion, with the concept of human (if not all) evolution rejected by many conservative faiths. As a result, research into human evolution is difficult, if not impossible, in those countries where the dominant religion rejects the concept on religious grounds, for example, Middle Eastern Islamic nations. The more widely accepted view of evolution is clearly articulated by the International Council of Museums Committee for Museums and Collections of Natural History (ICOM NATHIST), whose website asserts:

> ICOM NATHIST considers evolution the best current explanation for how the diversity of life around us came to exist. It remains the only scientifically compelling rigorous account of how life evolved on our planet for which a great deal of empirical evidence has been accumulated in natural history collections.
>
> (ICOM NATHIST, 2016)

Trends and influences on museum biological research

For most natural history museums, the foundation of biological research was, and for some still is, taxonomy, the order and classification of animals and plants, and the related field of phylogeny, the evolutionary history of organisms. Does taxonomy have a future in natural history museums? Is it still relevant? One of the key factors influencing taxonomic research in natural history museums is the question of just how many species there are. Is it reasonable to think that we could or should try to document a significant proportion of the species that live on our planet? Estimates concerning the total number of species are controversial and far-flung. Writing in *Nature*, Lee and Oliver state:

> The race to describe and archive the planet's dwindling biodiversity becomes even more urgent with the realization that the task's scale may be an order of magnitude greater than estimated... Dijkstra notes that we have so far named only about 1.2 million of Earth's estimated 8.7 million or so eukaryotic species... However, genetic analysis has revealed that many supposedly uniform morphospecies are complexes of multiple, reproductively isolated lineages, each of which constitutes a separate but cryptic species... The quoted estimate of the number of (morpho)species on Earth could therefore be just 10% of the true species number.
>
> (Lee and Oliver, 2016)

For those researchers whose work is based primarily on cataloguing biodiversity, this suggests that taxonomy should remain a key driver of natural history museum research, but a law of diminishing returns arguably exists in continuing to identify species while the very problems that threaten all species grow in scale and impact.

The great disruptor of the classical taxonomic world was the use of genetic markers to define species, which began in earnest in the 1980s and 1990s. There were the passionate early adopters of genetics and the equally passionate late defenders of morphological taxonomy. (See, for example, Hillis, 1987.) The work in high-volume sequencing pioneered by Craig Venter led to the ability to take a sample of something containing multiple organisms, like seawater, and use sequencing to extract those organisms whose genetic makeup is known and therefore have already been named, and equally to identify those that are different, the known unknowns. See, for instance, "Environmental genome shotgun sequencing of the Sargasso Sea" (Venter et al., 2004). The technique is increasingly rapid and low cost.

Does the debate surrounding morphology and genetics matter? This is a complex ongoing discussion that calls into question the concept of "species." There is not space here to do this debate justice, but I will explore some of its ramifications.

Genetic tools have increased the efficiency of species identification, so how does one explain the decline in the number of taxonomists? Based on my own experience as a leader of a botanical research organization and a natural history museum, I can see that several factors are at play. First, fewer students are opting to take taxonomy-related subjects at university. Second, universities have reduced their offerings in taxonomy. Third, the number of jobs available for taxonomists, which are mainly in museums and botanic gardens, have likewise diminished, often because of government funding cuts. Finally, and perhaps most tellingly to many prospective students, taxonomy is not seen as an attractive career or as addressing real problems, and is not perceived as having a future. Several aspects of the debate concerning whether taxonomy is declining (or, indeed, increasing) are explored in "Are we losing the science of taxonomy?" (Drew, 2011).

While the number of taxonomists has declined, in its place has been a growth in applications of taxonomic tools and knowledge to specific real-world problems, for example, biosecurity, ecology, understanding the impact of global warming, and managing invasive species. There is much written on this, and the work of Armstrong and Ball is typical:

> Molecular diagnostic tools provide valuable support for the rapid and accurate identification of morphologically indistinct alien species... This approach is a realistic platform on which to build a much more flexible system, with the potential to be adopted globally for the rapid and accurate identification of invasive alien species.
>
> (Armstrong and Ball, 2005, p. 1813)

Arguably, the two biggest threats to biodiversity are habitat loss through land clearing, and invasive species. The impact of global warming follows closely behind. Much of the future of natural history museum biological research is tied to aspects of these problems. Is the role of such research simply or primarily to describe the changes that are occurring or does it include predicting future impacts? More controversially, do natural history museums have a role or indeed an obligation to advocate for reduction in the harmful causes of species loss, to argue for changes in government policy, in resource exploitation? A strong advocate for, and example of, the activist approach is the entirely web-based "Natural History Museum" (Natural History Museum, 2016a), which is highly critical of museums it sees as too passive or, in its view, too dependent on corporate sponsorship.

As concern regarding human-caused global warming rose in the late twentieth century, museum biologists started to look at the impact of warming on species number and distribution. At first this comprised a dispassionate description of impacts, but has now progressed to more passionate calls for mitigation of what are increasingly frightening and likely outcomes. Typical of the response of some natural history museums is this statement on the Australian Museum's website:

> We don't research the causes or direct evidence of climate change, but focus on developing an understanding of the impacts of climate change on biodiversity and how best to implement conservation strategies for those ecosystems and species that will be impacted.
>
> (Australian Museum, 2016)

The availability of new analytical techniques has led to a reevaluation of the use and importance of museum collections for research. Rapid recent changes in habitats, species distributions, environmental pollutants, and climate have caused researchers to look anew at museum specimens collected over long time spans. While much emphasis has been placed on genetics, other new techniques are being developed.

One such technique is stable isotope analysis (SIA), the analysis of certain isotopes that are unchanging and preserved at different ratios at different points in time (one of them often being the death of an organism) and depend on many factors applicable at that point in time. While SIA has many uses, a typical museum example is that described by Turner et al. (2015). By studying museum fish specimens collected over a seventy-year period from the Rio Grande river system in the southwestern United States, they were able to conclude, "Overall, retrospective SIA of apex consumers suggests radical change and functional impairment of a floodplain river ecosystem already marked by significant biodiversity loss." SIA was thus able to further confirm the decline of the Rio Grande system.

Another technique is the use of museum collections of birds' eggs. Since the 1960s, they have been utilized to monitor the accumulation of the pesticide DDT in the environment, but the wider importance of these collections is now better recognized.

> Well labelled and reliable series of bird skins and eggs collected over long time-spans offer opportunities to determine environmentally induced changes in parameters of ecological interest, such as geographical range, the age structure of populations, clutch size, and the timing of breeding and migration... The value of museum collections for these purposes is sufficiently high for us to recommend the resumption of the systematic accumulation of avian specimens for long-term ecological research.
>
> (Green and Scharlemann, 2003, p. 165)

Most importantly, the authors note that this should only be done if it does not threaten the conservation status of the species being collected.

While collections are indeed being used more and in new ways, this presents problems in risk of damage or loss to specimens through mishandling or transport incidents. Increasingly, natural history museum researchers are providing, or being provided with, high-resolution scans of specimens with associated information, or very small tissue samples, rather than whole specimens. This reduces the risk and cost to the lending institution, and often means that much more information can be supplied and gained more quickly. (R. Johnson, Director, Australian Museum Research Institute, pers. comm., 29 Feb. 2016).

I refer above to the article by Green and Scharlemann (2003) on monitoring chemicals accumulated in birds, while not endangering wild populations. The authors have called on the booming field of citizen science to help solve this problem. They write:

> One example is the long-term scheme to collect specimens of birds of prey found dead by the public in the U.K., which has resulted in several valuable conservation-oriented applications.
>
> (Green and Scharlemann, 2003, p. 165)

Harnessing the passion of community members is both supporting natural history museum research, as well as changing it.

A more recent example of capitalizing on citizens' knowledge and willingness to act is the hunt for the giant rats of the Malaita, in the Solomon Islands. Lavery (2016) writes in the Australian Museum's science blog of working with the Kwaio people of East Malaita to find new species of large rodents and bats. The Kwaio have known of the giant rats for a very long time, but they are new to science. As in cases like this, recognizing and respecting local and traditional knowledge can open new doors for museum researchers.

Pulling it all together: the future of biological research in museums

A substantial number of factors are at play shaping natural history museum biological research. Classical taxonomy, in which a scientist based her or his career around one small group of organisms, is disappearing. In its place is an increasingly complex web of applications of taxonomy, usually in conjunction with partnerships and collaborations, and use of new genetic and analytical techniques. Massive computing power and digital access to collections are enabling a boom in bioinformatics. Placement of research students into museum research teams is benefitting students and museum researchers alike through the influx of new ideas and greater collaboration. Equally, collaboration with citizen scientists also brings fresh ideas, along with greater productivity and relevance to community needs.

The future of museum biological research is bright for those institutions that harness the opportunities and find new ways of building funds and resources, and engage fully with their communities. It is much less certain for those that cling to the past.

Trends and influences on museum geosciences research

Of all the natural history museum research areas, the geosciences are the ones most impacted by economic factors, in particular the mining industry. Geologists who might once have worked in museums—assuming there were jobs on offer—have instead been attracted to the mining sector. Growth in applied mining geology and associated remote sensing and geophysics has effectively removed the need for much museum-based research. Paleontology, on the other hand, is showing renewed potential.

Natural history museums were an important part of establishing the order and classification of rocks, and their rock and mineral collections were, and to some extent remain, key reference collections, but there are now few museum scientists working in classical geology except in the few very large natural history museums. However, as genetics changed biological taxonomy, so new analytical techniques have changed mineralogy.

Analytical techniques employed at the molecular level have enabled better understanding of mineral chemistry and of how minerals behave physically, for example, under seismic stress. These techniques infuse museum mineral collections with new significance, and present an opportunity for new areas of natural history museum research. Potential avenues of research are in the area of mine site remediation, for instance, in detoxifying uranium mine tailings (Prof. S. Miller, Chief Executive Officer, Queensland Museum Network, pers. comm., 4 May 2016).

The study of fossilized organisms has long been a mainstay of natural history museum research and collections. Knowledge of ancient organisms has obvious links to understanding current organisms, and new computer-based digital imaging techniques are giving newfound vigor to paleontology.

> In recent years, the discipline has been revolutionized by the emergence of powerful methods for the digital visualization and analysis of fossil material. This has included improvements in both computer technology and its availability, and in tomographic techniques, which have made it possible to image a series of 2D sections or slices through a fossil and to use these to make a 3D reconstruction of the specimen. As a consequence of applying these techniques, paleontological studies are often at the forefront of anatomical research.
>
> (Cunningham et al., 2014)

Current concerns regarding human-induced global warming have led to increased interest in ancient climates and the field of paleoclimatology. While much of this work is happening in universities, it represents a further area of potential natural history museum research, especially given the role of natural history museums in communicating climate change to the wider community. Museum fossil collections are of significance for such research. Elias (2013) writes:

> Fossil beetle research has led to many exciting breakthroughs in the understanding of the pace and intensity of climate change in terrestrial landscapes. In many ways, beetles are the ideal proxy for tracking terrestrial environmental change.

The great economic significance of the mining industry has notable consequences for natural history museum research. In several parts of the world, mining companies are key funders of museums, and this includes funded research positions, sometimes in partnership with universities. While the additional funding is good, it has also raised ethical questions surrounding the acceptability of mining industry money.

Organizations such as Greenpeace, and the (virtual) Natural History Museum have taken aim at mining industry support of museums. As recently as March 2016, the Natural History Museum website provocatively asks, "Is the Houston Museum of Natural Sciences a museum, or a PR front for the fossil fuel industry?" while this is "the central question" of *Mining the HMNS*, an exhibition of the Natural History Museum that "interrogates the symbiotic relationship between the Houston Museum of Natural Sciences and its corporate sponsors" (Natural History Museum, 2016b).

Pulling it all together: the future of geosciences in natural history museums

Concern in some areas of the community over how natural history (and other) museums are funded represents one aspect of greater community engagement with such museums, and this engagement is not unquestioning. While corporate funding—including mining industry funding—will enable expansion of museum geosciences research, museums will need to be thoughtful about ethical and reputational considerations in accepting such funding.

As with biological research, new techniques, greater engagement with communities, and more focus on global problems are bringing renewal to museum geosciences research. Through a combination of new imaging techniques and increased emphasis on climate change, paleontology is undergoing a resurgence in museum research, and this is likely to continue.

Trends and influences on museum anthropology and the study of indigenous peoples

Many of the world's longstanding natural history museums have extensive collections of materials created by indigenous peoples, and, in many cases, collections of whole bodies and body parts of such peoples. In Australia, New Zealand, the United States, and Canada, active and extensive programs of repatriating human remains have been undertaken. Progress on this has been much slower or in many cases nonexistent in Eastern and Western Europe.

The origins of these collections are as complex as the origins of anthropology itself, and reflect many factors at work amid the building of empires. Objects were added to anthropological or ethnographic collections for a wide range of reasons. Some were aesthetically appealing to a Western colonial eye; others were more prosaic and practical, including objects of daily life. Still others were weapons or fetish and ritual objects. These factors are summarized well in the introduction to *Objects and Others* (Stocking, 1988).

In the second half of the twentieth century, several developments began to challenge anthropological orthodoxy. Much of this was associated with the increasing demands from indigenous peoples for a greater say in what happened to material created by them and their ancestors. In parallel with this were challenges from within anthropology itself. In *Australasian Science*, anthropologist Kirrilly Thompson writes of early twentieth-century Polish anthropologist Bronisław Malinowski:

> Malinowski's personal diaries... show a man struggling between "us and them," between the old regime of a racism legitimating colonialism and asserting difference, and a new regime emphasizing sameness and questioning the superiority that any one culture has over another.
>
> (Thompson, 2016)

Both challenges had a significant impact on anthropological research and activities in natural history museums, most notably, the growing role of indigenous peoples in determining how they were studied and how their cultural heritage was treated and communicated with the wider world.

One factor more than any other seems to shape future collection-based museum research in anthropology. This is the shift in mindset on the part of some museums whereby they no longer consider the museum as "owning" the collections of the material culture of indigenous peoples, but, rather, as serving as custodians of the material, primarily for the creator communities and their descendants. Custodians have different and greater obligations than owners. Foremost is the obligation to involve those creator communities in key decisions pertaining to the use of collections, and the research conducted on them.

In this way, creator communities are seen as equals in the research, as collaborators, rather than merely the subjects of study. Given this, communities might be asked which elements of their cultural heritage they would like a museum to collect and hold. Major institutions in Australia and New Zealand, as well as the British Museum, work with Pacific communities to create objects that tell stories and preserve culture. A prime example of this is the Australian Museum's effort to commission works from the people of Erub (Darnley Island) in Torres Strait. Blog posts demonstrate the process by which the Erub people decided what stories to tell through the objects commissioned by the museum and made by them (Australian Museum, 2012).

A key question in anthropology is how modern humans migrated from Africa to the rest of the world. New and earlier dates for humans in various parts of the world, alongside better understanding of human genetics, suggest that the move out of Africa occurred in waves and was much more rapid than had previously been the case. By way of example is the ongoing uncertainty over how the first humans arrived in North, Central, and South America. Curry (2012) writes, "For decades, scientists thought that the Clovis hunters were the first to cross the Arctic to America. They were wrong—and now they need a better theory." In www.Smithsonian.com, on 21 July 2015, Helen Thompson writes of more recent genetic research:

> The prevailing theory is that the first Americans arrived in a single wave, and all Native American populations today descend from this one group of adventurous founders. But now there's a kink in that theory. The latest genetic analyses back up skeletal studies suggesting that some groups in the Amazon share a common ancestor with indigenous Australians and New Guineans. The find hints at the possibility that not one but two groups migrated across these continents to give rise to the first Americans.
> (Thompson, 2015)

The combination of ongoing specimen discovery and subsequent genetic work means that collections of early humans held in natural history museums have ongoing significance for such research, and museums have an obligation to keep pace with this rapidly changing field, and accurately represent levels of scientific uncertainty to their visitors.

One of the largest and most enduring museum anthropology programs is that at the American Museum of Natural History, whose research program manifests engagement not only with contemporary culture, but also with complex interdisciplinary issues. This is exemplified in a statement regarding a 2016 conference at the museum on the emergence of HIV:

> The conference presents international research on the biological, epidemiological, and social contexts of the emergence of HIV/AIDS. Bringing together specialists from the fields of virology and molecular biology, epidemiology and public health, and history and anthropology, this conference provides the context for cutting-edge, multidisciplinary insights into one of the most devastating global infectious disease pandemics of the twentieth century.
> (American Museum of Natural History, 2016a)

Anthropology and climate change are referenced in a description of a workshop held at the museum in 2013 and organized in conjunction with the National Museum of Australia. The workshop was charged with "explor[ing] how museums can engage communities in ways that foster understanding and help with adapting to processes of climate change" (American Museum of Natural History, 2013).

A logical extension of indigenous communities' greater influence in museums is those communities' creation of their own museums in Western countries. Such museums speak about indigenous cultures in the cultures' own words, rather than from the detached, usually non-indigenous voice of the science-based natural history museum. A groundbreaking example of this is the Smithsonian's National Museum of the American Indian. The existence of two major museums under the Smithsonian umbrella holding major collections of American Indian cultural heritage and associated research programs, the other being the National Museum of Natural History, has led to tensions based on their different research approaches. This is well summarized by Duarte (2012) in *Repatriation and the Smithsonian*. She writes:

> The Smithsonian Institution's involvement in the fight for control of indigenous history can be traced to many cases of disagreement between researchers and indigenous people throughout history, yet no other instance of its involvement has been more indicative of this larger debate than the Smithsonian's internal debate currently being enacted through the repatriation philosophies and practices of the National Museum of Natural History and the National Museum of the American Indian. While each museum has vastly different histories that have influenced their relationships with indigenous people, both choose to advance contrasting conceptions of property that purport either the political stance of science or that of indigenous peoplehood.

In the case of these two Smithsonian museums, the approach each has taken is consistent with their mission, goals and core values. The National Museum of Natural History is a fundamentally research based institution with a deeply seeded [*sic*] mission of providing access to knowledge to all mankind. The National Museum of the American Indian is the self-proclaimed, "Museum Different," and as such has intentionally deviated away from the traditional role of the museum seeking to serve indigenous communities and the greater public as an honest and thoughtful conduit to indigenous culture, present and past.

Perhaps the single most important aspect of the National Museum of the American Indian's philosophies and practices regarding the disposition of indigenous remains and cultural property is its focus on collaboration between indigenous people and researchers at every step of the process. This valuable aspect should be applied to the greater political debate over the control of indigenous history.

(Duarte, 2012, p. 41)

Pulling it all together: the future of anthropology in natural history museums

Of all the research areas in natural history museums, anthropology is in the process of the most profound change. While the subjects of biological and geological research do not have a voice (although in the case of animals, they certainly have human advocates), the subjects of anthropological research do have a voice and they are using it. Collaborative studies, such as using indigenous people's DNA to trace human migration, and collaborative addressing of problems, like the impact on indigenous peoples of global warming, are the way of the future.

Overall conclusions about the future of research in natural history museums

The successful natural history museum in the twenty-first century is revealed in up-to-date displays and a web presence that deals in a balanced but fearless way with contemporary issues. All staff, but most particularly research staff, are engaged with their work, their colleagues, and their institutions.

Those natural history museum researchers who embrace change, welcome collaboration, and work in partnership with their communities and stakeholders will thrive. They will be using new analytical techniques, harnessing the power of the digital realm, and collaborating with universities and citizen scientists. They will be focused on the problems of today and tomorrow. They will have engaged new funding partners who share their values, and distanced themselves from those who don't.

Research cultures will continue to evolve rapidly. Researchers who once saw themselves working for a discipline, or only with their peers in that same discipline, now see themselves as working for a museum and a community. A lifetime studying one animal group will be a thing of the past. Links between research, collections, and public engagement will be much stronger, but also innovative and adept. New ways of using collections will be found by researchers inside and outside museums. Communities will have a greater say in how those collections continue to grow. Digital access to and use of collections will grow exponentially.

Natural history museum research can and does have a bright future, one that is all about relevance, engagement, and collaboration.

Acknowledgments

In the preparation of this chapter, I have benefitted greatly from discussions with many people in and around natural history museums and like organizations in Australia, New Zealand, North America, and Europe, and I thank them for their insights, time, and patience.

References

Achenbach, J. (2015). Why do so many reasonable people doubt science? *National Geographic*, March. Available at: http://ngm.nationalgeographic.com/2015/03/science-doubters/achenbach-text [Accessed 12 Dec. 2016].

American Museum of Natural History (2013). *Collecting the Future: Museums, Communities, and Climate Change.* Available at: www.amnh.org/our-research/anthropology/news-events/collecting-the-future [Accessed 3 Aug. 2016].

American Museum of Natural History (2016a). *Histories of HIVs: Social Contexts of the Emergence of HIV/AIDS (May 20–22, 2016).* Available at: www.amnh.org/our-research/anthropology/news-events/histories-of-hivs [Accessed 28 July 2016].

American Museum of Natural History (2016b). *Museums and Climate Change Network.* Available at: www.amnh.org/our-research/anthropology/projects/museums-and-climate-change-network [Accessed 20 Sept. 2016].

Armstrong, K. F., and Ball, S. L. (2005). DNA barcodes for biosecurity: Invasive species identification. *Philosophical Transactions of the Royal Society, B.* 360, pp. 1813–1823. Available at: http://www.jstor.org/stable/30040928?seq=1#page_scan_tab_contents [Accessed 25 Sept. 2016].

Australian Museum (2012). *Ghost Net Art from Darnley Island (Erub).* Available at: http://australianmuseum.net.au/ghost-net-art-from-darnley-island [Accessed 1 Sept. 2016].

Australian Museum (2016). *Museum Research Related to Climate Change.* Available at: http://australianmuseum.net.au/research-related-climate-change [Accessed 18 Sept. 2016].

Castro, J. (2016). *Homo floresiensis*: Facts about the "hobbit." *Live Science.* Available at: www.livescience.com/29100-homo-floresiensis-hobbit-facts.html [Accessed 12 Dec. 2016].

Conniff, R. (2016). Our natural history, endangered. *New York Times*, 1 Apr. Available at: www.nytimes.com/2016/04/03/opinion/ournatural-history-endangered. html?_r=1 [Accessed 12 Sept. 2016].

Cunningham, J. A., et al. (2014). A virtual world of paleontology. *Trends in Ecology and Evolution*. Available at: www.cell.com/trends/ecology-evolution/fulltext/ S0169-5347(14)00087-1 [Accessed 18 Sept. 2016].

Curnoe, D., and Thorne, E. (2003). Number of ancestral human species: A molecular perspective. *HOMO: Journal of Comparative Human Biology* 53(3), pp 201–224. Available at: http://www.sciencedirect.com/science/article/pii/S001 8442X04700335 [Accessed 7 Dec. 2016].

Curry, A. (2012). Ancient migration: Coming to America. *Nature* 485, 30–32 (3 May 2012). Available at: www.nature.com/news/ancient-migration-coming-to-america-1.10562 [Accessed 3 Dec. 2016].

Drew, L. W. (2011). Are we losing the science of taxonomy? As need grows, numbers and training are failing to keep up. *Bioscience* 61(12), pp. 942–946. Available at: http://bioscience.oxfordjournals.org/content/61/12/942.full [Accessed 8 Dec. 2016].

Duarte, M. L. (2012). *Repatriation and the Smithsonian: An Examination of Repatriation at the National Museum of the American Indian and the National Museum of Natural History*. UCLA Electronic Theses and Dissertations. Available at: http:// escholarship.org/uc/item/4pt318pz#page-41 [Accessed 7 Aug. 2016].

Edis, T. (2009). Modern science and conservative Islam: An uneasy relationship. *Science & Education* 18, pp. 885. doi:10.1007/s11191-008-9165-3. Available at: http:// link.springer.com/article/10.1007/s11191-008-9165-3 [Accessed 10 Dec. 2016].

Elias, S. A. (2013). Beetle records: Overview. In: Scott Elias, ed., *Encyclopedia of Quaternary Science*. 2nd ed. Amsterdam: Elsevier.

Green, R. E., and Scharlemann, J. P. W. (2003). Egg and skin collections as a resource for long-term ecological studies. *Bulletin of the British Ornithologists' Club*. Available at: www.boc-online.org/PDF/124GreenEggAndSkin.pdf [Accessed 28 Aug. 2016].

Hillis, D. M. (1987). Molecular versus morphological approaches to systematics. *Annual Review of Ecology, Evolution, and Systematics* 18, pp. 23–42. Available at: www.zo.utexas.edu/faculty/antisense/papers/Hillis1987ARES.pdf [Accessed 1 Dec. 2016].

ICOM NATHIST (2016). *Evolution*. Available at: https://icomnathist.wordpress. com/evolution/ [Accessed 10 Nov. 2016].

Lavery, T. (2016). Through village gardens and into the mist. *Australian Museum*. Available at: http://australianmuseum.net.au/blogpost/amri-news/through-village [Accessed 12 Sept. 2016].

Lee, M. S. Y., and Oliver, P. M. (2016). Life on earth: Count cryptic species in biodiversity tally. *Nature* 534, pp. 621. Available at: www.nature.com/nature/ journal/v534/n7609/full/534621a.html [Accessed 8 Dec. 2016].

National Center for Science Education (2016). *Climate Change Denial Is Affecting Education*. Available at: https://ncse.com/library-resource/climate-change-denial-is-affecting-education [Accessed 11 Dec. 2016].

Natural History Museum (2016a). http://thenaturalhistorymuseum.org/ [Accessed 7 Sept. 2016].

Natural History Museum (2016b). *Mining the HMNS: An Investigation by the Natural History Museum*. Available at: http://thenaturalhistorymuseum.org/ events/mining-the-hmns/ [Accessed 31 Aug. 2016].

Network of European Museum Organisations (2016). *18% of Museums in UK Closed or Partly Closed in 2015/2016*. Available at: www.ne-mo.org/news/article/ nc/1/browse/1/topic/european-funding-for-museums/nemo/18-of-museums-in-uk-closed-or-partly-closed-in-20152016/376.html [Accessed 12 Dec. 2016].

Stocking, G. W., ed. (1988). *Objects and Others: Essays on Museums and Material Culture*. Madison, WI: University of Wisconsin Press.

Thompson, H. (2015). *A DNA Search for the First Americans Links Amazon Groups to Indigenous Australians*. Available at: www.smithsonianmag.com/ science-nature/dna-search-first-americans-links-amazon-indigenous-australians-180955976/#5LHlK7CkYdJHcAEb.99 [Accessed 18 July 2016].

Thompson, K. (2016). What does an anthropologist actually do? *Australasian Science*. Available at: www.australasianscience.com.au/article/science-and-technology/ what-does-anthropologist-actually-do.html [Accessed 28 Aug. 2016].

Turner, T. F., et al. (2015). Retrospective stable isotope analysis reveals ecosystem responses to river regulation over the last century. *Ecology*. Abstract. Available at: http://onlinelibrary.wiley.com/doi/10.1890/14-1666.1/abstract [Accessed 1 Sept. 2016].

Venter, C., et al. (2004). Environmental genome shotgun sequencing of the Sargasso Sea. *Science* 304(5667), pp. 66–74. Available at: http://science.sciencemag. org/content/304/5667/66 [Accessed 3 Dec. 2016].

5   The essential role of museums in biodiversity conservation

Felicity Arengo, Ana L. Porzecanski, Mary E. Blair, George Amato, Christopher Filardi, and Eleanor J. Sterling

Introduction

The complexity of forces threatening many of the most valued dimensions of the living planet is well recognized and compels a rich interplay between science that reveals the natural world and society's pathways to value and steward it (Rockström et al., 2009; Steffen et al., 2011). As collection-based institutions, natural history museums (NHMs) have long played a special role in the conservation arena. By documenting, cataloging, analyzing, and communicating the splendor and richness of life, NHMs immerse visitors in the natural world in a way they may otherwise not experience. The importance of this role is difficult to overstate—in a world where over 50 percent of people live in urban settings removed from natural systems that sustain us, NHMs can frame and maintain a collective sense of place, and root societal policy and values in the natural and cultural fabric that underlies them. NHMs provide a unique depiction of patterns of life across space and over time unavailable to any one person's perspective over their lifetime.

While the traditional role of museums has been to discover, interpret, and disseminate knowledge about the natural world, museums are ideally positioned to realize a broader and more relevant role in society: to promote informed engagement and stewardship of our biological and cultural heritage through pertinent research, institutional programming, and on-the-ground collaborations. Many NHMs have integrated biodiversity conservation into their mission and programs, and are leading the way in conservation-oriented research projects and collaborations, informing the public about issues concerning our planet's health, and promoting ecologically sustainable practices. In the 2015 Taipei Declaration on Natural History Museums and Biodiversity Conservation, the International Council of Museums Committee for Museums and Collections of Natural History (ICOM NATHIST) stated:

> Increased human activities have created catastrophic declines in biodiversity. Both ethics and logic point to a mandate to conserve vulnerable habitats and species. To achieve best practice, natural history museums take action to conserve natural habitats and populations.
>
> (ICOM NATHIST, 2015)

This role for NHMs is not new. While many NHMs have recently broadened their missions to strengthen their commitment to conservation issues, there is a deeper history to the role museums have played in recognizing and responding to threats to the richness of the living world. Over a century ago, Frank M. Chapman, a famously influential curator at the American Museum of Natural History (AMNH) in New York, promoted replacing Christmas bird "shoots" with the Audubon Society's Christmas Bird Count, one of the oldest citizen science programs in the United States, which has provided some of the most direct evidence of the impact of a changing climate on ecological communities. Chapman also saw firsthand the impacts of habitat degradation and hunting for meat and feathers on bird communities in the American Southeast and the Caribbean, and effectively used his position at the museum, and the respect for its science, to influence President Theodore Roosevelt to push market hunting limits and habitat conservation policy.

Chapman's career and conservation efforts embody the potential for NHMs to link their scientific power and reputation to fostering shifts in attitude, behavior, and political will. And there are numerous additional examples of how NHMs have made these links and influenced policy and action. For example, in the 1950s, high mortality and low reproductive success were recorded in many bird species. One hypothesis explaining these mortalities was that dichloro diphenyl trichloroethane (DDT), which was widely used as an insecticide since the late 1940s, had accumulated in adult birds and led to eggshell thinning. Scientists tested this hypothesis by comparing egg samples collected in the field with eggs deposited in museum collections prior to the widespread use of DDT. The results served as evidence to influence policy leading to the ban of DDT in the United States in 1972 (Ratcliffe, 1967, 1970; Anderson and Hickey, 1972).

In this chapter, we provide an overview of the roles that natural history museums (NHMs) have played in conservation, with a focus on collections-based work, including the long history of NHM expeditions and the contemporary trend toward museum-based genomics and bioinformatics. We also discuss innovative ways in which museums are able to contribute to conservation today, through diverse, interdisciplinary partnerships and conservation-oriented programming. Natural history museums have played a role in confronting societies' greatest ecological challenges, from species loss to tracking and responding to the impacts of climate change; we hope to illustrate how they can also lead society's approach to conservation issues into the future.

Collections and expeditions: their role in wildlife conservation

Direct observation through exploration, field research, and collections are integral components of museum science that support biodiversity conservation goals and actions. Collections are part of a museum's core scientific legacy, representing invaluable reference points for monitoring biological diversity, environmental change, and ecosystem health—available for use by multiple sectors, including science, health, and industry.

At the AMNH, scientists conduct between 50 and 100 field expeditions each year. As of 2016, the museum holds over 33 million specimens and artifacts in its collection; the Natural History Museum of London has over 80 million specimens; the Smithsonian National Museum of Natural History has over 145 million specimens; and the Field Museum of Natural History in Chicago has 23 million specimens and artifacts, just to name a few. The "heyday" of Western museum expeditions, from the 1880s to 1930s, during which well over 1,000 expeditions were sent to the remotest corners of the Earth, included, for example, the Whitney South Sea Expedition, which focused on collections for birds, plants, and other animal specimens on over 600 Pacific Islands. Modern expeditions have been reinvigorated through new initiatives such as AMNH's Explore21 program, which supports expeditions rooted in multidisciplinary partnerships and new technology, and seeks to intersect with biodiversity conservation goals through targeted explorations in regions with critically threatened habitats, or unknown diversity; an important aim given that the vast majority of the Earth's species remain to be described and studied.

The ethics and strategies guiding the collection of biological specimens and anthropological and archaeological artifacts for NHMs have been renewed and updated as the purpose of museums has evolved. Some have criticized biological specimen collection for scientific studies, claiming that collection has played a role in species extinction (Minteer et al., 2014). Modern collecting adheres to strict permitting and ethical boundaries, endeavoring to collect well below levels that would affect demography (Collar, 2000; Winkler et al., 2010; Rocha et al., 2014). Collection strategies can and should be grounded in partnerships and agreements with local resource stewards toward cogenerated biodiversity and biocultural conservation goals (for example, Housty et al., 2014).

Expeditions and collections continue to be invaluable for taxonomic and systematic study, leading to the discovery and description of new species or range extensions or contractions that inform biodiversity conservation actions and priorities. For example, AMNH's National Science Foundation–funded biotic inventory surveys in Vietnam from 1998 to 2001, led by its Center for Biodiversity and Conservation (CBC), brought together scientists and taxonomists from across the museum's scientific departments as well as from the Missouri Botanical Gardens and the Institute of Ecology and Biological Resources (IEBR) in Hanoi. These surveys resulted in the discovery of more than fifty new species, the rediscovery of species thought to be extinct, some of the first ecological research on rare and elusive species in remote areas of Vietnam, and contributions to the establishment, upgrade, or extension of protected area systems in Vietnam. The surveys also resulted in the most comprehensive and up-to-date review of Vietnam's mammal fauna at the time (Dang et al., 2008), which supported the incorporation of these frequently under-surveyed but abundant and diverse taxa into conservation strategies as indicators of ecosystem health.

There are many other examples where museum expeditions and collections have directly supported biodiversity conservation actions, such as the Rapid Biological and Social Inventories led by the Field Museum in Chicago, along with local experts. These inventories identify important biological communities in the region of interest and evaluate assets in local communities for long-term engagement. Since 1999, hundreds of local students and partners have been trained in field survey methods, and more than 150 species new to science have been discovered. The information is relayed to local and international decision-makers who set priorities and guide conservation. The inventories have supported the designation of over 32 million acres of protected wilderness in the Amazon headwaters, Cuba, and China (Field Museum, 2016).

In particular, local and regional museum collections provide fine-grained resolution and reference points for key questions concerning environmental change and pollutants, species, and ecosystem health (detecting the emergence and spread of Chytrid Fungus in museum specimens coinciding with amphibian declines; Cheng et al., 2011), emerging diseases (detecting the appearance of Lyme disease in museum tick collections; Persing et al., 1990), and climate change (testing the correlation of body size decline to climate change; Gardner et al., 2011).

Museum collections have played a critical role in local and global conservation policies related to the illicit wildlife trade. Museum specimens are ideal for providing vouchered reference specimens for scientifically and legally robust forensic identification of wildlife parts and products confiscated from illegal activities (Eaton et al., 2010). Fine-scale population assignment is particularly informative for wildlife trade management (Zhang et al., 2015). However, reference databases consisting of multiple sequences of trade-targeted species from across their range are typically lacking or impossible if derived only from the collection of a single museum. Thus, support of and collaboration among local and regional museums are critical to further these efforts and help clarify trade patterns and hot spots of trade activities or to identify populations with a high level of harvesting pressure.

New technologies now allow museum scientists to uncover growing layers of information on each specimen or artifact beyond anything that the original collectors could have foreseen, such as CT-scan tomography (Bi et al., 2013), stable isotope analysis, massively parallel sequencing, proteomics (Welker et al., 2015), ultra violet-visable (UV/VIS) spectrophotometry (Andersson et al., 1998), and machine learning algorithms for projecting species' distributions (Newbold, 2010; Peterson et al., 2011). Species distribution models (SDMs) use the relationship between observed specimen localities in geographic space and environmental variables such as climate to generate a map of suitable areas for species in a region. SDMs can help locate areas that may be suitable for a species but have not yet been surveyed, can inform the planning and designation of protected areas, and can project future changes in species distribution amid a changing climate (Peterson et al., 2011; Blair et al., 2012). Museum scientists have used specimens, remote sensing, and SDMs to improve understanding of local endemism in Madagascar, finding that multiple evolutionary processes interact to explain why so many species are restricted to small parts of the island (Pearson and Raxworthy, 2009; Blair et al., 2013). The work has important implications for conservation planning since improved understanding of ecological and evolutionary processes can improve predictions of where species are likely to be found, and hence help define which areas should be prioritized for conservation.

These new analyses and technologies are made possible in part because of advancing digitization of museum collections and increased open availability of these data sets through platforms such as the Global Biodiversity Information Facility (GBIF); SYNTHESYS, the Synthesis of Systematic Research project; as well as other global environmental and climate data sets such as WorldClim (Hijmans et al., 2005). Enhanced inventory, digitization of collections, and open sharing increasingly allow conservation scientists to leverage museum collections, new analyses, and technologies for their full potential toward informing conservation action. However, open sharing and digitization of global museum collections has also revealed some persisting gaps and challenges ahead; a GBIF task force on biodiversity data fitness convened at AMNH in 2015 stressed that the global gaps in primary biodiversity data are driven by taxonomic inaccuracies, backlogs in digitization, administrative obstacles to sharing or access, and biases in spatial coverage of data. Global natural history collections contain information on biodiversity from almost three billion specimens, all with great promise to be leveraged for wildlife conservation if remaining challenges can be addressed (Anderson et al., 2016).

Genomics research and its role in biodiversity conservation

Advances in genomics and bioinformatics have now made NHMs and their diverse collections even more valuable resources for biodiversity conservation. Traditional collections, which include vouchered specimens, provide a comprehensive and systematic sampling of genetic diversity through time and space. Specifically, historical collections capture changes in diversity over a crucial time for conservation research—spanning the duration of increased anthropogenic activity. In addition, analyses of historical, archaeological, and paleontological remains can contribute important information regarding the conservation of populations and species that cannot be obtained any other way (Leonard, 2008).

Collections contain a representation of extinct species, as well as reflect population diversity from areas where these species have been locally extirpated and artificially fragmented. For example, researchers have reconstructed genetic variation from the recent past using museum specimens of Dutch black grouse and alpine chipmunks to compare to current levels of variation, which can inform causes and effects of loss or gain of genetic diversity over time (Larsson et al., 2008; Bi et al., 2013).

Complementing these more traditional collections are new, frozen tissue repositories, which provide extraordinarily valuable specimens amenable to genomic research and other areas of conservation research. They can hold population-level samples collected less invasively, with critical examples represented by vouchered specimens. Collected and stored in ways that make them useful for high-quality deoxyribonucleic acid (DNA) and ribonucleic acid (RNA) extraction, these materials allow for examination of genetic diversity at unprecedented levels of detail including whole genome and transcriptome sequencing.

New technologies and natural history collections can be used for important conservation research through the ever-expanding field of conservation genetics and genomics (DeSalle and Amato, 2004). While originally focused on using molecular markers for resolving questions of uncertain taxonomy for determining conservation units and simple genetic threats such as inbreeding in highly fragmented populations, this field has expanded greatly. It now provides us with a better understanding of human impact on the evolutionary processes of whole ecosystems; facilitates discovery of important biological information on species that are difficult to observe directly; and uncovers molecular ecology and cryptic diversity, emerging diseases as a threat to biodiversity, as well as the complex interactions of the individual organism and its microbiome (McMahon et al., 2014; Gómez et al., 2015). The Sackler Institute for Comparative Genomics at the AMNH has engaged in a ten-year collaboration with the Panthera Foundation on an extensive large cat molecular ecology project focused on jaguars in Central and South America and tigers and snow leopards in Asia. Using fine-scale individual genotyping of noninvasively collected fecal samples, this program has constructed detailed, landscape genetics maps that provide information on the number of individuals in a population, genetic connectivity and use of corridors, and a rigorous testing of applied conservation management strategies in range countries (Caragiulo et al., 2015).

In other examples, genetic information from museum specimens has shown that northeastern beach tiger beetles were historically present across the northeastern United States, though they are currently only found in the state of Massachusetts (Goldstein and DeSalle, 2003). Genetic data from museums guided reintroduction efforts that would preserve the integrity of evolutionary significant unit boundaries for the brush-tailed rock wallaby in Australia (Paplinska et al., 2011). These areas of study require the extensive sampling strategies that are the historical and ongoing purview of natural history museums.

Another important area in which natural history collections and genomics combine to provide important tools for biodiversity conservation is the field of wildlife forensic science. Genetic and genomic tools allow museums to advance conservation through forensic investigations that link vouchers in collections to wildlife trade, allowing for better tracking of wildlife trade sources and supporting enforcement and management of a wide range of species. These museum-based wildlife forensics initiatives strongly augment the work of management authorities by offering a resource that would otherwise be unavailable in addressing global threats to biodiversity. Use of DNA barcoding for species identification has now become one of the most important tools for monitoring the illegal trade in wildlife and enforcing the laws governing its regulation (e.g., African bushmeat trade; Eaton et al., 2010; pangolin trade, Zhang et al., 2015). Without vouchered databases created from barcoding museum specimens, this would not have been possible.

No greater resource for biodiversity conservation genomics research exists than the historical and modern collections found in the world's NHMs. These collections increase in importance and value every day as new advances in genomics technologies and bioinformatics allow us to delve deeper into the processes responsible for the diversity of life on the planet—and the best ways to retain the greatest amount of that diversity into the future.

Museums as catalysts for conservation collaboration

NHMs also play a role in conservation action by catalyzing partnerships that transform the way conservation is envisioned, framed, and led. The diversity of disciplines in NHMs coalesces expertise in, for instance, earth sciences, paleontology, comparative biology, and anthropology, as well as education and communication, providing a robust, interdisciplinary platform for conservation problem-solving and innovation. Combined expertise in ancient DNA, paleontology, anthropology, and biology, along with new computational techniques and large data sets to study species distributions, have documented anthropogenic activity that has transformed ecosystems through millennia (Boivin et al., 2016). NHMs are ideal incubators for both interdisciplinary work and transdisciplinary work that convenes scientists, local communities, and other decision-makers. As one example, NHMs are ideal for framing biocultural approaches to conservation, which consider social-ecological systems as holistic units.

Because the role of museums in convening strategic partners, fostering local capacity, or guiding policy often underpins other, more visible actions, their catalytic impact can be underappreciated (McCarter et al., 2001). Yet conservation programs at museums are leading the way in innovative, long-term partnerships that connect diverse stakeholders across local and global communities and draw from multiple sources of knowledge for conservation action. These partnerships can take a diversity of forms and involve a variety of partnerships, ranging from short-term collaboration on expeditions to long-term relationships. A selection of examples is described in Table 5.1, taken from museums across the world.

Table 5.1 Selected examples of the diverse partnerships that natural history museums can convene and the conservation outcomes they catalyse

Institution	Program/project	Partners/stakeholders	Scale	Illustrative conservation outcomes (with key references)
American Museum of Natural History, New York	Center for Biodiversity and Conservation (CBC): Metropolitan initiatives	Museum scientists, state and city agencies, local communities	Local, regional	In the New York region, the CBC has been influential in the formation of the city's conservation policies and in New Yorkers' relationships to their environment, for example, by spearheading citizen monitoring programs and the integration of biodiversity conservation in the PlaNYC. (1)
	Center for Biodiversity and Conservation: Pacific Programs	Museum scientists, national agencies, indigenous and local communities	Global	In Melanesia, the CBC has catalyzed the development of a network of protected areas that includes the largest terrestrial protected area in the Solomon Archipelago. In the Great Bear Rainforest area of coastal British Columbia managed by the Heiltsuk First Nation, a joint research agenda in accordance with Heiltsuk customary law has allowed for more effective grizzly bear management. (2)
	Center for Biodiversity and Conservation: Grupo de Conservación Flamencos Altoandinos (GCFA)	AMNH scientists, academics, national and regional agencies, local communities, NGOs, industry, global conventions	Regional	The GCFA has convened local and regional stakeholders to coordinate research and monitoring of flamingos and wetlands. Long-term engagement with communities and agencies has resulted in the establishment of local and national protected areas, Ramsar sites, and Important Bird Areas. (3)

(Continued)

Institution	Program/project	Partners/stakeholders	Scale	Illustrative conservation outcomes (with key references)
California Academy of Sciences, San Francisco	Institute for Biodiversity Science and Sustainability	US and Filipino museum scientists, media professionals, educators, national agencies, local communities	Global	Collaborative expeditions in the Philippines that have included outreach, education, and discussion surrounding conservation policy; facilitating work with the local governments to conserve marine life; and advancing the establishment of new marine protected areas and the expansion of existing ones. (4)
Field Museum of Natural History, Chicago	Keller Science Action Center: Chicago Cultural Alliance, Calumet Stewardship Initiative, and Chicago Wilderness	Museum biologists, anthropologists, educators, geospatial analysts, governments, communities, landowners	Local and regional	Joint programs and alliances have fostered implementation of the Chicago region's climate action plans, engaged citizens in monitoring and learning, improved quality of life at the local level, and influenced broader networks and efforts for social and environmental change. (5)
	Keller Science Action Center: Rapid Inventories	US and local museum scientists, national agencies, indigenous and local communities	Global	Since 1999, the Rapid Inventories have discovered more than 150 species new to science, increased known ranges for more than 1,000 species, and fostered the protection of 32 million acres of wilderness in the Amazon headwaters, Cuba, and China. (6)

Institution	Department	Scope	Partners	Description
Museo Nacional de Historia Natural (MNHN) de La Paz	Zoology Department	Local and regional	Museum scientists, regional and local government, local and indigenous communities, fishermen associations	Since 2002, the MNHN has convened diverse partners to collaboratively assess and monitor freshwater fish populations across Bolivia, and fostered conservation and sustainable management programs that support both fish populations and local subsistence and livelihood. (7)
Vietnam National Museum of Nature, Vietnam Academy of Science and Technology, Hanoi	Department of Communications and Community Education	Local	Government ministries, Vietnam Association of Photographic Artists, Vietnam Forest Association, and nongovernmental and governmental organizations and Vietnam and international individuals	The museum in Vietnam has educational programs that merge science and art and raise awareness about the importance of protecting the natural environment and biodiversity, including photographic competitions and exhibitions such as *The Beauty of Natural Forests and Insects of Vietnam*. (8)

1—Kiviat and Johnson, 2013; 2—Filardi and Pikacha, 2007; Housty et al., 2014; 3—Marconi, 2007; Marconi et al., 2011; 4—Gosliner and Burke, 2013; 5—Zint and Wolske, 2014; Hirsch et al., 2011; 6—McCarter et al., 2001; 7—J. Sarmiento and S. Barrera, pers. comm.; 8—Vũ Văn Liên, pers. comm.

At the Center for Biodiversity and Conservation at the AMNH, for example, we aim to transform knowledge from diverse sources and perspectives—spanning areas of scientific research as well as traditional and local knowledge—into conservation action. We convene and connect diverse audiences or stakeholders, and establish collaborations centered on research and action and capacity development. Aiming to encompass the full cycle of conservation action—from identifying needs to implementing projects to adapting and broadcasting lessons learned—the CBC fosters long-term partnerships that can promote local ownership, and inspire replication and scalability (Housty et al., 2014; Sterling et al., 2016). The center's Network of Conservation Educators and Practitioners, for instance, has convened AMNH scientists, university educators, and conservation practitioners working on the ground to collaboratively develop more than 160 free conservation training modules in multiple languages, and offer training opportunities for over 4,500 conservation trainers and professionals in the United States, Latin America, Asia, the Pacific, and Africa (Bravo et al., 2016).

As these examples illustrate, NHMs have the expertise and skills to catalyze linkages between biodiversity surveys and protected area planning, between local management of natural resources and cultural dimensions of diversity. Through these collaborations, the conservation impact of museums also includes new, more diverse protected areas around the world, and participatory research that strengthens biodiversity management, local governance, and policy.

Inspiring action and developing capacity for conservation through education

A growing body of evidence indicates that the public learns much of what it knows about science outside the formal education system. From libraries, museums, and parks, to the Internet, friends, and family, a range of resources facilitates public science learning (Bell et al., 2009; Falk and Dierking, 2010; Falk et al., 2010). Given all the topics that need to be addressed in formal education, relatively little time can be devoted to conservation education in elementary, secondary, and university curricula, so natural history museums help to fill a crucial gap by making programs relevant to students and the general public (McCarter et al., 2001). Natural history and science museums are in a unique position as a venue for communicating science because of their high credibility ratings and level of trust they invoke in the public (Novacek, 2008).

NHMs have receptive and diverse audiences, and can raise awareness and engagement in conservation among their visitors through powerful experiences in permanent exhibit halls, thematic temporary exhibitions, public programming, and sustained mentoring and training programs. Millions of people visit natural history museums every year, and visiting museums is one of the most popular out-of-home leisure activities in the United States (American Alliance of Museums, 2016). For example, 60 percent of Los Angeles residents visited the California Science Center since its renovation in 1998, including residents of all races/ethnicities, neighborhoods, incomes, and education levels (Falk and Dierking, 2010). A personal visit to a museum allows for close encounters with specimens, dioramas, and artifacts as well as hands-on learning through interpretive visuals and interactive displays. In addition, through websites and social media, museums are offering science content through news and blog posts, online exhibitions, and even online courses for credit, reaching billions of people around the world (ICOM NATHIST, 2015).

Several museums have developed permanent galleries that showcase the extraordinary biodiversity of the planet; draw attention to recent declines, extinctions, and threats; and highlight actions and solutions using specimens and models, photos, videos, dioramas, and interactives. Some examples are the AMNH's Hall of Biodiversity, the Royal Ontario Museum's Life in Crisis: Schad Gallery of Biodiversity, the Field Museum's Abbott Hall of Conservation Restoring Earth, and Spain's Exhibition of Biodiversity in the Natural Science Museum of Barcelona. Smaller museums have also incorporated permanent conservation-focused exhibitions, such as the Interaction of Nature and Man hall in the National Museum of Nature and Science in Japan, and the Diversity of Life exhibition at the North Carolina Museum of Natural Sciences. However, some well-known and popular museums have more traditional permanent galleries that have not been revised to address conservation issues (McCarter et al., 2001). The updating of exhibitions, incorporating new and dynamic content and technologies in halls and exhibitions that are considered "permanent," is an ongoing challenge for museums.

One way that museums have addressed this is through temporary exhibitions dealing with current environmental issues; such exhibitions have proliferated in recent years (Novacek, 2008). Many museums have developed special exhibitions on climate change (*Climate Change: The Threat to Life and a New Energy Future* at the AMNH), species extinction (*Extinction: Not the End of the World* at London's Natural History Museum), resource management and sustainability (*H_2O = Life* and *Our Global Kitchen* at the AMNH), and protected areas (*Art of the Parks: Celebrating 100 Years of the National Park Service* at the Rockwell Museum, Corning, New York). Temporary displays are frequently designed to travel to various destinations around the world, offering content and messages of universal relevance, with some sections developed by local teams to include case studies or stories tailored to the local context.

To further engage the public in biodiversity research and conservation, many museums have developed citizen science programs, collaborations between scientists and citizen volunteers. These expand opportunities for scientific data collection; provide access to scientific information and opportunities to engage in the scientific process for community members; and equip the public with information, skills, and tools to make informed decisions regarding resource use and management. For example, several museums in the United States have led BioBlitzes, intense, twenty-four-hour sampling periods during which scientists, naturalists, and volunteers attempt to survey and record all living species in a region. The Natural History Museum of London's Big Seaweed Search program engages volunteers in plot surveys along the beach to record seaweed and help monitor change in the sea life due to sea level rise and ocean acidification, and to monitor for invasive species. Many more examples exist, and new projects are regularly being added to museums' public engagement offerings.

Finally, in addition to public programs aimed at general audiences, NHMs also provide advanced training in biodiversity science, curriculum development, and teaching strategies in conservation through site-based and online courses for students, teachers, and practitioners. Several national programs in the United States pair university students with museum scientists to develop applied research projects (for example, the Doris Duke Conservation Scholars Program, the National Science Foundation's Research Experience for Undergraduates). In 2013, the AMNH expanded its Science Research and Mentoring Program for high school students from across New York City to provide additional opportunities in conservation biology research. Evaluations show that students previously not familiar with the field of conservation biology plan on pursuing this as a career after participating in the program. The AMNH's NCEP works to improve the availability, quality, and access to high-quality, current educational resources for conservation teachers, professionals, and trainers around the world.

Promoting understanding, awareness, and stewardship of biodiversity to broad museum audiences requires a multidimensional strategy, using appropriate messages, approaches, and technology for effective communication. NHMs have a captive and diverse public and are well positioned to mobilize large audiences into the conservation fold (Novacek, 2008). While renewing content in permanent exhibitions is an ongoing challenge for museums, new digital technologies using mobile platforms, and approaches such as crowdsourcing, gaming, citizen science, and social media offer new and exciting ways to engage audiences around the world in NHMs conservation programs.

Engaging future generations in conservation action

Over the last three decades, compelling arguments have been made for NHMs to play a central role in research leading toward conservation of biodiversity, and to embrace their responsibility to inform stewardship of life on Earth (Alberch, 1993; Krishtalka and Humphrey, 2000; Pyke and Erlich, 2010). In the face of an increasingly urgent biodiversity and climate crisis, this role for NHMs becomes essential. Almost two decades ago, Krishtalka and Humphrey (2000) argued that to fulfill their potential into the future, NHMs needed to face challenges in four areas: deploying their information to address the biodiversity crisis, educating scientists and citizens to tackle complexity, engaging visitors in conservation action, and evolving their management culture. How far have we progressed on these, and what are our challenges moving forward?

NHMs have made progress on organizing, digitizing, sharing, and collaborative use of data. Emerging threats, like climate change, require that museum data systems remain flexible and alternative data sources be creatively repurposed (Johnson et al., 2011). New technologies and approaches are continuously generating more data, so this task remains an ongoing, high-priority challenge worthy of attention and resources.

In addition to the creation of conservation units or departments, some established institutions, such as the California Academy of Sciences, are now shifting the role of conservation and sustainability efforts to the core of their institutional mission, something more museums should contemplate. Newly established NHMs can be "born" with conservation units, such as the Department of Nature Conservation at the Vietnam National Museum of Nature, which was established in 2012. Tasked with producing research on restoration and conservation threat assessment and management, this department has developed in just a few years DNA assessment processes to identify species of tigers, white rhino, elephants, king cobra, five precious wood species, and some bamboo species, to inform wildlife trade mitigation efforts.

As NHMs look ahead, an emerging and important challenge is our growing understanding of biodiversity as a collection of dynamic systems linking biological and cultural components. Such a systems approach can provide a framework for understanding individual components and their interrelationships and result in more effective conservation actions (Sterling et al., 2010). A systemic view also requires a greater focus on the human element, and NHMs have traditionally tended to decouple nature and humans. The challenge then becomes how to communicate, investigate, and support the multiple ecological, cultural, and evolutionary processes that sustain biodiversity, and to promote a dynamic view of nature within the framework of museum collections and exhibit halls. However, since NHMs typically have a range of expertise in biology, anthropology, and education, they are ideally positioned to create multidisciplinary teams using systems approaches to tackle complex problems.

While NHMs have continued to innovate in the areas of education and engagement, how can they "inspire the citizenry to become the environmental conscience of the nation" (Krishtalka and Humphrey, 2000)? NHMs need to lower the barrier to conservation action by capitalizing on easy access to information through digital and virtual platforms, and the popularity of social media to promote solutions through specific, locally relevant, choices for action. NHMs can catalyze diverse communities to co-curate exhibitions, co-create educational materials, and even identify items for sale in their shops that resonate and inspire civic engagement and action. They need to expand their toolbox, for instance, to include the principles of conservation psychology, a growing field that studies the relationship between people and the environment and the factors that influence people's attitudes and motivates behavioral changes for better stewardship of the environment (Clayton et al., 2015). Additionally, NHMs need to think beyond their walls and work with communities and stakeholders to identify strategically where exhibitions will travel, targeting not only specific countries or regions but also diaspora communities around the world, for maximum outreach and impact. Finally, NHMs could amplify conservation messaging by working across collections-based institutions (other NHMs, zoos, aquariums, and botanical gardens) to design and evaluate programs that will reinforce what individuals can do (Sterling et al., 2007).

We agree with Krishtalka and Humphrey (2000) that updated management, administrative, and leadership training are necessary at all levels for NHMs to fulfill their mission to society. A core element of this should be a concerted effort to diversify the science and conservation workforce to achieve broad and lasting conservation outcomes. Complex issues such as biodiversity conservation are best addressed by diverse, inclusive groups of people. Research by organizational scientists, psychologists, sociologists, economists, and demographers show that socially diverse groups (those with a mixture of race, ethnicity, gender, and sexual orientation) are more innovative than homogeneous groups and are less likely to stall at suboptimal solutions (Page, 2007; Phillips, 2014). Further, biodiversity conservation depends on the support of a wide variety of citizens who may differ in their core values and beliefs. A more diverse and equitable museum workforce is key to generating research agendas, policies, and actions that achieve the goals of local and global biodiversity conservation (Hovardas and Poirazidis, 2007; Foster et al., 2014).

Moving forward, we believe NHMs will have to transform how we think of, exhibit, and interpret "natural histories," as well as our role and responsibility in the biodiversity crisis, and develop innovative and heterogeneous ways of bridging separation between nature and culture, local and global, colonizer and colonized, "us" and "them." Given their rigorous science, reputation, and place in local and global communities, NHMs are poised to be cutting-edge, transformative spaces for informing and engaging a diverse community in sustaining the world's biological and cultural diversity. If they boldly embrace this evolutionary potential, they can help us imagine and catalyze a multiplicity of success stories—models for a diverse, sustainable, and resilient society.

References

Alberch, P. (1993). Museums, collections, and biodiversity inventories. *Trends in Ecology and Evolution* 8(10), pp. 372–375.

American Alliance of Museums (2016). *Museum Facts.* Available at: http://aam-us.org/about-museums/museum-facts [Accessed 5 Jan. 2017].

Anderson, D. W., and Hickey, J. J. (1972). Eggshell changes in certain North American birds. In Voous, K. H., ed., *Proceedings of the XVth International Ornithological Congress*. Leiden: Brill.

Anderson, R. P., et al. (2016). *Final Report of the Task Group on GBIF Data Fitness for Use in Distribution Modelling*. Copenhagen: Global Biodiversity Information Facility (GBIF) Secretariat.

Andersson, S., and Andersson, M. (1998). Ultraviolet sexual dimorphism and assortative mating in blue tits. *Proceedings of the Royal Society of London B: Biological Sciences* 265(1395), pp. 445–450.

Bell, P., Lewenstein, B., Shouse, A. W., and Feder, M. A., eds. (2009). *Learning Science in Informal Environments: People, Places, and Pursuits*. Washington, DC: National Academies Press.

Bi, K., Linderoth, T., Vanderpool, D., Good, J., Neilsen, R., and Moritz, C. (2013). Unlocking the vault: Next-generation museum population genomics. *Molecular Ecology* 22, pp. 6018–6032.

Blair, M. E., Rose, R. A., Ersts, P. J., Sanderson, E. W., Redford, K. H., Didier, K., Sterling, E. J., and Pearson, R. G. (2012). Incorporating climate change into conservation planning: Identifying priority areas across a species' range. *Frontiers in Biogeography* 4, pp. 157–167.

Blair, M. E., Sterling, E. J., Dusch, M., Raxworthy, C. J., and Pearson, R. G. (2013). Ecological divergence and speciation between lemur (*Eulemur*) sister species in Madagascar. *Journal of Evolutionary Biology* 26, pp. 1790–1801.

Boivin, N. L., et al. (2016). Ecological consequences of human niche construction: Examining long-term anthropogenic shaping of global species distributions. *Proceedings of the National Academy of Sciences* 113, pp. 6388–6396.

Bravo, A., et al. (2016). Strengthening capacity for biodiversity conservation in the southern tropical Andes through partnerships of educators and practitioners. In: A. A. Aguirre and R. Sukumar, eds., *Tropical Conservation: Perspectives on Local and Global Priorities*. Oxford: Oxford University Press.

Caragiulo, A., et al. (2015). Presence of the endangered Amur tiger *Panthera tigris altaica* in Jilin Province, China, detected using non-invasive genetic techniques. *Oryx* 49(4), pp. 632–635.

Cheng, T., Rovito, S., Wake, D., and Vredenburg, V. (2011) Coincident mass extirpation of Neotropical amphibians with the emergence of the infectious fungal pathogen *Batrachochytrium dendrobatidis*. *Proceedings of the National Academy of Sciences of the USA* 108, pp. 9502–9507.

Clayton, S., et al. (2015). Expanding the role for psychology in addressing environmental challenges. *American Psychologist*. Available at: http://dx.doi.org/10.1037/a0039482.

Collar, N. (2000). Collecting and conservation: Cause and effect. *Bird Conservation International* 10, pp. 1–15.

Dang, C., et al. (2008). *Checklist of Wild Mammal Species of Vietnam*. Hanoi: Institute of Ecology and Biological Resources.

DeSalle, R., and Amato, G. (2004). The expansion of conservation genetics. *Nature Reviews Genetics* 5, pp. 702–712.

Eaton, M., et al. (2010). Barcoding bushmeat: Molecular identification of Central African and South American harvested vertebrates. *Conservation Genetics* 11, pp. 1389–1404.

Falk, J. H., and Dierking, L. K. (2010). The 95 percent solution: School is not where most Americans learn most of their science. *American Scientist* 98, pp. 486–493.

Falk, J. H., Mossouri, T., and Coulson, D. (2010). The effect of visitors' agendas on museum learning. *Curator: The Museum Journal* 41, pp. 107–120.

Field Museum (2016). *Rapid Biological Inventories.* Available at: http://fm2.fieldmuseum.org/rbi/results.asp. [Accessed 14 Oct. 2016].

Filardi, C., and Pikacha, P. (2007). A role for conservation concessions in Melanesia: Customary land tenure and community conservation agreements in the Solomon Islands. *Melanesian Geo* 5, pp. 18–23.

Foster, M. J., Blair, M. E., Bennett, C., Bynum, N., and Sterling, E. J. (2014). Increasing the diversity of U.S. conservation science professionals via the Society for Conservation Biology. *Conservation Biology* 28, pp. 288–291.

Gardner, J., Peters, A., Kearney, M., Joseph, L., and Heinsohn, R. (2011). Declining body size: A third universal response to warming? *Trends in Ecology and Evolution* 26, pp. 285–291.

Goldstein, P. Z., and DeSalle, R. (2003). Calibrating phylogenetic species formation in a threatened insect using DNA from historical specimens. *Molecular Ecology* 12, pp. 1993–1998.

Gómez, A., et al. (2015). Gut microbiome composition and metabolomic profiles of wild western lowland gorillas (*Gorilla gorilla*) reflect host ecology. *Molecular Ecology* 24(10), pp. 2551–2565.

Gosliner, T. M., and Burke, M. (2013). From parachutes to partnerships: An "integrated" natural history museum expedition in the Philippines. In G. C. Williams and T. M. Gosliner, eds., *The Coral Triangle: The 2011 Hearst Philippine Biodiversity Expedition.* San Francisco, CA: California Academy of Sciences.

Hijmans, R. J., Cameron, S. E., Parra, J. L., Jones, P. G., and Jarvis, A. (2005). Very high resolution interpolated climate surfaces for global land areas. *International Journal of Climatology* 25, pp. 1965–1978.

Hirsch, J., Phillips, S. V. D., Labenski, E., Dunford, C., and Peters, T. (2011). Linking climate action to local knowledge and practice. In H. Kopnina and E. Shoreman-Ouimet, eds., *Environmental Anthropology Today.* New York: Taylor and Francis Books.

Housty, W. G., et al. (2014). Grizzly bear monitoring by the Heiltsuk people as a crucible for first nation conservation practice. *Ecology and Society* 19(2), p. 70.

Hovardas, T., and Poirazidis, K. (2007). Environmental policy beliefs of stakeholders in protected area management. *Environmental Management* 39, pp. 515–525.

ICOM NATHIST (2015). *Taipei Declaration on NHMs and Biodiversity Conservation.* Available at: https://icomnathist.wordpress.com/taipei-declaration-on-nhms-and-biodiversity-conservation/ [Accessed 14 Oct. 2016].

Johnson, K. G., et al. (2011). Climate change and biosphere response: Unlocking the collections vault. *BioScience* 61(2), pp. 147–153.

Kiviat, E., and Johnson, E. (2013). *Biodiversity Assessment Handbook for New York City.* New York: American Museum of Natural History Center for Biodiversity and Conservation / Hudsonia.

Krishtalka, L., and Humphrey, P. S. (2000). Can natural history museums capture the future? *BioScience* 50(7), pp. 611–617.

Larsson, J. K., Jansman, H. A. H., Segelbacher, G., Höglund, J., and Koelewijn, H. P. (2008). Genetic impoverishment of the last black grouse (*Tetrao tetrix*) population in the Netherlands: Detectable only with a reference from the past. *Molecular Ecology* 17, pp. 1897–1904.

Leonard, J. A. (2008). Ancient DNA applications for wildlife conservation. *Molecular Ecology* 17, pp. 4186–4196.

Marconi, P. (2007). Proyecto Red de Humedales Altoandinos y Ecosistemas Asociados, basada en al distribución de las dos especies de Flamencos Altoandinos. In M. Castro Lucic and L. Fernandez Reyes, eds., *Gestión Sostenible de Humedales*. Santiago, Chile: Programa Iberoamericano de Ciencias y Tecnología para el Desarrollo (CYTED) / El Centro del Agua para Zonas Áridas y Semiáridas de América Latina y el Caribe (CAZALAC) / Programa Internacional de Interculturalidad, Universidad de Chile.

Marconi, P., et al. (2011). Fourth simultaneous flamingo census in South America: Preliminary results. *Flamingo* 18, pp. 48–53.

McCarter, J., Boge, G., and Darlow, G. (2001). Safeguarding the world's natural treasures. *Science* 294, pp. 2099–2101.

Mcmahon, B. J., Teeling, E. C., and Höglund, J. (2014). How and why should we implement genomics into conservation? *Evolutionary Applications* 7(9), pp. 999–1007.

Minteer, B. A., Collins, J. P., Love, K. E., and Puschendorf, R. (2014). Avoiding (re)extinction. *Science* 344(6181), pp. 260–261.

Newbold, T. (2010). Applications and limitations of museum data for conservation and ecology, with particular attention to species distribution models. *Progress in Physical Geography* 34(1), pp. 3–22.

Novacek, M. J. (2008). Engaging the public in biodiversity issues. *Proceedings of the National Academy of Sciences of the USA* 105, pp. 11571–11578.

Page, S. (2007). *The Difference: How the Power of Diversity Creates Better Groups, Firms, Schools, and Societies*. Princeton, NJ: Princeton University Press.

Paplinska, J. Z., Taggart, D. A., Corrigan, T., Eldridge, M. D. B., and Austin, J. J. (2011). Using DNA from museum specimens to preserve the integrity of evolutionary significant unit boundaries in threatened species. *Biological Conservation* 144, pp. 290–297.

Pearson, R. G., and Raxworthy, C. J. (2009). The evolution of local endemism in Madagascar: Watershed versus climatic gradient hypotheses evaluated by null biogeographic models. *Evolution* 63, pp. 959–967.

Persing, D. H., et al. (1990). Detection of *Borrelia burgdorferi* DNA in museum specimens of *Ixodes dammini* ticks. *Science* 249(4975), pp. 1420–1423.

Peterson, A. T., et al. eds. (2011). *Ecological Niches and Geographic Distributions*. Princeton, NJ: Princeton University Press.

Phillips, K. W. (2014). How diversity makes us smarter. *Scientific American* 311(4), pp. 42–47.

Pyke, G. H., and Ehrlich, P. R. (2010). Biological collections and ecological/environmental research: A review, some observations and a look to the future. *Biological Reviews* 85(2), pp. 247–266.

Ratcliffe, D. A. (1967). Decrease in eggshell weight in certain birds of prey. *Nature* 215, pp. 208–210.

Ratcliffe, D. A. (1970). Changes attributable to pesticides in egg breakage frequency and eggshell thickness in some British birds. *Journal of Applied Ecology 7*, pp. 67–115.

Rocha, L. A., et al. (2014). Specimen collection: An essential tool. *Science 344*(6186), pp. 814–815.

Rockström, J., et al. (2009). A safe operating space for humanity. *Nature 461*(7263), pp. 472–475.

Steffen, W., et al. (2011). The Anthropocene: From global change to planetary stewardship. *Ambio 40*(7), pp. 739–761.

Sterling, E. J., et al. (2016). *Measuring Impact: Stakeholder Engagement for Biodiversity Goals: Assessing the Status of the Evidence*. Washington, DC: Biodiversity Technical Brief, United States Agency for International Development (USAID).

Sterling, E. J., Gómez, A., and Porzecanski, A. L. (2010). A systemic view of biodiversity and its conservation: Processes, interrelationships, and human culture. *Bioessays 32*(12), pp. 109–1098.

Sterling, E., Lee, J. M., and Wood, T. (2007). Conservation education in zoos: An emphasis on behavioral change. In: A. Zimmermann, M. Hatchwell, L. Dickie, and C. West, eds., *Catalysts for Conservation: A Direction for Zoos in the 21st Century*. Cambridge: Cambridge University Press.

Welker, F., et al. (2015). Ancient proteins resolve the evolutionary history of Darwin's South American ungulates. *Nature 522*(7554), pp. 81–84.

Winkler, K., et al. (2010). The importance, effects, and ethics of bird collecting. *The Auk 127*, pp. 690–695.

Zhang, H., et al. (2015). Molecular tracing of confiscated pangolin scales for conservation and illegal trade monitoring in Southeast Asia. *Global Ecology and Conservation 4*, pp. 414–422.

Zint, M., and Wolske, K. (2014). From information provision to participatory deliberation: Engaging residents in the transition toward sustainable cities. In: D. Mazmanian and H. Blanco, eds., *The Elgar Companion to Sustainable Cities: Strategies, Methods, and Outlook*. Northampton: Edward Elgar.

Part 2

The future of natural history museum visitor experiences

6 Imagining the future of natural history museum exhibitions

Kara Blond

Introduction

Over the past century, natural history museum exhibitions have seen significant shifts in tone and approach—augmenting the tradition of labeled specimens with stories, context, and relevance. Yet the core of the visitor experience remains unchanged: audiences expect to feel wonder and curiosity as they marvel at amazing objects collected from around the world. The dynamic tension between celebrating iconic objects and giving them relevance is at the heart of imagining the future of natural history museum exhibitions.

So, what will the next wave of these exhibitions bring? The shifts will likely come from several directions. As the dual messages of biodiversity conservation and cultural preservation become ever-more-pressing rallying cries for natural history museums, the content and techniques of exhibits are likely to change to become more obviously relevant to the future of our planet and biodiversity—including us. As our audiences change, becoming younger, more global, and more tech savvy, our thinking about how we present content must also shift toward multilingual and multiperspective offerings, more accessible/universal design, and the integration of viewpoints from our audiences. As funds become more limited to support exhibitions, our strategies for exhibit development processes, fundraising, and partnerships will stretch in new directions as well, becoming more nimble and responsive. And as our audiences' expectations become ever more personal and digitally connected, we must continually reinvent our techniques to meet visitors where they are.

At the Smithsonian's National Museum of Natural History (NMNH), we are renewing our master plan for the first time in more than twenty years. And it's raising critical questions about the future of our public experience. How do we reinvent anthropology exhibitions to replace our now shuttered suite of traditional exhibitions devoted to individual cultures? How do we assess new strategies for showing off our behind-the-scenes spaces and collections to emphasize their value to understanding our planet? How do we explain the scientific processes behind emerging stories in the news, given the costs and timeline for developing exhibitions? How do we involve our audiences in the creation of our content—both through citizen science and participatory design? And perhaps most importantly, how do we emphasize stories of global change in a frank but optimistic way—one that invites broad conversation surrounding potential actions we can take as a human community without moving into advocacy? We, like other natural history museums, are at a crossroads. In conversations with natural history exhibitions teams, the refrains are the same: shrinking budgets, changing audiences and expectations, strategic and master planning on the docket. As our director, Kirk Johnson, often refrains: we are a nineteenth-century solution reinventing itself to address twenty-first-century problems. What does that mean for exhibitions?

Modes of interpretation

In recent decades, our conventional natural history exhibition techniques of objects in cases and dioramas modeling the natural and cultural world have been supplemented with multimedia and more in-depth interpretation pertaining to science, scientists, and the scientific process. In some ways, we've pushed visitors further from our collections—glass enclosures have replaced roped stanchions, and many sensitive type specimens have been taken off exhibit—but in other ways, we've drawn visitors in closer through touchable models, more inviting language in our labels, and more compelling and physically accessible graphics and three-dimensional designs. To explore where we've been and where we're headed, we'll look at the past and future of three techniques key to natural history museums: dioramas past and future, the display of specimens, and conversation prompts in exhibitions.

Dioramas

In the late 1800s, dioramas became a popular mode of interpretation, particularly for anthropological content. Miniature models debuted at the world's fairs of the day (Philadelphia, 1876; Chicago, 1893) and then made their way into museums halls as semi-permanent versions of a studied social/cultural life. Initially, the natural world was not part of the typical display; the focus was mostly on human life (architecture, archaeology, village life). Soon, though, full-sized models of natural landscapes, with and without human representation, became an integral component of the interpretive plan of natural history museums. Recently, due to scientific inaccuracies, social offenses, and challenging expectations concerning the level of detail, museums have begun to move away from traditional dioramas and are trying to find creative ways to display the complexities that make up our natural and cultural world.

At the Royal Alberta Museum in Edmonton, a debate flared up during the renovation of its exhibitions over the fate of the museum's historical dioramas. In the end, the team decided to relocate their dioramas to create a stylized, "vintage" entrance to the museum, a nod to nostalgia while recognizing the dioramas' limitations for interpretation. At the American Museum of Natural History in New York, the set of dioramas in its Hall of North American Mammals, originally built in the 1940s, were recently restored and updated with new interpretation and model work, doubling down on the powerful, visceral visitor response to standing alongside scenes of grizzly bears on the prowl. In 1998, NMNH gathered a team of expert museum professionals, scientists, artists, and exhibit fabricators to determine the future of the suite of historical dioramas in the North American Mammals Hall following a major planned renovation. After an assessment of the scenes using a defined set of criteria, the team decided that none of the twelve dioramas were of a quality worth preserving. Instead, modern stylized settings for the animal specimens were created to bring a new twist to the outdated hall. At NMNH, we have slowly removed all of our historical dioramas, most of which showed cultural scenes frozen in time. However, several, including iconic dinosaur dioramas from our Fossil Hall, have been carefully preserved—though they're no longer on exhibit.

In retrospect, the craft of diorama has remained relatively static. Model makers have long built large-and small-scale sets for visitors to peer into or walk through to re-create moments in time—active environments with modeled plants and taxidermy animals, mannequin people with traditional dress, and ceremonial objects from the collection. Backdrops are often painted murals intended to extend the background of the scene into the distance. Dioramas have grown more and more stylized in recent years, with abstracted ecosystems serving as foreground for collections objects rather than mixing reality with prop. In the *Deep Time* exhibition, currently in design at NMNH, we are planning a suite of intimate miniature dioramas to help visitors imagine particular scenes at particular times in prehistory. Callouts along the frames of these dioramas will help visitors focus their attention on key components, and remind them of the state of the planet at this time in history. We've discussed using augmented reality to enhance these scenes, but funding will tell whether that element comes to life.

As we look to the future, augmented reality and immersive virtual reality will give the time-honored diorama a run for its money, with lifelike scenes that immerse visitors in reconstructed worlds without seams, railings, and mannequins. Even traditional habitat dioramas could be put into motion or augmented with views of the same scene through time, and old-school collections displays can be brought to life and put into context, encouraging visitors to look more closely at the objects to understand how they might have moved or been made. At the California Academy of Sciences, a visual projection was added to their reconstructed zebra diorama to show a herd of elephants moving through the distance, adding a dynamic element to the static scene. Though both augmented and virtual reality have been tried in museum settings (as in the *Skin and Bones* app at the NMNH showing visitors what their vertebrate skeletons would look like moving with their feathers and fur), there's much work to be done to align the new-wave diorama approach with how visitors want to use their devices in museums.

Display of specimens

With collections at the core of the work we do, it's no surprise that their display has changed quite dramatically and will continue to evolve. Hands-on educational collections have become much more common, giving visitors the ability to touch and smell objects up close and examine them under microscopes as scientists do. The future of exhibitions will almost certainly include more objects that can be manipulated and examined, and more prompts for visitors to take that kinesthetic toolkit back into their neighborhoods as explorers of the natural world. Digitization and 3-D printing can now create convincing replicas of rigid items (bones, fossils, wood carvings); new technologies will likely allow the replication of invertebrates, jellyfish, and soft tissues with various textures, weights, and densities. This lends credence to the important role of both "real" and replica in exhibitions.

And despite the trend toward higher glass barriers and more steel protecting important specimens from public access, the future will probably reverse that trend, lowering barriers and inviting visitors to interact in respectful ways with collections. (Of course, this gives rise to the eternal battle between preservation of artifacts and specimens—as conservation standards become more stringent—and the desire to enhance learning through touch and close access.) Specimens will be posed in more active positions, giving clues about behaviors and context in a more intuitive manner. Open collections spaces may become more common, providing a window into the range of objects and artifacts stored behind the scenes. And those collections will likely be organized as a public story in terms of their interconnections and relevance, rather than according to their disciplinary divides. Both seem probable trends as we strive to communicate their value.

Active laboratory spaces on public view may also be reinvented as part of this movement, showing collections in use rather than encased. Examples like the Darwin Centre at the Natural History Museum in London and the deoxyribonucleic acid (DNA) Lab at the Field Museum in Chicago show promise but reveal significant challenges. Scientists are uncomfortable working in glass bubbles, with their every move on display—and often the work of collections manipulation is tedious to observe. As such, active on-exhibit collections work will have to be carefully thought through. Will digitization and 3D scanning of collections become part display, part citizen science? One trial at NMNH of a public presentation of 3D scanning of our new *T. rex* specimen led to frustrated visitors who expected to be able to participate, get closer to the action, and see the work's product. So, what will the appropriate compromise look like? Perhaps a combination of learning lab and professional work. Our new National Fossil Hall will include a working fossil preparation lab for staff and volunteers to prep collections for study, as well as a hands-on learning lab companion that will allow visitors to try their own hand at exploring fossils up close.

Exposing the museum processes, both scientific and exhibition development, will also progressively become more a part of the natural history museum experience. As you exit the NMNH temporary exhibition, *The Last American Dinosaurs*, you are given a peak into our paleontology department's world as you witness staff and volunteers working on identifying, cleaning, and sorting fossils from our collection. Nearby is a display documenting the evolution of the design of our permanent Fossil Hall, sharing updates as we establish the "look and feel," content, renovation, and reconstruction for the new gallery. This kind of "behind-the-scenes" experience surprises visitors and encourages them to consider museum careers.

Conversation in exhibitions

As natural history museum exhibitions become increasingly focused on ideas and relevance, rather than primarily on objects, exhibition teams and educators are keen to inspire robust, intergenerational conversation in exhibitions and post-visit activities. Exhibition techniques are following suit, with trained volunteers in the galleries who can help visitors navigate difficult, sometimes emotional content and offer visitors questions and alternative perspectives to consider. In the NMNH Hall of Human Origins, monthly "What's Hot in Human Origins" discussions give visitors opportunities to discuss evolution in the context of their religious faith and other related broader social issues. For the NMNH exhibition *Genome: Unlocking Life's Code*, the volunteer corps had the opportunity to have their own genomes sequenced and to express personal thoughts regarding the complex ethical and social questions that direct-to-consumer sequencing raises for them and their families. In other settings, teens have been specifically recruited to talk with other teens about relevant exhibit issues, and bilingual volunteers have been brought in to talk with visitors in their own language—prompting conversations and questions that might not otherwise emerge.

Other techniques have included role-playing with cue cards and conversation starters, question prompts in exhibit text, and, in one exhibit, *Race: Are We So Different?*, a school lunch table that invited visitors to sit with others to engage around critical topics.

In a study of NMNH's last decade of exhibition evaluation (National Museum of Natural History/Randi Korn & Associates, 2016), we found that several of our studies have investigated the question of whether visitors are conversing in the exhibits. And the numbers are high—in several studies, more than 75 percent of visitors reported talking with staff in the exhibit space, and one study showed a higher level of proficiency with exhibit vocabulary for those who spoke with staff in the gallery. Multilingual exhibits have the added benefit of welcoming a broader range of visitors into the conversation—often making marginalized groups feel more comfortable speaking their minds.

Use of social media in exhibition settings has also provided a forum for digital conversations, sharing intriguing moments from the exhibit experience with wide audiences and inviting comments. We've learned that, while visitors are keen to use their mobile phones to take pictures and post to their social media networks, the uptake of mobile apps for content (other than wayfinding and general information) has been very slim. "Visitors are largely not using museum-produced channels of mobile engagement, but are actively using mobile devices in museums in ways that reflect their general mobile usage preferences (e.g., Taking photos, sharing socially, browsing the web, searching organically, etc.)" (Chen, 2015). That opens opportunities for thinking about how to provoke conversations in ways that align with digital conversation channels. It also raises questions regarding the (museum's role in monitoring and correcting false "facts" and biases circulated via social media. Hashtags in exhibits have seen some success; texting from exhibit stations has seen fairly low use. The future will likely be an organic mix that depends on visitors to build their own paths, with tools provided by museums to spark new thinking and tinkering.

In the future, expect to see more opportunities for conversations and social interactions in exhibitions—gaming that requires input and collaboration between visitors who may not know each other, voting for a particular decision or to identify favorites, interactives that require crowdsourcing to synthesize a variety of perspectives, and even more of the simple techniques of Post-it notes and drawing tables that inspire social interaction and encourage critical thinking. These essential social and intellectual skills can be explicitly nurtured and practiced in the natural history museum setting.

Content

The content of natural history museums has remained relatively consistent until recently, with most major museums featuring halls focused on dinosaurs, taxa across the natural world—mammals, most commonly—and moon rocks, gems, and meteorites always on offer. Those natural history museums with anthropology collections have also shown treasures from native cultures as well as static views of cultural traditions and celebrations, usually with little context and often a Western take on the practices. Displays of human origins have lately come into vogue, as museums around the world are becoming more comfortable addressing the evidence of human evolution despite criticism from religious groups whose views conflict with those scientific themes. Live animals have made their way onto the scene, with insect zoos emerging in the 1970s, butterfly and spider pavilions in more recent decades, and exhibits featuring live fish, frogs, birds, and crocodiles more common.

But the shift now is away from the traditional "ologies" and toward interdisciplinary ideas that get visitors thinking across the natural and cultural world. We are no longer likely to represent a single culture, a single artist, or a single perspective, but instead, will reveal how interconnected the sciences are in terms of content and application. Our future will require presenting a range of perspectives that allow visitors to determine their own. In this vein, we're working to make content more relevant to visitors' lives. Taking these leaps must go hand in hand with understanding and reflecting visitor perspectives, challenging visitors' thinking while providing a safe space for testing out new ideas.

Interdisciplinary themes

At NMNH, where each department formerly "owned" a portion of the public floor space—paleontology, geology, vertebrate zoology, anthropology, and so on—we are now reinventing our approach through storytelling about integrated ecology and ecosystems. In recent years, we have focused exhibitions on broad themes like the ocean, stories of humans' place in the natural world (for example, our exploration of the genome), and a new view of anthropology through exhibitions of Arctic cultural/environmental themes and the cultural practices surrounding disease outbreaks. We now assess potential exhibits based on whether they intersect with multiple disciplines, rather than their pristine application of any one of them individually.

Co-curation has become a critical element of this renewal process, sharing first-person perspectives directly from people of cultures and social groups represented in exhibits, and the active users of objects selected for display (even "display" has become outdated nomenclature in many cases). The authoritative museum voice is shifting—we accept that we don't have all the answers, that we can't present definitive viewpoints. And nowhere is that more apparent than in anthropology exhibitions.

That change mirrors the move toward community journalism, removing a degree of objectivity and incorporating the first-person description as a critical part of the storytelling process. Journalism struggled with that balance in the 1990s as the Internet began to take hold, and museums are now at a similar crossroads. For example, the Smithsonian's National Museum of the American Indian works closely with many tribal community members and leaders to interpret the objects on display and tell the history of and modern perspectives on native peoples through their own voices. But they still work to maintain a curatorial voice that gives a broader perspective on any individual story. If the purpose of natural history museums is—as our mission purports—to understand the natural world and our place in it, then we need to examine the varieties of ways that people interpret the world around them and explore various relationships with cultural and biodiversity. A perfect example of a move in this direction is the conversation around urban ecology taking place as part of the natural history museum landscape. In exhibitions with this theme, visitors are encouraged to see nature not as a distant virgin landscape, but as part of the cityscape around us.

This interdisciplinary emphasis will also likely veer out of the sciences and into the arts—featuring exhibitions that combine both areas to craft a more impactful narrative and reach a broader audience. For example, an NMNH exhibition entitled *Hyperbolic Crochet Coral Reef*, in collaboration with the Institute for Figuring in Los Angeles, invited the museum community and audiences to build a sculptural reef out of crochet components, telling the story of ocean debris, environmental impacts on the ocean, and the mathematics of reef shapes. The resulting sculpture drew surprising audiences to the museum and introduced them to the sciences through the lens of art.

Global change

Another major change for natural history museum content has been a focus on global change, climate change, and human impacts on the environment. At the Smithsonian, in the wake of a public statement about human-caused climate change in 2014, the word "Anthropocene" has become a buzz word for conversation and a focus of exhibition content. Themes have focused on the dramatic changes people have wrought on the planet, and the choices our human community will have to make to find a sustainable balance with the planet's resources into the future. The central theme of our National Fossil Hall looks at how scientists study the past to understand our planet today and plan for its future. An entire gallery encouraging conversation surrounding humans' impact on the planet will invite visitors to become more planet savvy, discuss sustainable strategies, and take part in activities that contribute to the health of our natural world. Emlyn Koster's thinking on this topic is instructive:

> The profound changes that have lately occurred in aquariums and zoos, including an increase in conservation efforts for endangered species, offer an instructive analogue... What becomes of the interpretational responsibility of museums as the contents of display cases and dioramas outlive the last breathing representatives in the wild?
>
> (Koster, 2006, p. 203)

Museums are no longer attempting to avoid this potentially charged content, or maintain a neutral tone in the face of conversations regarding climate change. The Museums and Climate Change Network is moving that conversation forward apace. Expect to see new takes on the Anthropocene in natural history museums around the world—from examples such as the Deutsches Museum's special exhibition *Welcome to the Anthropocene: The Earth in Our Hands* (Mollers, 2015), to projects that allow artists to provide their take on global change themes. Of course, the biggest challenge in this vein is to inspire thinking and optimism while addressing difficult, often depressing content. What is the right mix of candid gloom and doom and hopeful optimism? How should we frame the types of actions that visitors might take, thinking big while offering realistic next steps? How do we invite all visitors into these conversations by supplying familiar entry points for a variety of perspectives without engaging with anti-science sentiments? These are ongoing conversations for museums around the world—encouraging a stronger alignment between museums and other cultural organizations including zoos and aquaria, libraries, community centers, universities, and the like.

In many ways, this will become the critical core of the future of natural history museums. Their success in solving this puzzle may determine their relevance and survival into the future. We hold in perpetuity a remarkable record of the natural world—how can it help us as we approach this global challenge? In a conference entitled "21st Century Learning in Natural History Settings" held at NMNH in 2012, the following became a central tenet of the discussion: "Natural history museums have the opportunity to play a pivotal role in addressing critical challenges like climate change and the biodiversity crises and in communicating these concerns to a wide audience" (National Museum of Natural History, Smithsonian, 2012). Exhibitions, of course, are only one output—but a critical one.

Stories in the news

Exhibition content must also reflect the stories our visitors hear in the news, and we must be prepared to deconstruct complicated science, show relevance, explain phenomena, dispel myths, and uproot unfounded fears. This means that exhibitions will need to be updatable and flexible enough to respond to emerging stories—and allow for a quick turnaround on the floor. Kit-of-parts exhibits that can be quickly assembled, digital signage that can be modified easily, and flexible exhibit teams that can respond in the moment to news are all part of the future of this type of content. Natural history museums aren't known for their nimbleness. But our visitors have grown to expect responsiveness and relevance—and museums must work hard to meet that expectation.

Recent exhibits around the world have explored natural disasters in affected communities, themes such as infectious diseases in response to Zika and Ebola, stories like the opening of relations between the US and Cuba, and the $1,000 sequencing of the human genome. In each case, visitors have armed themselves to participate actively in conversations on science and culture in new ways. Science careers are often featured, and visitors see why collections are relevant to the scientific process. For example, historical collections are now being used to identify modern diseases, and genomics of ancient species help us explore modern ancestry and human migration across the planet.

Design and audience trends

Our thinking about exhibition design has been strongly influenced by changes in our audiences' expectations and demographics (in particular, new thinking in regard to how to reach millennials and teens), our desire for inclusivity (universal design and accessibility has become a critical element of our thinking), and our options related to sustainability, recycling, and use of materials. Design thinking reflects new approaches to free-choice learning and visitor-centered design, providing visitors with opportunities to socialize and create memories with family and friends.

The rise of science centers and their collections-free, audience-first approach has put natural history museums on their toes (or is it their heels?). We see ourselves as clearly distinct from the entertainment culture of Walt Disney and its theme parks (although we integrate clear lessons for visitor services and amenities), but we see many smart moves in science centers that are relevant and urgent for us to adopt in a way that's our own. The hands-on, participatory, compact experiences from science centers have become critical strategies in our wheelhouse and will comprise a growing presence in natural history museum experiences.

Redefining exhibition spaces

At many large museums, a new, intense focus on audience has called for the blurring of educational and exhibition spaces into experiential zones that combine the two. Butterfly pavilions and insect zoos provide examples of this, and the future may see more developments along those lines. Fossil "digs," planting gardens, cultural activities in exhibit spaces, DNA testing labs, and a wide-ranging reinvention of education centers will all be part of this trend. Designated "risk-taking zones" on the floor where museums can try out new approaches in a way that telegraphs their experimental nature to visitors will give natural history museums latitude to try new techniques in exhibit halls—virtual reality goggle experiences, theater elements like detective shows (for example, the theater space in the American Museum of Natural History's *Poison* exhibition), citizen science project participation such as pinning bugs or sorting microfossils. At places like the Exploratorium in San Francisco, participants in these zones are often part of active research projects and are videotaped to understand what they learn from the experience.

Reimagined education centers are popping up across the country— Nature Lab at the Natural History Museum of Los Angeles County; Q?rius at NMNH in Washington, DC; and an in-design space at the American Museum of Natural History in New York. As Strager and Astrup write, "Informal learning centers like museums may have an advantage in generating interest and learning; the mere fact that museums are 'not school' is what makes them attractive to many" (2014, p. 324).

At NMNH, Q?rius opened in December 2013 as an experimental free-choice learning space in the museum specifically targeted at teens. While the museum has long had a small early childhood learning space, Q?rius was the first to target the ten-to eighteen-year-old set with six thousand touchable collection objects, digital field books for collecting and organizing information, and activities including high-end scientific equipment that lets visitors try their hand at being scientists. Part collections vault, part do-it-yourself (DIY) garage, part classroom, part community center, Q?rius was designed with all components (tables, chairs, screens, and so on) on wheels for flexibility and responsiveness to visitor needs. While not a traditional exhibition space, the project originated as a joint effort between the exhibition and education departments during its conception and development. With a small theater, lounge, classroom, high-end laboratory, and open space for exploration, Q?rius attracts its target audience by bringing scientists and researchers into the space to work with students and answer their questions. While Q?rius doesn't realize the same audience numbers as major exhibitions, it sees longer dwell times, indicating deep investment—a significance achievement. It also allows for integration across platforms, creating an active experience in the space as well as in classrooms and at home.

The inherent contradiction in learning about the natural world inside of a building (often a historical one with thick walls and little natural light) will also become more apparent as natural history museums evolve their thinking regarding exhibitions. Museums will increasingly integrate the outside experience with the inside one, planting learning gardens and different species of plants (that, for example, can help tell the story of pollination or the evolution of flowers and food). The Natural History Museum of Los Angeles took their once-urban exterior and turned it into a learning space with access to its Nature Lab, creating a more fluid connection between inside and out. The Natural History Museum in London has plans to do the same as part of their new master plan, reinventing their exterior spaces as exhibitions connected with the content inside. "The grounds will be an elegant and sensitive setting... [to] reinforce the narratives of Origins and Evolution, Diversity of life and Sustainable futures, powerfully expanding the public offer of the Museum" (Natural History Museum, London, 2016).

Finally, natural history museums are likely to go the way of the library, setting aside deliberate gathering spaces for socialization and discussion, rather than filling every available space with content. These "Hang Out, Mess Around & Geek Out" (HOMAGO) spaces (Ito et al., 2010) require the museum proper to get out of the way of learning—less planning, more opportunities for spontaneous reflection and exploration. In our selfie culture, giving teens, in particular, the tools (but not the direction) to integrate themselves into the story will play a critical role in our success.

Accessibility

Accessibility, or, more broadly, universal design, has become a buzzword in exhibition design and planning over the past decade—with the goal of connecting with learners of every kind, visitors with a variety of physical or mental abilities, speakers of many languages, and underserved audiences. Traditional modes of thinking about accessibility have led to design standards for physical access—legibility of text, color contrast, cane detection, wheelchair access, simple interactives for grasping, captioning for film audio, and the like. The Smithsonian and US National Park Service, among several other institutions, have published their accessibility standards, which have been adopted broadly. More recently, museums have given careful thought to access for the visually impaired specifically, with efforts to include an audio description of exhibition content and design, braille headings, and touchable maps and objects to help interpret content.

But the future of access in museums will go much further than addressing physical abilities. Multilingual exhibitions, which have become the norm in some parts of the world, will become the expectation—and technology solutions will broaden the language options for visitors. Multisensory exhibit elements including smell, sound, taste, and temperature will help visitors experience places and cultures they've never visited, and broaden access to a variety of audience learning types and ages. Personalized tours of exhibitions through mobile devices will assist visitors with specific needs (NMNH has created a tour specifically for visitors on the autism spectrum, for example) and help visitors experience the museum content in a way that meets their needs.

The accessibility themes also extend to reaching underserved audiences. Natural history museums will need to adapt and evolve to serve our diverse public. We must become places that are welcoming, familiar, comfortable, and safe for all visitors, especially those traditionally underserved or underrepresented in the museum, both as staff and visitors. Natural history museums have to be aware of the social histories that created them in order to look forward and create relevant exhibitions attentive and sensitive to all who come through the doors. From an exhibit development perspective, multiple languages, diverse people represented in exhibit graphics and films, locally focused examples, and co-curation/co-development with target audiences can help make the museum more broadly accessible.

Structure and process

Not only will the content, techniques, and design of natural history museum exhibitions change as we move into the future, but the process that puts exhibits on the floor will also shift. As we evolve our approach, we'll likely reconsider how we choose new projects, how we fund them, how we develop content, and how we assess our success. These behind-the-scenes elements of exhibit making are critical to our mission, and shrinking waistlines for museum budgets will make smarter planning all the more essential.

Exhibit development process

As audience needs have been increasingly prioritized on a par with content goals, the exhibit development process has grown ever more challenging—a drawn-out negotiation between complex content from expert scientists and audience priorities as defined by exhibit developers and educators. Exhibit writers have, in many cases, replaced curators as the label writers for the text on the wall, and interpretive planners have been added to the process to help focus messaging and organize content around accessible themes. The future of exhibit development will likely lean toward more audience accessibility and engagement, and away from the curator as the last word. In the process, exhibit teams will hopefully shorten the timeline and complexity inherent in the process for teams and reviewers alike.

At NMNH, we begin our exhibition process by developing a statement of purpose to develop clear definitions of audiences, messages, and exhibit tone and experience. In the future, expect to see more stakeholder participation in the development of this and similar documents, particularly regarding target audience involvement, so that the process turns inside out to some degree. This has always been a slippery slope for exhibition teams, and scientific expertise will continue to be owned by the museum, but a more open policy will likely become a necessary component of buy-in and success.

The audience-first approach will also become more of an element in the selection of new exhibitions, as we incubate new exhibit ideas and assess their feasibility. Fewer exhibits will hew strictly to the science emerging from particular natural history museums, and more will connect the strands of that basic collections research to applied fields outside the natural history industry.

> The consequence is that museums almost everywhere have, in essence, shifted from a "selling" mode to a "marketing" one. In the selling mode, their efforts have been concentrated on convincing the public to "buy" their traditional offerings. In the marketing mode, their starting point instead is the public's own needs and interests.
>
> (Weil, 1999, p. 173)

Evaluation and prototyping

Setting goals and later testing against them are the bedrock of strong exhibition development—and a summative evaluation of particular exhibits has become a critical component of most grants and financial awards. But the future of exhibit development will include much more formative testing and rapid prototyping, taking cues from product design and the design thinking landscape. Rather than putting all our eggs (in the form of dollars) into summative evaluation, exhibit leaders recognize the value in studying visitor responses early on in the process and adjusting the design to reflect how they respond. The high-tech evaluation that tracks visitors' facial expressions and movements will also make evaluation cheaper, less labor-intensive and easier to analyze, ensuring a place for these vital elements that often get cut from exhibit budgets.

Evaluation will also likely become more consistent across natural history museums and more broad in its perspective, looking at key components across different exhibitions to understand their impact. At NMNH, we recently undertook a study of our past decade of one-off exhibition evaluation, looking at the trends and outliers from more than twenty evaluation and visitor studies. We looked carefully at the audience (who?), content (what?), components (how?), and influence (so what?) of our exhibits in order to identify emergent themes and areas for further study to begin to build institutional knowledge. We realized that throughout this time we've been asking similar questions in different ways, and have been consistently inconsistent in our tracking studies and in how we gauge success. This process helped us begin to understand why some exhibit elements have been successful and others less so, and to frame new questions about the museum experience. Emerging from this process is a new "reporting tool" that will standardize how we collect critical audience demographic data and enable us to sort our project goals under consistent headings of higher-level museum objectives. For example, we have defined targets for audience awareness, engagement, attitude, behavior and skill building in exhibitions, and will ask our exhibit developers to identify project goals within these categories. This tool will also allow us to build our learning around particular exhibition techniques, visitor behavior/activity in the galleries, and recurrent content themes.

Funding

And so, it comes down to money, as do so many conversations about the future. Natural history museum models for exhibition funding vary widely, from ticketing that supports new project development to grants, gifts, and partnerships that provide seed funding to move forward. One consortium of science centers in the United States, the Science Museum Exhibit Collaborative, has developed a model in which each of the five to eight museums in the group takes turns producing traveling exhibits on a wide range of topics. The museums pay annual dues to support the early development of exhibit concepts, including topic research, focus groups, exhibit development workshops, and collaborative activities among exhibit developers, educational program developers, and marketing staff of the member institutions. From that effort, thirty exhibitions have been developed, and each museum in the consortium hosts the exhibit for no lease fee. The American Museum of Natural History in New York, the Natural History Museum in London, and the Field Museum in Chicago, among many other museums, ticket their temporary exhibitions, then tour them internationally and sometimes sell them at the end of their run. But it has become clear that very few of the group's museums see significant returns on traveling exhibitions, and thus other sustainable funding models will need to be developed. Perhaps a more collaborative model will emerge (spurred by foundation or National Science Foundation support) that encourages natural history museums to provide open-access exhibition designs to broaden their content reach significantly.

Other questions are on the table in the discussion around funding. How many temporary galleries are required to meet audience needs? How often do they need to change? Can we design exhibits that can be repurposed flexibly for future shows with new content? Can we develop smaller, pod-like exhibits that allow us to tell brief stories (in the news, as above) or feature startling objects, rather than massive ones that require significant up-front investment? Where is sustainable design in all of this—recycling of old components, energy-efficient lighting, more black box galleries that require less renovation for new shows? Where will natural history museums draw the line in terms of who they accept gifts from and how they recognize those donations in the exhibition context? Will product placement and sponsored content become part of the business plan, as it has for radio, newspapers, and magazines? For free museums like NMNH, will licensing our content help us pay the bills? What business model will move exhibitions from reactive to proactive? The future is largely guesswork in this domain.

Conclusion

It's clear that public trust is one of the most fundamental characteristics that make natural history museums vital and essential for helping people interpret the world around them. How do we maintain that trust while incorporating new, experimental exhibition techniques, complex, sometimes-controversial content, and democratic design approaches—all as we reinvent how we do our work and how we pay for it? As the NMNH 2016–2020 strategic plan makes clear, we face two major challenges as a natural history museum field generally and as our museum in particular: (1) determining our role in addressing the challenges of our rapidly changing planet; and (2) firmly establishing our sometimes flailing field as a critical tool for future research and outreach (National Museum of Natural History, 2015). Our exhibitions will reflect those urgent challenges and help us as an industry achieve progress on both fronts.

As we begin to chart a course for our future through our master plan, we are asking the same questions that so many others are pondering. What can we offer to the world? Where do we want to grow? What story do we want to tell? Our overall goals are to ensure that NMNH remains relevant, forward-looking, and exciting to visit, and to make the museum's science and collections more visible, connected, and accessible. We want to help our visitors understand the fundamental stories of life and the planet, and invite them to see their role in the Earth's past and future. Our exhibitions, therefore, have a big job to do. But their future will necessarily be a more integrated aspect of the museum and cultural landscape writ large, closer to education, closer to the science, closer to current events, and closer to our audiences.

Acknowledgments

Thank you to Lauren Kibbe and Junko Chinen for their extensive research and support.

References

Chen, C. (2015). *Mobile Research Report.* Unpublished.
Ito, M., et al. (2010). *Hanging Out, Messing Around, Geeking Out: Kids Living and Learning with New Media.* Cambridge: MIT Press.
Koster, E. (2006). The relevant museum. In: G. Anderson, eds., *Reinventing the Museum: The Evolving Conversation on the Paradigm Shift.* 2nd ed. Lanham, MD: AltaMira Press.
Mollers, N., Schvagerl, C., and Trischler, H. (2014). *Welcome to the Anthropocene.* Munich: Deutsches Museum.
National Museum of Natural History, Smithsonian (2012). *21st Century Learning in Natural History Settings Conference.* Washington, DC: National Museum of Natural History, Smithsonian, 12–15 Feb. 2012.
National Museum of Natural History, Smithsonian (2015). *Strategic Plan, 2016–2020: Natural History in the Age of Humans: A Plan for the National Museum.* Unpublished.
National Museum of Natural History, Smithsonian/Randi Korn & Associates (2016). *National Museum of Natural History: Meta-Analysis of Exhibition and Experience Evaluations* (working title). Unpublished.
Natural History Museum, London (2015). *The Natural History Museum Strategy, 2020.* Unpublished.
Strager, H., and Astrup, J. (2014). A place for kids? The public image of natural history museums. *Curator* 57, pp. 313–327.
Weil, S. E. (1999). From being *about* something to being *for* somebody: The ongoing transformation of the American museum. In: G. Anderson, eds., *Reinventing the Museum: The Evolving Conversation on the Paradigm Shift.* 2nd ed. Lanham, MD: AltaMira Press.

7 Teaching in natural history museums

Colette Dufresne-Tassé and Pierre Pénicaud

Teaching in natural history museums

Today, formal teaching and diffusion of culture are clearly separated, but this was not the case in the past, especially where natural history museums were concerned. The diffusion of culture is among the primary missions of all museums, but academic teaching, which has often been at the origins of natural history museums, is still very present.

Academic and formal teaching

The Muséum National d'Histoire Naturelle

The Jardin du Roi in Paris owes its existence to the rivalry between the professors at the Sorbonne's School of Medicine and the king's doctors, mainly trained at the prestigious University of Montpellier. In 1635, Louis XIII ordered the creation of the Royal Garden of Medicinal Plants, as suggested by his personal physician, Guy de la Brosse, who desired a place for the cultivation of plants with medicinal uses and the teaching of medicine and pharmacy (Barthélemy, 1979). This new institution's free lectures were open to the public but did not lead to a degree. The original disciplines tended toward various fields of natural history: botany; zoology; vegetal, animal, and human anatomy; chemistry; and mineralogy. During the eighteenth century, the Comte de Buffon increased the size of the garden and transformed the ancient Droguier into the Cabinet of Natural History, in order to present numerous and varied collections to the public (Bernard and Couailhac, 1842). Amid the French Revolution, the two institutions merged, and the newly formed entity was known as the Muséum National d'Histoire Naturelle. With the opening of a menagerie, the institution for the first time united the three collections that would form the basis for research and the teaching of the natural sciences in France: living vegetal collections, living animal collections, and collections of natural objects. Throughout the nineteenth and twentieth centuries, the museum continued to evolve with the creation of new university chairs, some without collections, including new disciplines concerned more with mechanisms than with objects: comparative physiology, organic chemistry, ecology, and ethology. The collections were widely displayed to the public both at the Jardin des Plantes and outside the museum (for example, in the Musée de l'Homme and the Zoo of Vincennes), and scientific expeditions were on the rise (Lemoine, 1935).

Several centuries later, still struggling with the universities, the museum could not grant a university degree and appears to have been neglected by the authorities, with the buildings and collections in a decrepit state after World War II. In the late twentieth century, the museum benefitted from the successive reforms of the French university system. It was now able to award postgraduate degrees (PhDs). The museum's integration into a university network that included about ten establishments now comprises its higher education system. Although comprising only approximately 500 researcher-teachers and 500 students, the museum is in direct contact with 5,800 teachers and researchers and the 59,000 students of this community. This higher education system relies on the largely interdisciplinary doctoral program "Natural and Human Sciences: Evolution and Ecology" and on the master's program, where one of the specialties is museology (Muséum National d'Histoire Naturelle, 2016). Following a three-hundred-year tradition, the museums host public lectures on natural and human sciences, based on field research and its impressive collections, from gardening to ethnomusicology to the discovery of sea life in its maritime sites, recently doing so through online lectures.

The example of the Clermont–Ferrand museum in the provinces

Throughout the nineteenth century, museums were created in many provincial towns in France. Today, the nation is home to nearly fifty institutions with zoology, botany, and geology collections, and in some cases, prehistory and ethnology have been indebted to developments in local scientific research and the discovery of new continents and their ecosystems (OCIM, 1991). From the start, the museums of natural history handled the conservation and diffusion of scientific culture, but in the provinces, research and higher education at the national museum are directed by the universities.

The origins of the Muséum d'Histoire Naturelle in Clermont-Ferrand may be found in the late eighteenth century, when the volcanic nature of the Auvergne mountains was unearthed, attracting scientists from all over Europe and encouraging local naturalists. In 1795, the revolution prompted the opening of central schools to replace the old ones, one of which was created in Clermont-Ferrand with a small font of collections to permit the teaching of natural sciences. The institution was closed in 1802, and the municipality decided to pursue the teaching of natural sciences by offering public lectures based on the collections of a specific museum. In 1826, Henri Lecoq was named municipal professor, director of the botanical garden, and curator of the museum. The University of Clermont-Ferrand was inaugurated in 1856, and Lecoq became the first holder of the chair in Natural History. The collections were deposited at the university; they were still used for educational purposes but were not open to the public. Lecoq, who had become rich thanks to his career as a pharmacist, installed in his private residence his private collection, fruits of his research on the geology and botany of the Massif Central and the variability of the species. At his death, he bequeathed his collections to the city of Clermond-Ferrand, which opened the Museum Henri Lecoq in 1873. However, relations between the municipal museum and the university slowly became strained (Pénicaud, 2002). In 1997, the new scientific team of the Lecoq museum decided to improve relations with the university and welcome back the students. This decision was guided in part by the need to update the institution's holdings, and to clean and prepare an inventory after restoring and documenting over six hundred thousand specimens of the collections. An agreement was signed between the municipality and the university to organize a partnership headed by the museum. This agreement concerned the management of the university collections, part of which belonged to the 1856 accession; it also addressed the work on the collections and especially the creation of a teaching unit, co-directed by the university and the museum.

The teaching unit proposed an annual course in museology for twenty students and a seventy-hour-long phase during which they would handle, clean, and develop an inventory of a small group of objects. This way, every year students would have the opportunity to explore the collections and the museum. This partnership encouraged students to visit the exhibitions and attend the conferences they had abandoned in the past. Indeed, regional museums in France, which are not university institutions, can and must have a close relationship with higher education and research. On the other hand, all museums are concerned with the training of high school teachers and undergraduate professors.

Informal education: the dissemination of scientific culture to the public

Informal education, which occurs outside the normal rubric and is addressed to a diverse public and largely noncaptive audiences, takes many forms: exhibitions, whether permanent or temporary; mediation; cultural events; and online lectures and other resources. Dissemination means that all of these activities, along with further developments natural history museums, are closely tied to these institutions' collections (Pénicaud, 2002; Figure 7.1).

A   In cabinets of curiosities, the products of nature and humankind are shown without any order or distinction. Given their combination of reasoning, observation, and superstition, these do not yet make use of sciences. Cabinets' collections tend to illustrate a world where the temporal and spatial dimensions remain to be explored.

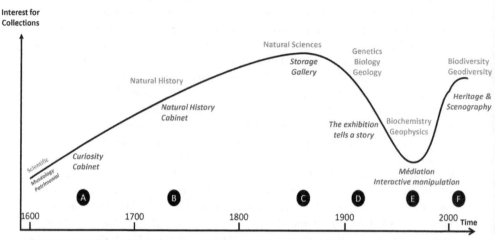

Schematic curve of scientific interest *(clear grey)* and museology and patrimonial interest for the natural history collections *(dark grey and italics) over a period of time.*

Figure 7.1 A brief, comparative account of the spread of culture, collections, and science.

B   Curiosity cabinets are replaced by the cabinets of natural history that eventually become museums. These collections provide support to the study of natural history that defines the three "kingdoms" of nature. They are also used for the education of doctors and chemists, initially carried out in botanical gardens.

C   The golden age of museums begins during the French Revolution with the creation of the Muséum National d'Histoire Naturelle, featuring professors who teach, research, and enhance the collections. The collections are divided into various specialties of the natural sciences and are presented to the public in comprehensive galleries. This model reflects the systematic approach that, in 1889, leads to the construction of the zoological galleries of the national museum, a temple to the science of classifications and a reserve available to researchers and a broad public (Schaer, 1993).

D   New sciences appear following Charles Darwin's articulation of the theory of evolution and the better understanding of the functions of organisms, from the cell to the ecosystem. In 1899, the galleries of comparative anatomy and paleontology are established. From the collection, the curators choose those items that could best tell the story of evolution in line with the science of the time: demonstrating the relationship between vertebrates and the evolution of life on Earth. A new type of exhibit—the diorama— also emerges, which shows naturalized specimens placed, as in life, in their environment, an early indication of the new science of ecology (Lafon, 1999; Pénicaud, 2004a).

E   The evolution of the natural sciences in the twentieth century nearly proves fatal to museums of natural history. Outside some disciplines such as paleontology, which continue to be based on specimens, the "modern" sciences take precedence over the collections. At the same time, and stemming from the creation of the Palais de la Découverte, science museology moves in the direction of mediation and experimentation, followed by the Cité des Sciences et de l'Industrie, which, by proposing modern, interactive devices, relegates the showcases of specimens to oblivion. The collections are no longer seen as presenting a scientific or pedagogical, much less aesthetic interest (Poirier, 2016). Natural history museums' divorce from other museums is consummated in 1959 when the latter is placed under the authority of the newly formed Ministry of Culture. As for natural history museums, they remain under the aegis of the Ministry of Education, reduced to the slightly denigrated role of children's museums. Perhaps fittingly, schoolchildren and their families remain faithful to the museums that had developed them as audiences, although this does not stop certain collections from becoming obsolete or galleries from closing.

F   The end of the twentieth century witnesses a revival of natural history museums and their collections, largely due to the influx of new ideas such as bio-and geodiversity, environmental sciences, and the newfound awareness of the fragility of our planet. In this light, naturalist collections appear as a font of irreplaceable information. The galleries of the Muséum National d'Histoire Naturelle in Paris are renovated, starting with the Grande Galerie de l'Evolution, and followed by many provincial museums such as those in La Rochelle, Toulouse, Lyon, and Bordeaux. In the early twentieth century, the new law on national heritage strengthens the ties between natural history museums and other types of museums. The numerous collections of former are again considered a vital part of the French national heritage (Pénicaud, 2004b; Rainette et al., 2008).

At the dawn of the new millennium, natural history collections receive newfound appreciation as instruments for scientific research, tools for the transmission of knowledge, aesthetic objects, and as the heritage of humanity. The following three examples show that even if museology is now assisted by modern technologies, the collections remain the core element of exhibitions of natural history museums.

The staging of the collections at the Grande Galerie de l'Évolution

Although preserving its magnificent nineteenth-century interior architecture, the renovation of this gallery revolutionized museology of the natural sciences by introducing a theatrical scenography (OCIM, 1991; Eidelman and Van Praët, 2000; Figure 7.2). On a large central stage, animals from the African savanna are disposed in a caravan that leaves room for the imagination and aesthetic pleasure while defining relations between the species of a biotope. In 2014, twenty years after the renovation, the introduction of dynamic lighting

Figure 7.2 La Grande Galerie de l'Évolution © B. Faye – MNHN.

and sound, possible thanks to computerized techniques and control of energy, create a suggestion of movement. The objects are magnified by mobile projectors and by the old glass roof that revolves like the sky. Environmental sound is realized by the positioning of speakers throughout the gallery and near the specimens. Hour-long shows for the public present an existing image of a day in the African savanna, while adding a temporal element.

Scenography designed as a three-dimensional open book in the Tree of Life exhibition at the Clermont–Ferrand museum

Completed in 2006 in an environment limited in both size and budget, *Tree of Life* was the first presentation of the concept of phylogenetic classification in France (Figure 7.3). The museum's scientific team had a relatively small, seventy-five-square-meter space to realize a permanent exhibition that was based on up-to-date information and could also enhance the collections. In *Tree of Life*, the visitor is placed in the center of a three-dimensional tree whose branches represent about 450 species, from the hummingbird to the orchid, from the coelacanth to the fly and the jellyfish. The visitor may also find oneself in a mirror, beside a chimpanzee. This presentation allows each visitor, whatever his or her level of education, to understand the place of all living beings in the tree and to learn, through their phylogenetic relation, the characteristics of the different branches. In addition to being geared toward the general public, this exhibition was also conceived as a pedagogical took for primary and secondary school students.

Figure 7.3 La Salle de l'Arbre du Vivant © P. Pénicaud – Muséum Henri Lecoq, Ville de Clermont-Ferrand.

Explaining research at the Balcon des Sciences at the Musée de l'Homme

The Balcon des Sciences, which opened in October 2015, was conceived in the context of the museum's renovation (Figure 7.4). The objective of this "museum-laboratory," inspired by Paul Rivet, is to encourage the public to discover the work of researchers and their tools and thereby create a link between the visitor and the actuality of science (Guerry and Pénicaud, 2017). To permit the regular updating of scientific research, it was necessary to create interchangeable units whose contents could be changed rapidly and automatically—text panels, small digital showcases, and multimedia— along with a feature allowing museum personnel to integrate new informa- tion (texts, photos, videos, soundtracks). These units introduce visitors to the actors in the museum-laboratory, the various stages of research, and the disciplines that comprise the field of anthropology, whether cultural or bio- logical, modern or ancient. The various stages of research are shown—the collecting of material and nonmaterial specimens, followed by their return to the museum for analysis, and the instruments needed for this purpose. The exhibit also presents the laboratories and technical platforms and, finally, the dissemination of the interpretation. In addition, it gives researchers an opportunity to present their recent findings. The space uses mainly digital supports, but researchers and mediators are often on hand to meet the public.

The history of French natural history museums reveals that formal or informal education and instruction of the public have always been among

Figure 7.4 Le Balcon des Sciences © J.-C. Domenech – MNHN.

their greatest missions, certainly to a higher degree than in museums less concerned with the collecting of data and basic research. This history also shows that these collections' role has changed in accordance with the evolution of science, but that it remains fundamental for the learning of scientific culture; the latter is a source of great interest to the visitor, especially when presented using tools of modern scenography. Collections are the essential material support to scientific questioning and the conducting of research. They are part of the new pedagogies based on digital technologies, and on public participation that is found in many museums. Multimedia terminals encourage public participation toward achieving a better understanding of content. The public becomes the actor inside the inventorying the species or the deciphering program of the collections' archives (Les Herbonautes).

Learning as a response to teaching

In the eighteenth century, when Antoine-Laurent de Jussieu was at the Jardin du Roi teaching the classification of plants based on their morphology, he was addressing a wide audience of students and amateurs interested in the natural sciences. For these two types of audience members, learning meant different things: for the students, it meant remembering what they were hearing, because they would have to reuse it later; and for the amateurs, learning simply connoted the pleasure of understanding and discovery. In both cases, the institution presented the same information, but the listeners benefitted from it in different ways. Today, of course, natural history museums still play their educational role through teaching, but mainly do so through programs and exhibitions designed for science lovers and the public at large. The rest of this paper will deal only with exhibitions, because they are now the primary vehicle for museum adult education.

Two views on learning

Adult education became an important concept for the international museum community in the aftermath of World War II, giving rise to two contrasting views on the subject. The first, observed largely in the Francophone countries, has been articulated by a small number of authors with mainly theoretical and critical concerns (Dufresne-Tassé, 1991; Eidelman and Van Praët, 2000).[1] These researchers have been primarily interested in the learning process and secondary phenomena such as the possible discrepancy arising between knowledge acquired and level of satisfaction derived from a museum visit (Burigana and Caucat, 2003; Langlois, 2010*).

The second position predominates in the Anglo-Saxon countries, and recently seems to have gained almost worldwide acceptance, becoming dominant and almost paradigmatic. It is thus the one studied here. Seven major texts published during the last twenty-five years set forth the main elements of this position: the conception of the museum's educational role, learning as the visitor's response to the museum's actions, and the instruments used for identifying and measuring learning. Since a study of these various aspects of the Anglo-Saxon view seems to produce less than satisfactory results, an alternative approach will be explored, namely that of producing meaning on the part of the visitor.

Learning as seen by the Anglo-Saxons

The educational role of the museum

The museum's educational role concerns not only individuals but also society as a whole (AAM, 1992; Anderson, 1997; Hein, 2005). When it comes to society, the museum, in collaboration with other institutions, promotes democracy, human rights, and tolerance for diversity (AAM, 1992; Hein, 2005; UNESCO and Ukrainian Committee of ICOM, 2012). As far as individuals, the museum's mission should be to foster their development (Anderson, 1997; Hein, 2005) through the enhancement of a series of skills, such as exploration, observation, contemplation, study, synthesis, problem-solving, criticism, creativity, and collaboration (American Association of Museums [AAM], 1992; Anderson, 1997; Institute of Museum and Library Services [IMLS], 2009). In short, the Anglo-Saxon writers conceive of the museum's educational role in an all-encompassing and generous manner.

Learning as the public's response to museum education

However, the museum's very worthy ambition is confined to the promotion of the visitor's learning. This reduction may be explained by the intervention of the following three factors: museums' desire to evaluate rigorously their contribution to people's development (Tobelem, 2010*; Daignault, 2011); the pressure by the state in demanding clear evidence of the return on its investment in the museum sector (Hooper-Greenhill et al., 2003); and the absence of instruments that can accurately quantity other repercussions of the museums' educational action (Bournival, 2013; Jacobsen, 2016*).

A definition of learning

Two of the seven authors mentioned above offer a formal definition of learning. For Hooper-Greenhill et al. (2003, p. 9), learning is a process of active engagement with experience. It is what people do when they want to make sense of the world. For Hein (1998, p. 22), learning is a transformation of the schema in which the learner plays an active role and which involves making sense of a range of phenomena presented to the mind.

Although contemporary, these constructivist concepts of learning are problematic when applied to an adult, for not all an adult's attempts to give meaning to his or her experience of the world necessarily lead to learning. For instance, when I, as an adult standing at a street corner and seeing a green light, infer that I can cross safely, I learn nothing even though I give meaning to what I see. Moreover, learning does not necessarily cause a change of schema. Indeed, if I learn that there are two species of osmonds, the cinnamon osmond and the royal osmond, but I do not know what an osmond is, I cannot change my schema of an osmond because I do not yet have one. Thus, it is better to stay with Pritchard's position (2006): learning necessitates that the meaning given to an experience be new, that the accuracy of this meaning be verified, and that it be subject to an effort of memorization to enhance its chances of entering a person's long-term memory, where it will be retained.

When an adult—especially one who visits museums infrequently—visits an exhibition, what that person sees is mostly new for him or her; but the person does not need to check the accuracy of the information received since he or she can trust the veracity of the contents offered by the curator. However, this person must control the accuracy of what he or she makes of this information. A study of several exhibitions with over five hundred visitors (Dufresne-Tassé, 2010) showed that adults rarely make this last check, any more than they try to memorize the information they collect or produce. Consequently, production of meaning for adult visitors rarely means learning in the strict sense of the word. A better term for what takes place is probably "discovery."

Tools for identifying adult learning in a museum setting

For the last twenty-five years, the main tools used to identify learning acquired by adults in exhibitions are the tracking method, the questionnaire, and the interview (Hein, 1998). As we shall see, each of these presents problems.

Tracking

Observation of the visitor's behavior without his knowledge is useful for identifying the objects[2] that attract or retain his attention. However, neither the fact of approaching an object nor the fact of lingering over it constitutes a reliable indicator of learning. Indeed, the fact that a visitor approaches an object may mean that it is seen as interesting or intriguing, but not necessarily as a source of new information to be remembered. As for lengthy examination of an object, that may mean the visitor is accumulating information and learning, but also that he is struggling with a problem that prevents him from understanding and acquiring knowledge. Information obtained by tracking, therefore, suffers from a serious problem of validity.

The questionnaire

The author of a questionnaire cannot imagine everything a visitor learns and even less so about a group. The author, therefore, limits his or her questions to the learning that corresponds to the aims of the exhibition designer and thus leaves out an unknown quantity. Moreover, the comparison between a visitor's knowledge before and after the visit may well overestimate what he or she has learned during the visit, for the sight of certain objects may awaken dormant knowledge. "Reawakened," this shows up at the exit and falsely increases the amount of knowledge actually acquired during the visit. In short, the questionnaire supposedly used to obtain the most objective data possible may also underestimate as well as overestimate the learning acquired.

The interview

An interview carried out once the visit is over should enable a visitor to express him- or herself freely, offering the opportunity to describe everything he or she has just learned. But this is not the case, at least for the following reasons: (a) if the visit to the various galleries takes more than a few minutes, so many things are thought of during that time that it is impossible to remember all of them; (b) as it accumulates, the information grasped by the visitor is transformed, so that upon leaving the exhibition, what the person says differs markedly from what he or she has acquired during the visit. In short, the interview offers a picture of learning distorted by various types of bias.

Hein (1998) adds a few more tools to track learning in exhibitions, such as the comments book or the focus group. The study of these tools, like those of the three described above, would likewise reveal their lack of validity.

Overview

The tools discussed above are therefore of doubtful validity. Moreover, the extension of the learning concept is not sufficiently marked; it imprudently reduces the role of museum education, and raises embarrassing questions such as, "When visiting exhibition galleries, does the visitor only learn?" "If not, what else does he or she do?" "Is it without value?" "Is it unrelated to the person's psychological development?" "To the museum's educational action?" Even if we attribute outcomes such as enhanced knowledge, understanding, skills, change in attitudes and values, enjoyment, inspiration, creativity, or action (Hooper-Greenhill et al., 2003), one should show that these consequences are due solely to learning, and that the rest of the psychological activity manifested by the visitor in the exhibition plays no role in it at all.

The first attempt to understand the consequences of the museum's educational action, learning, and the tools that identify or measure it, suffer from significant weaknesses. The situation, therefore, seems ripe for what Kuhn (1962) calls a paradigm shift: the development of an alternative concept.

An alternative approach: the visitor's production of meaning

This section offers a definition of the production of meaning, a means of identifying it, as well as the validity of the means and several advantages of its use.

A definition

For an adult visitor, to produce meaning is to put into words—whether communicated or not—what one is conscious of,[3] one's experience as it unfolds.[4] In an exhibition, this experience corresponds to what the visitor thinks or feels: that person's response to the museum's educational action. Thus, as understood here, a visitor's minute-by-minute production of meaning has a far greater scope than for the Anglo-Saxon researchers. It is not limited to learning, to the apprehension of the new information that the visitor seeks to memorize, and, if necessary, whose accuracy he or she tries to verify.

A means of identification

The proposed means is an adaptation of a technique developed by Ericcson and Simon (1993), validated for use in a museum context (Dufresne-Tassé et al., 1998a,b) and termed "Thinking Aloud" or "Telling One's Experience" (Dufresne-Tassé et al., 2014). It consists of asking a visitor entering the museum to visit the galleries as he or she wishes while thinking out loud, in other words, expressing what goes on in that person's mind as he or she goes along without holding back or justifying the contents. What this person expresses constitutes a "discourse" that delivers the following equivalent phenomena: (1) the visitor's production of meaning; (2) what he or she thinks or feels; (3) that person's experience moment by moment; (4) the visitor's treatment of what he or she is seeing—in other words, the meaning he or she attributes to it.

A researcher accompanies the visitor throughout, without intervening but simply to record the person's "discourse." Once the visit is over, the discourse is entered into a computer and then analyzed in written form.

An example of producing meaning

It is impossible to reproduce entire discourses here, as they would take up too much space.[5] The following is merely an extract that illustrates some phenomena continually observed in the discourses of a sample of ninety visitors (Dufresne-Tassé, 2010). This extract was taken from that of a forty-year-old architect visiting the greenhouses of the Montreal Botanical Garden. These greenhouses are organized as follows: a central one offers basic information on plant physiology; it, in turn, leads to two series of greenhouses in which nine collections of exotic plants are displayed.

Discourse extract

The visitor walks through the central greenhouse without stopping, saying that he had already read what was written there during a previous visit. He then enters the greenhouse featuring tropical rain forest plants. He next visits four other greenhouses, but the extract from his discourse presented here will cover only what he said in the first two.

Tropical rain forest greenhouse

1 "It's humid in here." He then reads in a low voice a panel concerning the three levels of vegetation in a rain forest.
2 He looks at a plant and reads: "*Nidularium*, Bromeliaceae, Brazil." "Even though I know a bit of Latin, amo, amas, amant (laughs), that's not much help."
3 Goes to another plant, muttering, "*Alcantara imperial*, Bromeliaceae," then reads the plaque accompanying the plant and explaining why it is called imperial. "Bromeliaceae, I'll try to remember to tell that to my mother-in-law. She has one like it."
4 Looks at a plant, then reads: "Moses' cradle, blah, blah, blah." "It looks like the other one."
5 Looks at a plant, then reads: "*Nidularium*, Bromeliaceae, Brazil." "It's got water in the middle. The other one didn't. That's interesting."
6 Looks at a plant, then reads: "Bat plant, *Tacca* something, Taccaceae." "Where is it? There are so many different plants in the corner; I don't know which one it is."

7   Looks at a plant, then reads: "Spider lily, Amaryllidaceae, Tropical America." "It's very pretty."

8   "It's a bore. You look, then you read bromeliaceae, cacadacaea, pigad-acaea, machinadacaea, all-you-want-adacaea!!"

9   Looks at a plant, then reads: "Impatience." "I thought so, I know that one."

At this point, the visitor reaches the far end of the greenhouse and enters the next one.

Tropical food plants greenhouse

10 While continuing to walk, he says: "These are things like spices, pine-apple, coffee, banana, mangoes, etc."

11 Then, in front of a clump of banana trees, he reads: 'Banana tree, Musa, yeah, Musaceae, horticultural origin." "I've seen banana plantations in Colombia, and Garcia Marquez talks about them."

12 "It's fun to see them up close."

13 "The little one, you can see how it grows and develops, with a stalk in the center."

14 "I've already seen other plants that grow like that."

15 "It's pretty, the light green, a bit of blue with white, lots of white."

16 "That reminds me of certain Thai celadons."

17 "The leaves aren't too big' you can see stripes, little parallel lines."

18 "It's very pretty."

19 "How does it develop?"

20 "The leaf, the shoot, comes from the trunk."

21 "So the trunk has to grow as the plant grows."

22 "It's touching... apart from being intriguing!"

23 "That's fragile."

24 "How can that become strong enough to bear a whole bunch?"

25 "A bunch of banana, this is really heavy."

26 "Because I've seen men carrying them. They're not laughing. Their shoulders are all bent."

27 "I'd like to find information about that."

28 "I'd like to know how it develops, how it becomes strong."

29 "I like trying to understand what's complicated."

30 "I feel like a researcher."

31 "And then things become so fine... so interesting."

32 "It's really wonderful!"

33 "It makes such a difference between seeing a banana plantation from a distance and seeing three or four banana trees up close!"

34 "It all becomes so interesting when one... when one... puts down the phone and just starts to look, really look!"

35 "I'm leaving them... ahead, I see the ferns."
36 "But I'd like to go on."
37 "It's like taking a deep breath."
38 "It feels really great, understanding... what's beautiful... Finding beauty... that one understands!"
39 "I must think about that... in my work."

A question concerning validity

Reading the above extract, one realizes that the "Thinking aloud" technique can provide a lot of information, but can this information be trusted? To answer this question, two sub-questions must be answered: (1) Does the fact of speaking modify the visitor's psychological functioning and, consequently, his production of meaning? "Thinking aloud" does not disturb this functioning (Ericcson and Simon, 1993; Kukan and Beck, 1997*). Such would be the case if the visitor had to "talk about what he thinks." Yet this is not the case, for when he "tells his experience," the visitor merely "expresses directly" what comes into his mind; (2) Does the researcher's presence cause the visitor to modify what he has to say? More precisely, does it cause him to say more, other, or less than he really thinks? The visitor cannot say more or something else because he must think it in order to say it.[6] But he can choose not to say things, especially when what he might say contravenes norms or taboos. However, such cases are mostly predictable and easy to detect, so that the general validity of a visitor's discourse should not be questioned.

Advantages

Just as we have seen only an extract of a discourse, for the sake of brevity, we shall now read a brief analysis aimed simply at emphasizing some of the advantages of the production of meaning for knowledge of the visitor's functioning and as useful information for the curator.

Knowing how the visitor functions

Identification of the contents learned

The visitor's discourse reveals not only the learning achieved (remark 3 above), but also indicates its content, the effort made to remember this content, and even the motivation behind it. A careful study of the rest of the discourse also reveals that the visitor learns nothing else despite the twenty-eight remarks devoted to the banana trees (remarks 11–39 included); but, it also shows that learning is not necessarily related to a large number of remarks, nor to lengthy observation of the object considered.

Observation of several forms of affective functioning

The content of the extract presented above permits further examination of the two following beliefs related to emotion: (1) Emotion is a powerful factor for learning in an exhibition. However, learning about the Bromeliaceae does not seem to be preceded or accompanied by emotion; moreover, the lengthy passage about banana trees does reflect several emotions, but no learning; (2) Emotion is *the* affective phenomenon of an adult's visit to a museum. However, in the extract cited, emotions are certainly observed (6, 19, 24; curiosity in all cases), but also a whole range of other affective phenomena:[7] affectively connoted sensations (1, 12, 37, 38); estimative reactions (5, 8, 23, 33); pleasure, either aesthetic (7, 15, 18) or intellectual (22); empathy (26); self-projection (30, 31, 32, 34), desire (27, 28, 36); and the expression of personal tastes (29).

Evocation of past knowledge or experience

The visitor's recourse to his knowledge or experience (10, 11, 14, 16, 26) is probably as useful as the acquisition of new knowledge. Indeed, in the above extract, it plays several roles: identifying (plants) without having to consult the information provided in the exhibition (10), deepening or completing what the visitor produces as meaning (11, 16, 26), and situating as similar or different what he sees and what he already knows (19). In short, these evocations help to lighten the visitor's load, enriching or clarifying his production of meaning, in other words, the meaning he attributes to what he observes. Moreover, these evocations help bridge the gap between the visitor's discoveries and his personal universe and integrate them into this universe. Lastly, among adults forty years of age and over, they the maintenance of knowledge and memories in the great storehouse of the long-term memory.

Distinguishing two types of experience

The first type of experience, which takes place in the rain forest plant greenhouse, is characterized by the collection of data to identify the plants on show (2, 4, 5, 6, 7), each followed by a rapid and simple reaction. Moreover, these collection-reaction twinnings are disjointed from each other so that a real repetition can be seen of the same sort of functioning. This is considered boring by the visitor himself (8).

   The second type starts like the first, by a collection of information aimed at identifying what the visitor is viewing (11). But this identification leads to an important and diversified production, totally different from what we have seen above. Participant elements are phenomena already analyzed such as the evocation of knowledge and experiences, emotions, and affectively connoted feelings. To these phenomena are added numerous observations

(13, 15, 17, 20, 23), questions (19, 24), explanations (21, 26), and a lengthy return on the preceding production of meaning (29, 30, 31, 32, 33, 34, 37, 38). Moreover, instead of being disjointed, the remarks that correspond to this production of meaning fit into each other so that meaning develops and is built up. The result is a small unified semantic whole and a visitor who expresses pleasure and desire.

The production of meaning, as soon as it reaches a certain critical mass and is articulated as seen above, produces what might be called an intense or psychological immersive experience (Dufresne-Tassé, 2014). Numerous studies show that such an experience contributes greatly to the visitor's psychological development (Engeser, 2012*). Furthermore, it lowers his or her mental fatigue and stress level (Hartig et al., 1997; Packer and Bond, 2010*), thus, directly fostering that person's mental health (Chatterjee and Noble, 2013*); and by having a positive impact on the visitor's cardiac and immune functions, it indirectly supports his or her physical health (Steptoe et al., 2015).

Benefits for the curator

The production of meaning as seen here provides the curator with a considerable amount of detailed information concerning the reaction of one or more visitors to the exhibition. More precisely, it informs the curator about the visitors' reactions in his or her galleries—in this case, greenhouses— and their modalities: the places they stop, their way of dealing with what they encounter, the possibility of producing meaning merely by observation. Moreover, they inform the curator about the use of texts and museography, and the way in which such elements help—or hinder—the visitor's ability to make sense of what he or she sees. This information enables the progress of the visit to be followed and, as we have seen above, to distinguish very different types of experiences.

A new response to teaching

The subject of this text, teaching and learning, may suggest that these concepts conflict or that there is at least considerable tension between the two: the curator wishing to transmit knowledge, the visitors disappointing him or her by the little they learn. However, opposition or tension disappear if visitors' production of meaning is substituted for learning. Indeed, this production provides the curator with a font of information that he or she lacks to identify accurately the learning and to adapt his or her "teaching" to the characteristics of the visitors' psychological functioning. But it also provides the curator access to the "rest" of the visitors' production, namely, their imaginary and affective reactions, their escapes into their own world to consolidate or modify their projects, but also their emotions and feelings, the empathy they show to "living" things, their pleasures and their desires. Thus, this comprises a whole set of elements that contribute to the visitors' psychological development and well-being. All in all, the visitors' production of meaning offers information on all these benefits to the curator and shows him or her the places of an exhibition that could be improved. It is then up to the curator to experiment and to retain those changes that seem the most fruitful!

Notes

1 An asterisk (*) indicates a large number of references to a particular subject, and that those cited are given as examples.
2 The term "object" here refers to any item displayed in a natural history museum: plant, instrument, cast, model, and so on.
3 This way of conceiving the production of meaning corresponds to that proposed by Hirtle (2013). As to consciousness, this is understood as suggested by Dennett (1993).
4 The experience in question here is what Rogers (1966) and Garneau and Larivey (1983) describe as immediate, and that Jantzen (2013) calls "experiencing." It should be distinguished from the overall visit experience (Falk and Dierking, 1992; Gottesdiener, 1992), namely the impression left by the visit when it is over.
5 A discourse corresponding to a half-hour visit may represent from 3 to 8 or 9 pages of text at 1.5 spacing.
6 This position does not contradict the well-known French maxim "Saying one thing but thinking another," for in this case, "what one thinks" means saying what one knows or believes, or the values to which one adheres.
7 For a definition of each of these phenomena, see Dufresne-Tassé et al., 2013.

References

AAM (1992). *Excellence and Equity: Education and the Public Dimension of Museums*. Washington, DC: AAM.

Anderson, D. (1997). *A Common Wealth: Museums and Learning in the United Kingdom*. London: Department of National Heritage.

Barthélémy, G. (1979). *Les Jardiniers du Roy*. Paris: Le Pélican.

Bernard, P., and Couailhac, L. (1842). *Le Jardin des Plantes*. Paris: L. Curmer.

Bournival, M. T. (2013). *L'évaluation de la performance dans les institutions muséales au Québec: Étude spécifique déposée au Groupe de travail sur l'avenir du réseau muséal québécois*. Quebec: Ministère de la culture et des communications.

Burigana, P., and Caucat, M. (2003). *Projet de réaménagement de la serre des plantes tropicales économiques du Jardin botanique de Montréal: Enquête sur les attentes des visiteurs, recherches et propositions muséographiques*. Montreal: Jardin botanique de Montréal / Université de Montréal.

Chatterjee, H. J., and Noble, G. (2013). *Museums, Health, and Well-Being*. Farnham: Ashgate.

Daignault, L. (2011). *L'évaluation muséale: Savoirs et savoir-faire*. Quebec: Presses de l'Université du Québec.

Dennett, D. C. (1993). *La conscience expliquée*. Paris: Éditions Odile Jacob. (P. Engel translation of *Consciousness Explained*. London: Little, Brown, 1991.)

Dufresne-Tassé, C. (1991). L'éducation muséale: Son rôle, sa spécificité, sa place parmi les autres fonctions du musée. *Revue canadienne de l'éducation* 16(3), pp. 251–258.

Dufresne-Tassé, C. (2010). *Le public adulte: Fonctionnement psychologique et éducation muséale; Notes de cours.* Paris: École du Louvre.

Dufresne-Tassé, C. (2013). Optimal functioning of the visitor and principles of temporary thematic exhibition development. In: I. V. Chuvilova and O. N. Shelegina, eds., *Innovations in the Museum World: Collection of Scientific Articles.* Novosibirsk: Publishing Center of Novosibirsk State University (published in Russian).

Dufresne-Tassé, C. (2014). Experiencia intensa e experiencia de imersão: Relatório de observações diretas. *Museion: Revista do Museu e Arquivo Histórico La Sallem* 19, pp. 27–42.

Dufresne-Tassé, C., O'Neill, M. C., Sauvé, M., and Marin, D. (2014). Un outil pour connaître de minute en minute l'expérience d'un visiteur adulte. *Revista Museologia & Interdisciplinaridade* 3(6), pp. 187–204.

Dufresne-Tassé, C., Trion, E., Barucq, H., Sauvé, M., and O'Neill, M. C. (2013). Entre l'apprentissage et la délectation: Les émotions du visiteur adulte de type grand public. *Journal of Arts and Cultural Management* 6(2), pp. 121–169 (published in Korean).

Dufresne-Tassé, C., Sauvé, M., Weltzl-Fairchild, A., Banna, N., Lepage, Y., and Dassa, C. (1998a). Pour des expositions muséales plus éducatives, accéder à l'expérience du visiteur adulte: Développement d'une approche. *Canadian Journal of Education* 23(3), pp. 302–316.

Dufresne-Tassé, C., Sauvé, M., Weltzl-Fairchild, A., Banna, N., Lepage, Y., and Dassa, C. (1998b). Pour des expositions muséales plus éducatives, accéder à l'expérience du visiteur adulte: Élaboration d'un instrument d'analyse. *Canadian Journal of Education* 23(4), pp. 421–438.

Eidelman, J., and Van Praët, M. (2000). *La muséologie des sciences et des publics.* Paris: Presses Universitaires de France.

Engeser, S., ed. (2012). *Advances in Flow Research.* New York, Dordrecht, Heidelberg, and London: Springer.

Ericcson, K. A., and Simon, H. A. (1993). *Protocol Analysis.* Cambridge: MIT Press.

Falk, J., and Dierking, L. (1992). *The Museum Experience.* Washington, DC: Whalesback Books.

Garneau, J., and Larivey, M. (1983). *L'auto développement: Psychothérapie dans la vie quotidienne.* Montreal: Les éditions de l'Homme / Le Centre interdisciplinaire de Montréal.

Gottesdiener, A. (1992). La lecture de texte dans les musées d'art. *Public et Musées* 1, pp. 75–91.

Guerry, E., and Pénicaud, P. (2017). Le Balcon des sciences au Musée de l'Homme. *La Lettre de l'OCIM* 169.

Hartig, T., Korpela, K., Evans, G. W., and Gärling, T. (1997). A measure of restorative quality in environments. *Scandinavian Housing and Planning Research* 14(4), pp. 175–194.

Hein, G. E. (1998). *Learning in the Museum.* London: Routledge.

Hein, G. E. (2005). The role of museums in society: Education and social action. *Curator: The Museum Journal* 48(4), pp. 357–364.

Hirtle, W. (2013). *Making Sense out of Meaning*. Montreal and Kingston: McGill-Queen's University Press.

Hooper-Greenhill, E., et al. (2003). *Measuring the Outcomes and Impact of Learning in Museums, Archives, and Libraries*. Leicester: Research Centre for Museums and Galleries, Department of Museum Studies, University of Leicester.

IMLS (Institute of Museum and Library Services) (2009). *Museums, Libraries, and 21st-Century Skills*. Washington, DC: IMLS.

Jacobsen, J. W. (2016). *Measuring Museum Impact and Performance: Theory and Practice*. Lanham: Rowman & Littlefield.

Jantzen, C. (2013). Experiences in everyday life. In: J. Sundbo and F. Sorensen, eds., *Handbook on Experience Economy*. Cheltenham: Edward Elgar.

Kuhn, T. S. (1962). *The Structure of Scientific Revolutions*. Chicago: University of Chicago Press.

Kukan, L., and Beck, I. L. (1997). Thinking aloud and reading comprehension research: Inquiry, instruction, and social interaction. *Review of Educational Research* 67(3), pp. 271–299.

Lafon, M.-F. (1999). *Philippe, duc d'Orléans*. Paris: Boubée.

Laissus, Y. (1995). *Le muséum national d'histoire naturelle*. Paris: Découverte Gallimard 249.

Langlois, A. (2010). *La motivation et l'apprentissage dans les musées*. Paris: Mémoire de Maîtrise de psychologie cognitive appliquée présenté à l'Université Nanterre Paris ouest La Défense.

Lemoine, P. (1935). *Le Muséum National d'Histoire Naturelle: Son histoire, son état actuel*. Paris: Masson.

Muséum National d'Histoire Naturelle (2016). *Rapport d'activité, 2015*.

OCIM (1991). *Guide des musées de l'éducation nationale*. Nantes: Ouest éditions.

OCIM (1994). La Grande Galerie du Muséum National d'Histoire Naturelle. *La Lettre de l'OCIM* 33.

Packer, J., and Bond, N. (2010). Museums as restorative environments. *Curator: The Museum Journal* 53(4), pp. 421–432.

Pénicaud, P. (2002). Henri Lecoq: Les fortunes d'un naturaliste à Clermont-Ferrand. *Mémoires de l'Académie des Sciences* 59.

Pénicaud, P. (2004a). *Chasses Royales: Regards scientifiques sur les collections du Domaine royal de Randan*. Clermont-Ferrand: Muséum d'histoire naturelle Henri Lecoq.

Pénicaud, P. (2004b). Musées de France et collections d'étude. *Musées et collections publiques de France* 242, pp. 8–13.

Pénicaud, P. (2015). Collections et itinérances des expositions. *La Lettre du Comité Français de l'ICOM* 39, pp. 46–51.

Perrier, E. (1908). *Le Muséum National d'Histoire Naturelle*. Paris: Éditions de la Revue Politique et Littéraire.

Poirier, P. (2016). *Histoire de la culture scientifique en France*. Dijon: Éditions Universitaires de Dijon.

Pritchard, D. (2006). *What Is This Thing Called Knowledge?* Abingdon: Routledge.

Rainette, C., Cornu, M., and Wallaert, C. (2008). *Guide juridique sur le patrimoine scientifique et technique*. Paris: L'Harmattan.

Rogers, C. R. (1966). *Le développement de la personne*. Paris: Dunod. (E. L. Hébert translation of *On Becoming a Person: A Therapist's View of Psychotherapy*. New York: Houghton Mifflin, 1961.)

Schaer, R. (1993). *L'invention des musées*. Paris: Gallimard–Réunion des Musées Nationaux.

Steptoe, A., Deaton, A., and Stone, A. A. (2015). Subjective well-being, health, and aging. *Lancet* 385(9968), pp. 640–648.

Tobelem, J. M. (2010). *Le nouvel âge des musées*. 2nd ed. Paris: Armand Colin.

UNESCO (United Nations Educational, Social, and Cultural Organization) and Ukrainian Committee of ICOM (International Council of Museums) (2012). *Role of Museums in Education and Cultural Tourism Development*. Kiev: Ukrainian National Committee of ICOM.

Web resources

La Grande Galerie de l'Évolution, www.grandegaleriedelevolution.fr/

La Salle de l'Arbre du Vivant, www.clermont-ferrand.fr/-L-arbre-du-vivant-.html
Le Balcon des Sciences du Musée de l'Homme, www.museedelhomme.fr/fr/visitez/espaces/balcon-sciences.

Le Muséum d'Histoire Naturelle Henri-Lecoq à Clermont-Ferrand, www.clermont-ferrand.fr/-Museum-Henri-Lecoq-41-.html.

Le Muséum d'Histoire Naturelle Henri-Lecoq à Clermont-Ferrand, www.clermont-ferrand.fr/.

Le Muséum National d'Histoire Naturelle, Paris, www.mnhn.fr/.

Les Herbonautes, http://lesherbonautes.mnhn.fr/.

Vigie nature, http://vigienature.mnhn.fr/.

8 The Natural Futures Museum

Interactivity and participation as key instruments for engaging audiences

Christopher J. Garthe

Introduction: natural history museums and the challenges of the twenty-first century

Natural history museums are among the world's most valued cultural institutions, but many are currently struggling to find their relevance in the twenty-first century. Although there are countless inspiring and impressive examples, numerous natural history museums are stale institutions, or, as Evans baldly put it: "A great many natural history museums are the dreariest of all the museum family and consist of long, echoing galleries filled with glass cases" (Evans, 2014, p. 35). This current state of many natural history museums is in stark contrast to the ever-faster-evolving world around them, be it through technological developments or multiple global crises. Indeed, many natural history museums are failing to address issues of contemporary relevance and urgency (see, for example, Janes, 2009). Thus, from the perspective of a wide audience, they are increasingly losing their relevance—for both prospective visitors and society as a whole. Against this background, it becomes obvious that natural history museums have a critical need to redefine their role in society. At the core of this process will be "a reconceptualization of visitor learning and engagement" (Dillon et al., 2016, p. 1).

Although some have argued that the most pressing global problems are not technological or political but primarily biological (Evans, 2014, p. 36), in the age of the Anthropocene (Davies, 2016) all global challenges inherently concern humans and are thus complex, interconnected problems involving biology, ecology, culture, technology, economics, and politics. These global challenges of the twenty-first century are characterized by the uncertainty of existing knowledge as well as conflicts surrounding underlying values. Such complex circumstances have been described as "messy situations" (Garthe, 2015, p. 4) or "wicked problems" (Balint, 2011, p. 2).

Amid this uncertainty of knowledge, it follows that knowledge and, more importantly, the production thereof—namely, science—become increasingly significant. At the same time, current concepts of science incorporate stakeholders in all stages of the research process (see Hirsch Hadorn et al., 2008). Museums have traditionally combined research with communication activities and are thus ideally poised to serve as sites not only for communicating knowledge but also for interaction and participation in the setting of a knowledge society (Silvestrini, 2013). In this way, they can act as facilitators of communication and collaboration between scientists and laypeople on complex global challenges.

The central challenges of the twenty-first century, whether pertaining to climate change, food security, intellectual property, or traditional knowledge, all have interconnections with the natural sciences. Additionally, as humankind is part of the natural world and all global challenges innately concern humans, natural history museums are—especially as compared to other museums—perfect places to learn about, and address, the issues of the twenty-first century.

As research in the knowledge society becomes ever more complex and resource-intensive, and communication in the digital world resides increasingly in the hands of the prosumer (Fois, 2015), museums can play a major role in enabling exchange and collaboration between these two worlds. In this context, museums' mission to provide opportunities for appreciation and understanding of heritage (International Council of Museums [ICOM], 2006, p. 4) takes on increasing importance and could arguably be prioritized over research objectives. As such, the formulation of visitors' code of ethics, developed from the perspective of the audience, might be an important avenue to pursue.

Having outlined some of the obstacles facing natural history museums, we will now turn to the "Natural Futures museum": a new vision for museums with natural history collections. What form will the natural history museums of the future take? The Natural Futures museum will be the first place that comes to mind when a citizen wants to learn or think about, discuss, or act upon the future of the planet. As the complex challenges that face us are accompanied by a great deal of uncertainty, this museum will focus on multiple possible futures. The broad topic of the Natural Futures museum will be the relationship between humankind and nature.

Although the Natural Futures museum will not describe the past, it will draw upon the wealth of knowledge that can be derived from analyzing the history of the planet, for example, by using specimen and natural science collections. This museum will illustrate global change, promote the discourse on this change through interaction and participation, and conduct research that can reveal paths to a sustainable future. It will not adhere to an object-focused presentation but will instead adopt a problem-centered approach, which could have implications for the traditional method of subdividing exhibitions. A Natural Futures museum will use an integrated perspective on objects and phenomena, placing them in a network of interpretations and interconnections (Sampson and George, 2004, p. 283). As future problems are encompassing the human-nature interface, they also call for the inclusion of social sciences. Traditional natural history museums are thus challenged to embrace this broad perspective and incorporate more social science research into their exhibitions and programs (Garthe and Peter, 2014, p. 16).

When coping with such complex problems on a global scale, the goal is not to reach an objectively correct and possibly non-existent solution. Rather, tackling these kinds of issues can be conceived of as a process of social learning, realized by negotiation and collaboration (Collins and Ison, 2009, p. 365). If a museum is called on by society to implement a more participatory approach, an institution that deals predominantly with these kinds of problems must reflect this development. Thus, "natural history institutions need to... take advantage of... participation and co-creation" (Dillon et al., 2016, p. 7).

This view signifies a shift from communicating knowledge and pushing messages to fostering a visitor who is self-contained and extracts meanings and constructs interpretations from his or her museum experience. To realize such a visitor, different kinds of interactive exhibition experiences alongside opportunities for participation as citizen scientists are necessary. The result is a natural science museum that uses interaction and participation as seminal instruments to engage its audience.

Numerous natural history museums around the world are addressing global challenges as relevant topics for their exhibitions. However, curating exhibitions on these topics is in itself not sufficient to help solve these challenges. Approaches to visitor learning and engagement must consider this new vision and acknowledge the need to reconsider the objectives of museum visitors. To play a pivotal role in a global societal transformation, museums need to equip visitors with the necessary skills to react to future challenges, to change their values as well as influence their behaviors and lifestyles. The concept of education for sustainable development seems to be an ideal model, as it goes beyond addressing issues of sustainability, aiming to empower people to cope with future challenges (De Haan, 2006, p. 22). The first steps on how to implement the concept of education for sustainable development in museum practice have already been outlined (Garthe and Peter, 2014, p. 14).

While concepts such as public understanding of research, transdisciplinary research, and citizen science, and institutions like open research labs are gaining increasing importance, the knowledge society is developing into a new participatory scientific society. The Natural Futures museum will define itself as a core institution of this society by actively connecting researchers, volunteers, and laypeople. As such, museums' self-image will change drastically compared to that of traditional museums: the Natural Futures museum will need to share some of its authority with the public.

To tackle the challenges of the twenty-first century, a great societal transformation is in order (see Schellnhuber, 2010). The Natural Futures museum will play a major role in developing potential solutions in a knowledge-based society. It cannot be stressed enough that a museum's mission does not end with achieving the learning objectives of its audiences. Another central element is problem-solving—one of the key ethical responsibilities of museums. Problem-solving in natural history museums must mirror the specific resources and expertise of these museums (Janes, 2013, pp. 375–382).

Interaction and participation in natural history museums

The practice of interaction and participation in natural history museums varies greatly. Many museums in North America along with other well-known institutions with considerable resources can be described as pioneers in this area, offering diverse opportunities for interaction and participation. However, most natural history museums are still dominated by collection objects as material only to look at. Collection items are usually presented within display cases, which separate the visitors from the objects. These museums are also dominated by text as the prevailing vehicle for the conveying of knowledge, rarely providing opportunities for visitors to engage with the collection objects. On the other hand, interactive experiences are regularly included in traveling exhibitions or exhibitions specifically designed for children. Interactive exhibits and activities for self-regulated learning are more common in visitor or interpretation centers, and in specially themed centers on natural history. This discrepancy solidifies the impression that natural history museums are lagging behind somewhat in creating opportunities for interactivity and participation.

Cutting-edge participation in museums often comes down to the use of impressive architecture, immersive scenography, state-of-the-art media, artistic installations, storytelling, emotional triggering, gamification, or personalization. Although each of these approaches can be used effectively in natural history museums, they are applicable to all museum types and arguably do not adequately take into account the specifics of museums with natural history collections.

Because of an ongoing popularization of the museum sector, many exhibitions feature elaborate scenography or media exhibits that are less and less directly related to their collections. This can be illustrated by observing the exhibition concepts at work in the Natural History Museum in London, where exhibitions usually start out with a focus on specimens, subsequently introduce graphics, and later incorporate touchscreen and media exhibits in the Darwin Centre.

In line with their longstanding role as stakeholders of learning, museums have customarily focused on fostering the understanding of science and, more recently, the understanding of research. However, it must be acknowledged that natural science collections offer vast resources to generate crucial knowledge to solve the problems of the future. This is regularly underestimated and poorly understood by society (Cotterill, 2002, p. 272). Whether collections are held for exhibition or research, collection objects have often been used to illustrate a state of knowledge or the results of research. For example, collection objects are increasingly presented as aesthetic art objects (Nicholls, 2012, p. 36). In an interactive natural history museum, these objects would be used to tell new and exciting stories with the objects, while at the same time being employed by visitors for experiments. In this way, visitors learn about the research process itself and the creation of meaning that is connected to it. By engaging visitors with the collection objects, natural history museums can evolve from a mission of promoting public understanding of science and research to one of promoting a "Public Understanding of Collections" (PUC).

Object-related interactions

Among the biggest challenges to enhancing interactivity is that collection objects need to be stored in an environment in which preservation is a major concern. Due to fragility, value, or toxicity, objects in natural history museums are usually displayed in cases, removed from possible interaction with visitors. Finding new methods for using, modifying, or directly integrating these items into the visitor experience remains one of the most important steps to increase engagement in natural history museums. Interactions with natural history objects should be based on and connected to actual research conducted within the museum or on natural history research in general. These interactions could feature the identification, description, or classification of living beings. By extracting data from objects, visitors can come closer to the collection. The interactions mimic research processes using description and lead to an increased awareness of biological characteristics while involving the production of digital data.

Basic, non-destructive methods to describe objects include the writing of text, the taking of photographs, microscopy, or drawing. More advanced processes for extracting data, which depend on a museum's infrastructure comprise, 360° photography, 3D scanning, and other specialized measuring techniques, among them the use of color temperature meters, X-rays, genetic analysis, or magnetic resonance imaging. In using such techniques, visitors can develop an ongoing database of user-generated data on collection objects. They can also bring data produced prior to the visit, such as photos or sound recordings, which they can then analyze during the visit and incorporate into the database thereafter. Future visitors can work with this database, and scientists can potentially use the information for their own research, if requirements for successful citizen science activities are met, such as rigorous quality control over the produced data (Dickinson et al., 2010, p. 166) as well as consideration of the fact that such data is more suitable for showing general patterns and less so for answering closely focused research questions (Bonney et al., 2009, p. 981). As the database expands, visitors can begin to work with the object-related information in different ways. They can use the descriptions to draw objects, comparing the results with the original objects and possibly even helping to refine the original characterization, thereby increasing their knowledge of the importance of specific attributes. They can also use the information in the database for other purposes, such as identifying objects in the museum or virtually assembling digital skeletons.

Visitors can also gain a deeper insight into the research process by characterizing collection objects, for instance, being asked to weigh in on an object's most characteristic trait. The goal is to empower visitors to identify traits and compare objects based on these traits. Similarities can be grasped through different characteristics, and visitors possibly invited to make their own connections and identify the most similar objects in a collection or an exhibition area. The exploration of similarities does not have to be focused on the object but can occur by means of photos or drawings. A smartphone app might allow visitors to take photos anywhere in the museum; the app would show similar photos (with comparable objects) from the collection.

Visitors can also be empowered to categorize collection objects, learning about classification systems, variety, and evolution through an interactive and fun identification key. This can be done using jigsaw puzzles, quizzes, or dedicated smartphone apps to identify collections objects, in the manner of currently available plant or bird identification apps. A comprehensive identification app for all displayed objects could even replace traditional labels. An identification key can be a social learning experience, for example, by projecting an intersection of an identification key on the ground, with visitors voting for a branch by stepping on it. Working on classification and identification is an ideal opportunity to create situations that provoke astonishment or require explanation, such as an unknown composition of characteristic traits or an inability to incorporate an object into an existing classification system.

Digital data derived from museum collections create new possibilities for visitors to interact with museum resources (Merritt and Katz, 2013, p. 16). The basic idea is that, given the existence of a comprehensive digital collection, visitors may browse through the collection objects and choose one. In a "MakeNatureSpace"—a fab lab and a high-performance 3-D printing workshop—visitors can print replicas of the chosen collection items, even if the item is housed in another museum, as long as the digital data are available. A MakeNatureSpace could be considered a key facility for every museum based on the collection of three-dimensional objects.

Using these replicas, visitors can discover new ways of interacting with a collection, directly engaging with objects and their replicas, respectively. These engagements include touching the traditionally separated objects and playing with these replicas, for instance, by building a whole skeleton out of replicated bones—a very demanding task. Visitors can also use these replicas for experiments, allowing detailed examination and interpretation. In this way, the collection objects finally move out of the display case. Visitors might even take a printed object with them, and will thus have a souvenir of the museum (as available in the souvenir shop of the Natural History Museum in London) or can use it for further examination.

Visitors will only value collection objects if they can be incorporated into a familiar context and take on personal meaning. Toward this end, it is essential to establish relationships between a collection object and visitors' everyday lives; these relationships must also be widened to show the relevance of these objects for global challenges. Integrating models of environmental conditions into the interaction process with objects offers the chance to address these questions. For example, visitors can explore how animals morphologically and behaviourally adapted to the environment or learn about the impact of changed conditions on species, by visualizing the changes in environmental conditions and connecting them to morphologically different objects or digital representations thereof.

Open digital data and natural history collections

In many museums, only a very small part of the collection can be on display. By creating digital collections, a much larger percentage of a collection can be presented to the audience and be accessible to visitors. The addition of other digital data can further enrich and contextualize collection objects; audio, touch screens, and projections alongside mobile devices are promising tools if adapted to the learning experience in natural history museums.

But it is important to realize that mobile devices are only useful in this context when they offer place-specific content and services. Place-based services and similar technical solutions vary in several ways. First, they differ in the number of people involved and the type of experiences offered, ranging from personal or solitary experiences to shared and social ones. Second, they differ in the place on which they focus, either enhancing users' immediate surroundings to transporting them to a different space or place (Joseph, 2015). If interaction is one key paradigm, museums would obviously not wish to separate visitors from one another; it seems contradictory to the notion of a museum visit that visitors would use mobile devices to experience a virtual space unrelated to the museum environment at hand. Thus, technical devices that enable social experiences and enhance the immediate surroundings are especially suited to a museum setting.

Digital collections offer visitors the possibility of experiencing the museum before and after the visit while leading to new types of visitor engagement. By browsing in a topic-structured digital environment that uses associative links between objects, visitors can discover things they were not looking for. Enhanced information such as text, images, audio, or video is easy to incorporate into digital collections and offer a way to display and discuss diverging interpretations of displayed objects.

At the same time, digital collections afford museums an opportunity to become institutions of the sharing economy. As collection objects are rarely all accessible at the same time, digital collections enable visitors to access these objects independent of time and location (Merritt, 2014, p. 45), while offering future business perspectives by means of subscription-based models. Data contained in digital collections or produced by visitors can be relevant to scientists around the world (Cameron and Robinson, 2007, pp. 185–187), contributing to the advancement of knowledge to develop solutions to global challenges. By inviting the free culture movement to use digital collections, museums could share their data in a comprehensive open access policy (Norris and Butts, 2014, p. 113).

The "Build a Dinosaur" feature on the website of the Melbourne Museum, Australia, represents a playful approach to digital collections data. Visitors can create their own digital prehistoric animal by combining different aspects like skin color or skeletal structure, and when they are finished, they can print out their copy as a postcard or send it by email. In addition to the creativity involved, visitors learn about the uncertainty scientists face when constructing images of dinosaurs.

Alongside their own websites, institutions can connect to, and exchange data with, highly frequented sites such as *Biodiversity Library Exhibition*, *Biodiversity Heritage Library*, *Encyclopedia of Life*, *Barcoding of Life*, or the *Tree of Life Web Project*. This puts data in the open access realm and makes museums' information available to a broader public. A comprehensive open access policy, where it exists, creates new opportunities for visitors while supporting the open culture movement in the form of museum-hosted data jams or hackathons (Vos et al., 2014).

Co-creating the museum of the future

Enhancing visitor participation can be achieved to varying extents by means of different methods. One approach, involving the audience in a broad sense, could be described as co-creating the museum. It comprises the co-creation of exhibition content, both the co-curating of exhibitions as well as the co-development of museum activities (Figure 8.1).

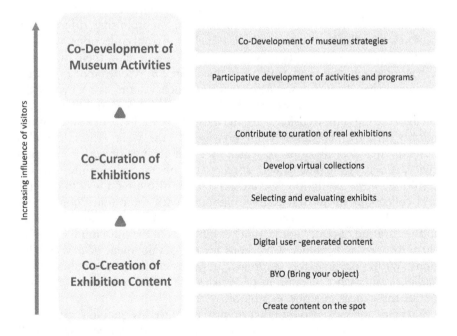

Figure 8.1 Three levels of co-creation in the Natural Futures museum.

Different models of co-created exhibition content exist (Simon, 2010). One is to encourage visitors to create content in situ, that is, on the spot, while they are visiting an exhibition. This can be done in multiple ways: by surveys whose results are shown directly in an exhibition; by sharing personal experiences (a well-known instance being the Pledge Wall in the United States Holocaust Memorial Museum in Washington, DC); by the production of text for new exhibit labels; or by using visitor tracking, the results of which are then meaningfully integrated and displayed in an exhibition. Visitor-generated content can also be more elaborate, such as the recording of audio in a small microstudio (as at the Friedrichshain-Kreuzberg Museum in Berlin, where visitors can share their stories about specific locales in the city), or the production of videos (as at the Rijksmuseum in Amsterdam). Another possibility is to invite visitors to bring their own objects to display in an exhibition: photos or personal or historical items, as are often used in participatory museums of local history. A successful example of a museum whose collection consists entirely of donated objects is the Museum of Broken Relationships in Zagreb, Croatia. A further option is to incorporate digital content, either produced by visitors at home or in another context, such as in a citizen science project. The challenge for museums is to present this digital content in an accessible, appealing, and interactive way.

Co-curating gives visitors the opportunity to participate in the activities of museum and exhibition professionals. Participation in curatorial practices could be as low-key as asking visitors to vote for exhibits or selecting the best exhibit of a collection. As with other options for promoting visitor engagement discussed thus far, digital data is again promising, offering various new models for co-curating. These include virtual collections, whereby visitors can choose objects they favour and then develop their own such collections; a widely-used example of this is the *Encyclopedia of Life*, with its impressive *Beautiful Sea Monsters*, in which visitors can view all the holdings of their personally curated collections on a screen and then upload them to the museum website. After the museum visit, they can also view and modify their own collection from anywhere on the Web. Visitors can also develop virtual exhibitions, in which they can arrange objects in a digital space, enriching the objects with content and subsequently maintaining the resulting online exhibition. Virtual exhibitions also offer a way to connect real collections in natural history museums with the online *Biodiversity Library Exhibition*. By becoming virtual curators, visitors can contribute to the curating of real, "nonvirtual" exhibitions in the museum by inviting them to open stakeholder workshops for the development of new exhibitions. With a participatory approach, curators can learn a lot about their audience and their expectations prior to an exhibition and thereafter incorporate these ideas in a new exhibition.

Participation can also be taken to a higher level by enabling visitors to contribute to the governance of the museum, in the co-development of museum strategies and programs. Engagement on this basic level will instill in visitors a sense of ownership of the museum as a publicly funded institution. But such audience involvement will come at a price: natural history museums will need to share some of their authority with their audience and in the process, readjust their self-perceptions. This level of participation would also lead to the need for new museum infrastructures as well as new staff positions with different skill sets.

Natural history museums as forums for research, discussion, and action

One of the core areas of expertise of natural history museums has long been the research carried out by its science staff. Within a participatory scientific society, natural history museums are especially conducive to evolving into institutions that mediate and facilitate interchange between scientists, volunteer experts, and laypeople. In doing so, they can lower the threshold for the general public's participation in science (Bandelli, 2016a, pp. 138–142). As discussed above, natural history museums' communicative role is no longer about disseminating scientific findings and topics, but about fostering audiences' understanding of the research process itself. Apart from a focus on a public understanding of collections, the general background for this communication strategy is the concept of public understanding of research (Powell and Field, 2001). Implementing this concept in the realm of museum practice includes approaches of transparent, playful, and participatory research; open interpretation and discussion; and participation in the application of results.

The demand to open the so-called back of the house to visitors is a well-trodden path. Although transparent research methods encompass similar approaches, they offer more direct interaction for visitors, starting with personal contact with scientists in predefined settings, such as lectures, discussions, or personal interviews with researchers. Transparency can go further by allowing the public to see research activities within the museum by means of videoconferencing or video blogs, whereby visitors communicate with researchers in their work environment or via guided visits and scientist-led tours.

In its ultimate form, transparent research is conducted in open research laboratories, in which the knowledge acquired throughout the exhibition can be applied to an immediate and actual situation. The National Museums Liverpool is an example of an open research lab (Watts et al., 2008). Visitors to open research labs can observe ongoing experiments and talk directly with scientists while the latter is performing research. Open research labs also yield considerable benefits for scientists, as they can gain insights into social and cultural contexts underpinning the perceptions of their research. This, in turn, contributes to a deeper reflection of the process of research in general and their own field of research in particular (Hix and Heckl, 2011, p. 379). To alleviate the considerable challenges for the scientists working in open research labs, it is important to ensure both the authenticity of research carried out in the lab (in contrast to student labs) and interaction on equal terms for visitors and scientists.

Visitors can encounter actual research operations by proposing possibilities for playful research, among them traditional student labs as well as "sciencetainment" events like the well-known worm-charming or artistic research approaches. Sciencetainment takes edutainment to the next level by focusing on scientific content and contributing to a public understanding of research. Playful research can also include inviting visitors for self-experiments on biological parameters. Other opportunities for participatory research in natural history museums are crowdsourcing approaches, transdisciplinary research, and citizen science projects (Irwin, 1995). Citizen science projects can be carried out inside the museum itself, in the context of outreach events or by using Web portals or smartphone apps. Using an online interface enables volunteers to collect and produce data no matter their location. A citizen science approach is especially appropriate in projects that entail crowdsourcing or monitoring. Inside the museum, visitors can even be involved in data evaluation, in the analysis of samples and photos, or in the preparation of graphs and tables. Successful examples of this approach include BioBlitz, Project Noah, iSpot, or iNaturalist. Natural history museums can also act as pioneers in transdisciplinary research by engaging all relevant stakeholders in the process of regular scientific research projects (Garthe and Peter, 2014, p. 16). A museum's implementation of participatory research suggests not only that it operates as an educational institution, but that it is also reliant on citizens, for example, with regard to the collecting of data covering a large area.

All these approaches necessarily result in the adoption of new requirements for museum staff. These include the hiring of staff devoted to the enlisting, training, and supervising of volunteers as well as the content they are providing, or the creating of new positions such as Wikipedian in residence or curator of community engagement (Merritt and Katz, 2012, p. 7). Transdisciplinary research also challenges the authority structure of natural history museums, thereby having the same effect on museums' self-perception as co-curating.

By implementing a public program that offers and facilitates conversations and discussions among both visitors and museum staff, natural history museums can become forums for dialogue. By way of example is a project carried out at the Natural History Museum in London that tackled the topic of evolution, regularly prompting discussions among visitors with faith-based world views (Gay, 2012, pp. 101–103).

Communication in museums traditionally involved the disseminating of established and accepted knowledge. The global challenges facing the world today have given rise to a new role for natural history museums: negotiators of uncertain knowledge "in the making" between the public and other stakeholders involved in the scientific process (Bandelli, 2016b).

The application of scientific results to address these challenges regularly involves efforts in conservation and sustainability, efforts that require a love for nature. Amid the rise of alienation from nature (Louv, 2008, p. 34), the role that natural history museums as cultural institutions could play to overcome this condition and nourish a love for nature is debatable. In fact, natural history museums exhibit dead things—which would not appear to provide a good starting point for love and engagement. As such, they must evolve from institutions presenting dead nature to those making connections with living nature, something that will only be possible if they develop a greater sense of place and focus on the immediate surroundings. In the process, they will more and more come to resemble visitor centers in national parks. At the same time, natural history museums must seek to avoid imitating theme parks, falling into the well-documented trend of "Disneyfication," a pitfall they can avoid by maintaining a focus on collections.

It is also important that natural history museums support local communities in their efforts to tackle pressing concerns by applying scientific results and contributing toward solutions. Toward this end, museums are already employing outreach programs and are contributing to community work (Garthe and Peter, 2014, p. 15); such is the case of the Miami Science Museum, which uses social media and land art (Smithson, 1979) to engage volunteers to restore coastal habitats. By tailoring research projects and their conclusions to local problems, both the objects exhibited and the work performed in museums can become even more meaningful to the public.

Conclusion: how interaction and participation will change the role of natural history museums

Given their traditional focus on their collections and the conclusions that can be drawn from their study, many natural history museums are struggling to stay relevant in the twenty-first century. A reconceptualization thus seems in order, one that defines the natural history museum as a future-oriented institution that is the place to address global challenges and the future of the planet.

Since addressing these complex problems involves uncertain knowledge and value conflicts, interaction and participation will be the main instruments of this new type of natural history museum. Furthermore, as a core institution in a participatory scientific society, natural history museums will reprioritize their communications mission, thus facilitating the interchange between scientists and laypeople and offering diverse opportunities for participation. This, in turn, will necessitate the development of new infrastructures and new staff positions throughout institutions. As global problems become increasingly challenging, natural history museums will likewise be challenged to embrace the responsibility of contributing toward the formulation of solutions to pressing concerns (Figure 8.2).

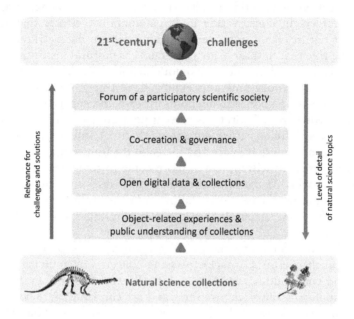

Figure 8.2 Interaction and participation in the Natural Futures museum.

In taking the first steps in implementing this reconceptualization, it must be kept in mind that small regional museums operate with different resources and amid conditions from large national ones, and that the instruments and participatory formats must be adapted to the specific situation. Although national museums have more resources to implement many of these instruments, smaller museums are frequently better connected to communities by local activities and can, therefore, play a seminal role in realizing the responsibility of contributing to solutions to tackle the challenges of the twenty-first century.

References

Balint, P. J. (2011). *Wicked Environmental Problems: Managing Uncertainty and Conflict*. Washington, DC: Island Press.

Bandelli, A. (2016a). *Visitor Participation: Science Centers as a Platform for Scientific Citizenship*. PhD dissertation, Vrije Universiteit, Amsterdam.

Bandelli, A. (2016b). Where citizens go to become scientific citizens. *Spokes* 19. [online] Available at: www.ecsite.eu/activities-and-services/news-and-publications/digital-spokes/issue-19-0#section=section-indepth&href=/feature/depth/where-citizens-go-become-scientific-citizens [Accessed 10 Oct. 2016].

Bonney, R., Cooper, C. B., Dickinson, J., Kelling, S., Phillips, T., Rosenberg, K. V., Shirk, J. (2009). Citizen science: A developing tool for expanding science knowledge and scientific literacy. *BioScience* 59(11), pp. 977–984.

Cameron, F., and Robinson, H. (2007). Digital knowledgescapes: Cultural, theoretical, practical, and usage issues facing museum collection databases in a digital epoch. In: F. Cameron and S. Kenderdine, eds., *Theorizing Digital Cultural Heritage: A Critical Discourse*. Cambridge: MIT Press, pp. 165–191.

Collins, K., and Ison, R. (2009). Jumping off Arnstein's ladder: Social learning as a new policy paradigm for climate change adaptation. *Environmental Policy and Governance* 19(6), pp. 358–373. [online] Available at: http://dx.doi.org/10.1002/eet.523 [Accessed 10 Oct. 2016].

Cotterill, F. (2002). The future of natural science collections into the 21st century. In: Diputación Foral de Alava, ed., *Actas del I Simposio sobre el Patrimonio Natural en las Colecciones Públicas en España*. Vitoria: Departmento de Cultura Diputación Foral de Alva, Vitoria.

Davies, J., (2016). *The Birth of the Anthropocene*. Berkeley, CA: University of California Press.

De Haan, G. (2006). The BLK "21" programme in Germany: A "Gestaltungskompetenz"-based model for education for sustainable development. *Environmental Education Research* 12(1), pp. 19–32.

Dickinson, J. L., Zuckerberg, B., and Bonter, D. N. (2010). Citizen science as an ecological research tool: Challenges and benefits. *Annual Review of Ecology, Evolution, and Systematics* 41(1), pp. 149–172.

Dillon, J., DeWitt, J., Pegram, E., Irwin, B., Crowley, K., Haydon, R., King. H., Knutson, K., Veall, D. and Xanthoudaki, M. (2016). *A Learning Research Agenda for Natural History Institutions*. London: Natural History Museum.

Evans, J. W. (2014). The functions of natural history museums. *Museum International* 66(1–4), pp. 35–38.

Fois, V. (2015). The prosumer: The key player of the museum of the future. In: K. Ng, ed., *Conference on Electronic Visualisation and the Arts*. London: EVA London, pp. 291–297.

Garthe, C. J. (2015). *Erholung und Bildung in Nationalparken: Gesellschaftliche Einstellungen, ökologische Auswirkungen und Ansätze für ein integratives Besuchermanagement*. Hamburg: Kovac.

Garthe, C. J., and Peter, M. (2014). Education for sustainable development as a concept for science centres and museums: Engagement for a sustainable future. *Spokes* 4, pp. 12–17. [online] Available at: www.ecsite.eu/sites/default/files/spokes6_0.pdf [Accessed 10 Oct. 2016].

Gay, H. (2012). Talking about evolution in natural history museums. *Evolution: Education and Outreach* 5(1), pp. 101–103. [online] Available at: http://dx.doi.org/10.1007/s12052-012-0402-5 [Accessed 10 Oct. 2016].

Hirsch Hadorn, G., Hoffmann-Riem, H., Biber-Klemm, S., Grossenbacher-Mansuy, W., Joye, D., Pohl, C., Wiesmann, U., Zemp, E., eds. (2008). *Handbook of Transdisciplinary Research*. Dordrecht and New York: Springer.

Hix, P., and Heckl, W. M. (2011). Public understanding of research: The Open Research Laboratory at the Deutsches Museum. In: D. J. Bennett and R. C. Jennings, eds., *Successful Science Communication: Telling It Like It Is*. Cambridge and New York: Cambridge University Press.

ICOM (2006). *ICOM Code of Ethics for Museums*. Paris: ICOM.

Irwin, A. (1995). *Citizen Science: A Study of People, Expertise, and Sustainable Development*. London and New York: Routledge.

Janes, R. R. (2009). *Museums in a Troubled World: Renewal, Irrelevance, or Collapse?* London and New York: Routledge.

Janes, R. R. (2013). *Museums and the Paradox of Change: A Case Study in Urgent Adaptation.* 3rd ed. London and New York: Routledge.

Joseph, B. (2015). *Mooshme Matrix of Place-Based Augmented Devices.* [online] Available at: www.mooshme.org/2015/03/augmented-wearables-and-the-future-of-museums/ [Accessed 10 Oct. 2016].

Louv, R. (2008). *Last Child in the Woods: Saving Our Children from Nature-Deficit Disorder.* 1st ed. Chapel Hill: Algonquin Books.

Merritt, E. E. (2014). *TrendsWatch 2014.* Arlington, TX: American Alliance of Museums.

Merritt, E. E., and Katz, P. M. (2012). *TrendsWatch 2012: Museums and the Pulse of the Future.* Arlington, TX: American Alliance of Museums.

Merritt, E. E., and Katz, P. M. (2013). *TrendsWatch 2013: Back to the Future.* Arlington, TX: American Alliance of Museums.

Nicholls, H. (2012). Museums: A natural evolution. *Nature* 484(7392), p. 36.

Norris, C. A., and Butts, S. (2014). Let your data run free? The challenge of data redaction in paleontological collections. *Collection Forum* 28(1–2), pp. 113–118. [online] Available at: http://dx.doi.org/10.14351/0831-4985-28.1.113 [Accessed 10 Oct. 2016].

Powell, P., and Field, H. (2001). Public understanding of science versus public understanding of research. *Public Understanding of Science* 10(4), pp. 421–426.

Sampson, S. D., and George, S. B. (2004). Reinventing a natural history museum for the 21st century. In: A. E. Leviton et al., eds., *Museums and Other Institutions of Natural History.* San Francisco, CA: California Academy of Sciences.

Schellnhuber, H.-J. (2010). *Global Sustainability: A Nobel Cause.* Cambridge: Cambridge University Press.

Silvestrini, G. V. (2013). Toward knowledge societies. In: A.-M. Bruyas and M. Riccio, eds., *Science Centres and Science Events: A Science Communication Handbook.* Milan: Springer.

Simon, N. (2010). *The Participatory Museum.* Santa Cruz, CA: Museum 2.0.

Smithson, R. (1979). A sedimentation of the mind. In: N. Holt, ed., *The Writings of Robert Smithson.* New York: New York University Press, pp. 82–91.

Vos, R., et al. (2014). Enriched biodiversity data as a resource and service. *Biodiversity Data Journal* 2, pp. e1125.

Watts, S., Abbott, D., Crombie, D., Gunn, A., and La Pensée, A. (2008). Science revealed: The hidden story of objects. *Studies in Conservation* 53, pp. 146–150.

Part 3
Interfaces

Part 3
Interface

9 Natural history museums, zoos, and aquariums

Gerald Dick

Zoos and aquariums as living collections

The keeping of animals for various purposes is a practice that originated in ancient times. The oldest zoo in the world still in existence is the Tiergarten Schönbrunn in Vienna, Austria. It was built in 1752 on the order of Holy Roman Emperor Francis I, husband of Maria Theresa of Austria, to serve as an imperial menagerie as part of Schönbrunn Palace. The modern history of zoos basically started in the nineteenth century (Penn et al., 2012). At that time, living natural history cabinets had a taxonomic focus, showing the variety of life, sometimes referred to as "stamp collections." In the twentieth century, zoos evolved into living museums; the ecological context emerged as the central theme, and animals were presented largely in dioramas. As societies changed and the threats to species and nature became more and more dire, zoos made conservation their primary mission and evolved into conservation centers. In the twenty-first century, the environment, biodiversity, and the human impact on nature became predominant themes, and exhibits were immersive in order to provide the visitor with a nature-like experience. The first public aquarium was opened at London Zoo in 1853, and the earliest scientific stand-alone aquarium, the Oceanographic Museum in Monaco, in 1910. Zoos became increasingly involved in joint breeding programs and reintroduction projects, such as those of the Californian condor, the Przewalski horse, the American bison, and the Arabian oryx, are outstanding success stories of the zoo community (Dick and Gusset, 2013). Today, zoos have four primary functions: education, conservation, research, and public recreation. They are especially well-equipped to do all of these and are often called open-air museums, arranging permanent and temporary exhibits in cooperation with living nature itself.

When talking about interfaces, it is useful to begin by examining the meaning of the word. In computer science, "interface" refers to hardware linking one device with another. In a broader context, however, the word also stands for facts, problems, considerations, theories, and practices shared by two or more disciplines, procedures, or fields of study. There are many elements in common when translating this to the realm of museums and zoos, for example, maintaining collections, performing research, and informing the public through education. There are also aspects of info-tainment or edutainment and conservation, interfaces of growing potential. Collections in museums represent an invaluable asset for our understanding of biodiversity, including genetics. Deceased animals in zoos often end up in museums for necropsy and further research.

Why, then, are there differences that should be better linked? In other words, what are the common denominators in the meaning of interface as shared fields of study that could create a win-win situation for natural history museums as well as zoos and aquariums? The rising challenge of a growing human population and the threats to the natural world provide the answers. Increased sharing of knowledge and collaborating on conservation can strengthen like-minded institutions and the positive impact for species and their habitats. The International Council of Museums Committee for Museums and Collections of Natural History (ICOM NATHIST) declaration of Taipei (2015) states: "Increased human activities have created cata-strophic declines in biodiversity. Both ethics and logic point to a mandate to conserve vulnerable habitats and species. To achieve best practice, natural history museums take action to conserve natural habitats and populations" (ICOM NATHIST, 2015). The World Association of Zoos and Aquariums' (WAZA's) World Zoo and Aquarium Conservation Strategy, "Committing to Conservation" (2015), asserts: "As zoological professionals who care for animals as our core function, it is critical that we give the highest priority to increasing our commitment to the conservation of wild populations" (Barongi et al., 2015). By combining the power and outreach of museums, zoos, and aquariums, we may achieve our goals in a much more effective way.

The disconnecting of scientific society: from universalism to specialization

At the origin of modern universities are the principles of *universitas magistrorum et scolarium* (community of teachers and students), stemming from the oldest continuously operating university, founded in Bologna, Italy, in 1088. Studies there comprised a *studium generale*, directed at gaining a holistic overview of science (*universitas litterarum*). Since then, the increasing complexity of science and the associated diversification led to the establishment of discrete disciplines and departments. Among the most important of the splits that ensued was that between the natural and the cultural (or historical) sciences and the related disputes concerning methodology (the so-called *Methodenstreit*). The philosopher Wilhelm Windelband (1848–1915), arguing from the premise that reality is indivisible, proposed an a priori logical distinction between the natural and social sciences on the basis of their methods. The German philosopher Wilhelm Dilthey (1833–1911), on the other hand, contrasted the natural sciences (*Naturwissenschaften*) and the human sciences (*Geisteswissenschaften*) in terms of their subject matter. This division follows logically from the concept that reality can be segregated into autonomous sectors—a fundamental distinction being that between the realms of "nature" and of "human spirit"—with each sector being the prerogative of a separate category of Sciences (Marshall, 1998). Many articles have appeared on these different perspectives, their various scientific methods, the competition for resources, and the fact that they often do not talk to one another as a matter of principle (Rickert, 1986; Tool, 2007).

This split in the academic world has a long history and seems to have intensified due to increasingly diversified fields of science. Hence, it seems a bit ironic that the new standard-setting procedure in the European Union is called the Bologna Process (European Higher Education Area, 2003–2015), in stark contrast to the idea of *universitas litterarum*. In order to realize unified criteria for a harmonized academic education in Europe, encompassing increased quality control and better comparability between universities, academic freedom was drastically reduced, a more rigorous school-like schedule established, and research and teaching separated.

Of tribes and silos

Research has identified small human groups as the core functional units of hunter-gatherer societies (Hamilton et al., 2007). Most generations of human beings have lived in those conditions, and some basic human behavior still appears to stems from those early times. What worked well in prehistoric societies may not, however, be as productive amid modern structures, larger entities, and a globalized world. It is often difficult to establish contacts and even work together across disciplines, and this applies as well to departments in zoos or museums such as education, marketing, or science. These different areas are often referred to as different "tribes," and their discrete operations as "thinking in silos." Even in closely related fields, such as natural history, biology, ecology, and environmental science, it is often very hard to overcome barriers. So, what is the interface between natural history museums, zoos, and aquariums? How can the barriers between them be removed, and what can be the big win-win situation for all?

The allure and threat of biodiversity: a bridge for the future?

Focused on the variety of natural phenomena and driven by the desire to understand nature, both museums and zoos started out as collections. In the early days of zoo history, menageries had the prevailing function of satisfying the curiosity of visitors by exhibiting then-unknown exotic species. Amid growing scientific interest, the collections evolved in a taxonomic, "stamp-collection" fashion. In museums, a similar allure led to special exhibits that were called *Wunderkammern*, or cabinets of curiosities. For

Krishtalka and Humphry (2000), many museums still resemble Victorian cabinets, while the business is the science of biological diversity. With an estimated three billion objects of irreplaceable natural heritage in museums worldwide, there is an immense potential for connecting the museum-based collections with science and conservation (ICOM NATHIST, 2012).

Museums are becoming the last remaining stronghold of taxonomic expertise. This discipline is increasingly regarded as outdated, with most universities having ceased the teaching of biological taxonomy. In reality, taxonomic knowledge forms the basis for the conservation of biodiversity, and as such, organismic biology needs to be strengthened in teaching as well as research. Zoos have recently undergone a substantial shift, intensifying their scientific interest and involvement in conservation (Zimmermann et al., 2007). More and more, the presentation of animals takes the ecological situation of the species into consideration, and educating visitors has become one of the central functions of a modern zoo, alongside recreation, conservation, and research (Figure 9.1). One of the oldest aquariums, the Oceanographic Museum of Monaco, also known as the "Temple of the Sea," is even called a museum, and has had a focus on both art and science since its founding in 1910. Aquariums have a shorter modern history than zoos but are catching up in their outward focus, increasingly serving as leaders in education and involved in marine rehabilitation and other conservation projects (Penning et al., 2009).

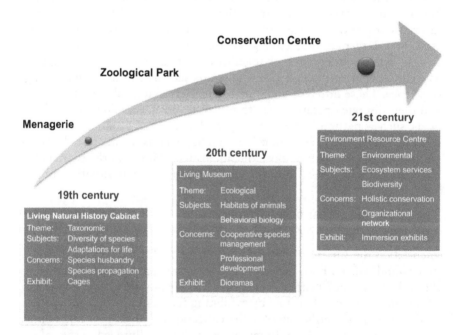

Figure 9.1 Evolution of Zoos © WAZA, modified after CZS 1992.

Natural history museums, zoos, and aquariums share many core elements: all exhibit natural objects, be they alive or mounted by taxidermists; and all aim to educate visitors and use their collections for scientific research and the conservation of biodiversity. In addition—and unfortunately—they also share a concern regarding the negative trends in global biodiversity (Convention on Biological Diversity, 2014). These alarming developments, combined with society's increasing awareness of those trends and the expertise situated in natural history museums, zoos, and aquariums, call for cooperation and a better use of limited resources. A first such attempt, internationally, occurred with the sharing of materials of WAZA's global campaign "Biodiversity Is Us" with members of the zoo and aquarium communities as well as members of the International Council of Museums (ICOM). These materials included movies, designs for displays, an app for smartphones and tablets, and social media activities desired to trigger action in visitors' daily lives. Yet there is still much room for individual institutions to intensify their cooperation on a scientific basis.

Zoos as museums and museums as zoos?

Among the utmost concerns for both natural history museums and zoos are the world's biodiversity and the survival of our living planet. In support of its members, ICOM's Committee for Museums and Collections of Natural History (NATHIST) has put forward the Taipei Declaration on Natural History Museums and Biodiversity Conservation (ICOM NATHIST, 2015). Similarly, WAZA has stated the importance of wildlife conservation in its World Zoo and Aquarium Conservation Strategy (Barongi et al., 2015). In order to enhance mutual support and information exchange, WAZA and ICOM NATHIST entered into a partnership via a formal memorandum of understanding. Attending each other's conferences has been a good start to strengthen the connection between the two communities (Taipei, 2015; Milan, 2016; Puebla, 2016). WAZA's Biodiversity Is Us campaign, the support of conservation projects of WAZA members, the awarding of small grants for conservation and education projects, and communication efforts (press releases, web stories, social media and policy work) are examples of WAZA's activities. In cooperation with the secretariat of the Convention on International Trade in Endangered Species of Fauna and Flora (CITES) and the Trade Record Analysis of Fauna and Flora in Commerce (TRAFFIC),[1] WAZA supports activities that combat the illegal wildlife trade, as well as the listing of species threatened by trade on CITES appendices. It holds formal memorandums of cooperation with both organizations.

As most natural history collecting institutions have biodiversity conservation at the heart of their mission, museums, zoos, and aquariums should likewise have this goal as their raison d'être (Miller et al., 2004; Barongi et al., 2015). Special exhibitions in museums try to highlight

Figure 9.2 Hall of Biodiversity, American Museum of Natural History, New York
© Anagoria.

certain aspects of the natural world (Figure 9.2), and zoos and aquariums
often seek to integrate their living creatures in museum-like exhibitions.

In some cases, the integration is so complete that it is difficult to tell whether
you are in a museum or a zoo—in fact, a museum can at the same time be a
zoo, and vice versa (Figures 9.3 and 9.4; Steiner, 2011). The Natural History
Museum in Vienna even runs the "National Park Institute" on the Danube
River and organizes boat tours, excursions, and workshops, all of which can
be booked on the museum's website (www.nhm-wien.ac.at). Similar programs are offered by zoos and aquariums in many countries (for example, the
Virginia Aquarium, United States; Fundación Temaikèn, Argentina).

Examples of recent collaborations between museums, zoos, and aquariums
can be seen among a wide variety of institutions. The Australian Museum
Research Institute and the Regional Zoo Association in Australia (Zoo and
Aquarium Association Australasia; ZAA) have entered into a partnership
with a focus on genetic services for ZAA-managed programs: the implementation of molecular genetics in species management, biobanking facilities
for ZAA members, forensic genetics to reduce wildlife trafficking, and new
acquisitions in the Australian Museum collection. Helping customs officials, a low-cost, rapid molecular species identification tool for seized "rhino
horn products" has been developed. In international trade, animals are often declared as captive-bred, which for several species is simply not possible,
either because of lack of breeding facilities or complex behavior that makes
captive-breeding impossible. For the broad-headed snake *Hoplocephalus
bungaroides*, molecular genetics have been used to show the differences in
known captive-bred individuals from those wild origin specimens seized by

Figure 9.3 Hall of Giants, Magic Mountain at Budapest Zoo, with displays on polluting overfishing and overhunting the oceans as well as 1:10 models of the ten largest whale species with an interactive game and a twenty-meter-long life-size statue of a sperm whale © Budapest Zoo.

Figure 9.4 Lowland River Exhibit at Landesmuseum Niederösterreich, St. Pölten, Austria © Gerald Dick.

the New South Wales Office of Environment and Heritage (OEH). For the short-beaked echidna (*Tachyglossus aculeatus*), a number of zoos have provided samples to enable the development of forensic genetic techniques that will be validated by known pedigree relationships. The outcome will be a tool enabling regulatory authorities to globally ascertain the validity of claims of captive-bred wildlife (Chris Hibbard, personal communication to the author).

National Museums Scotland has been collaborating with zoos for more than twenty-five years. At first, these collaborations took the form of providing specimens for exhibitions, but as sample sizes increased, opportunities for research quickly arose. Among them: using these specimens as a source of fresh, non-fragmented DNA for phylogenetic and taxonomic research, with samples corroborated by preserved specimens to confirm identification. In-house research has included investigating the effect of captivity on the flight capability of the fruit bat (*Pteropus* spp.), studying the impact of feeding gum arabic to callitrichid monkeys as a source of calcium, and developing dental and skeletal pathologies in bears and other large mammals. The museum has also been involved in studies of population genetics of captive species, such as the Asiatic lion (*Panthera leo persica*) and the mountain bongo (*Tragelaphus eurycerus isaaci*), compared with other captive or wild populations. These kinds of research are important for zoo managers because they provide crucial new information concerning captive husbandry and allow for improvements in captive welfare (Kitchener, 1997; Gippoliti and Kitchener, 2007). Captive animals are also highly sought-after for anatomical and functional morphological studies developed as collaborations with universities around the world. Above all, museums retain archives of specimens enabling future researchers to interrogate the research of their predecessors and facilitate long-term studies of changes in wild and captive populations.

A recent partnership between the Natural History Museum of London and the Zoological Society London (ZSL) focused on the research and husbandry of caecilians (*Gymnophiona*; Tapley et al., 2014), demonstrating the first case of lethal chytridomycosis in a caecilian amphibian (Gower et al., 2013). The team subsequently arrived at a chytrid treatment protocol for caecilian amphibians, alongside husbandry requirements. The museum personnel also ran training sessions for the ZSL veterinary team. By using preserved specimens, they substantiated unique aspects of caecilian morphology while reviewing the structures via ultrasound on living specimens.

In another noteworthy development, an exciting exhibition has been installed in the Texas State Aquarium in collaboration with OCEARCH, the Houston Museum of Natural Science, and the Harte Research Institute for Gulf of Mexico Studies. Visitors can see and feel white-spotted bamboo sharks (*Chiloscyllium plagiosum*), horn sharks (*Heterodontus francisci*), and epaulette sharks (*Hemiscyllium ocellatum*), as well as stand inside a life-size underwater diving cage. An online shark tracker allows visitors to track great whites in real time (www.ocearch.org).

Conclusion

Clearly, the interface as shared field of study of natural history museums, zoos, and aquariums is biodiversity: awareness raising thereof, research, and conservation (Krishtalka and Humphry, 2000; Dick and Gusset, 2010). Some of the most recent buildings in zoos and museums also underline this claim with extraordinary architectural highlights, such as the tropical Gondwanaland in the Leipzig Zoo or the Confluence Museum in Lyon (Figure 9.5).

For zoos, the role and responsibility for the future have been articulated and repeatedly proclaimed by various authors (Croke, 1997; Conway, 2003; Hutchins and Smith, 2003; Mallinson, 2003; Fraser and Wharton, 2007; Conway, 2010, 2011; Dick, 2015; Gross, 2015). Their contribution and impact through conservation projects, outreach to about seven hundred million visitors worldwide (Gusset and Dick, 2010a,b), and awareness raising for biodiversity conservation has been demonstrated (Smith et al., 2008; Moss et al., 2014). Partnering with the UN Decade on Biodiversity, WAZA was able to develop the global campaign Biodiversity Is Us. Using modern technology (social media, an app for tablets and smartphones available in seven languages) and movies and posters with QR codes, the zoo and aquarium community, received a unique set of tools that enable individual institutions to connect the local situation with visitors and the international cause of biodiversity loss. Through a formalized cooperation with ICOM, museums also started to use this material, among them the Natural History Museum Rijeka in Croatia.

Figure 9.5 (a) Musée des Confluences, Lyon, France © Gerald Dick; (b) Asian Village among Giant Trees in 1.7 ha (16,500 m²) big rainforest hall, Gondwanaland, Zoo Leipzig, Germany © Zoo Leipzig.

The interface is not only a shared field of study but is increasingly becoming a shared field of action. The time is ripe for more interaction and joint activities, in the hope that we can move past the traditional borders that separate our tribes and foster the establishment of silos. To best serve the joint mission of connecting science with conservation, making use of synergies and saving resources will be the way of the future.

Note

1 TRAFFIC is itself a joint venture of the World Wide Fund for Nature (WWF) and the International Union for Conservation of Nature (IUCN).

References

Barongi, R., Fisken, F. A., Parker, M., and Gusset, M., eds. (2015). *Committing to Conservation: The World Zoo and Aquarium Conservation Strategy*. Gland: WAZA Executive Office.

European Higher Education Area (2003–2015). *European Higher Education Area and Bologna Process*. Available at: www.ehea.info [Accessed 3 Apr. 2016].

Convention on Biological Diversity (2014). *Global Biodiversity Outlook* 4. Available at: www.cbd.int.

Conway, W. (2003). The role of zoos in the 21st century. *International Zoo Yearbook* 38, pp. 7–13.

Conway, W. (2010). Buying time for wild animals with zoos. *Zoo Biology* 29, pp. 1–8.

Conway, W. (2011). A growing role for zoos. *Wildlife Professional* 5(4), p. 8.

Croke, V. (1997). *The Modern Ark*. New York: Simon & Schuster.

Dick, G. (2015). Current challenges to the zoo and aquarium community: Leadership – responsibilities – diplomacy – animal welfare – public perception – activists. *WAZA News* 3(15), pp. 2–4.

Dick, G., and Gusset, M., eds. (2010). *Building a Future for Wildlife: Zoos and Aquariums Committed to Biodiversity Conservation*. Gland: WAZA Executive Office.

Dick, G., and Gusset, M. (2013). Conservation biology. In: M. Irwin, J. B. Stoner, and A. M. Cobaugh, eds., *Zookeeping: An Introduction to the Science and Technology*. Chicago and London: University of Chicago Press.

Fraser, J., and Wharton, D. (2007). The future of zoos: A new model for cultural institutions. *Curator: The Museum Journal* 50, pp. 41–54.

Gippoliti, S., and Kitchener, A. C. (2007). The Italian zoological gardens and their role in mammal systematic studies, conservation biology, and museum collections. *Hystrix: The Italian Journal of Mammalogy* 18(2), pp. 173–184.

Gower, D. J., Doherty-Bone, T., Loader, S. P., Wilkinison, M., Kouete, M. T., Tapley, B., Orton, F., Daniel, O. Z., Wynne, F., Flach, E., Müller, H., Menegon, M., Stephen, I., Browne, R. K., Fisher, M. C., Cunningham, A. A., and Garner, T. W. J. (2013). *Batrachochytrium dendrobatidis* infection and lethal chytridiomycosis in caecilian amphibians (Gymnophiona). *EcoHealth* 10, p. 173.

Gross, M. (2015). Can zoos offer more than entertainment? *Current Biology* 25, pp. R391–R408.

Gusset M., and Dick, G. (2010a). "Building a future for wildlife"? Evaluating the contribution of the world zoo and aquarium community to in situ conservation. *International Zoo Yearbook* 44, pp. 183–191.

Gusset, M., and Dick, G. (2010b). The global reach of zoos and aquariums in visitor numbers and conservation expenditures. *Zoo Biology* 29, pp. 1–4.

Hamilton, M. J., Milne, B. T., Walker, R. S., Burger, O., and Brown, J. H. (2007). The complex structure of hunter-gatherer social networks. *Proceedings of the Royal Society B* 274, pp. 2195–2203.

Hutchins, M., and Smith, B. (2003). Characteristics of a world-class zoo or aquarium in the 21st century. *International Zoo Yearbook* 38, pp. 130–141.

ICOM NATHIST (2012). *Vienna Statement, Platform 2022: Global Initiative on the Wise Use of Nature.* Available at: http://www.platform2022.org/ [Accessed 3 Apr. 2016].

ICOM NATHIST (2015). *Taipei Declaration on NHMs and Biodiversity Conservation.* Available at: https://icomnathist.wordpress.com/taipei-declaration-on-nhms-and-biodiversity-conservation/ [Accessed 3 Apr. 2016].

Kitchener, A. C. (1997). The role of museums and zoos in conservation biology. *International Zoo Yearbook* 35, pp. 325–336.

Krishtalka, L., and Humphry, P. (2000). Can natural history museums capture the future? *BioScience* 50(7), pp. 611–617.

Mallinson, J. J. C. (2003). A sustainable future for zoos and their role in wildlife conservation. *Human Dimensions of Wildlife* 8, pp. 59–63.

Marshall, G. (1998). Geisteswissenschaften and Naturwissenschaften. In: *A Dictionary of Sociology. Encyclopedia.com* (12 July 2015). Available at: www.encyclopedia.com/doc/1O88-GstswssnschftnndNtrwssnsc.html [Accessed 3 Apr. 2016].

Miller, B., et al. (2004). Evaluating the conservation mission of zoos, aquariums, botanical gardens, and natural history museums. *Conservation Biology* 18, pp. 86–93.

Moss, A., Jensen, E., and Gusset, M. (2014). Evaluating the contribution of zoos and aquariums to Aichi Biodiversity Target 1. *Conservation Biology* 29, pp. 537–544.

Penn, L., Gusset, M., and Dick, G. (2012). *77 Years: The History and Evolution of the World Association of Zoos and Aquariums, 1935–2012.* Gland: WAZA.

Penning, M., et al. eds. (2009). *Turning the Tide: A Global Aquarium Strategy for Conservation and Sustainability.* Gland: WAZA.

Rickert, H. (1986). *Kulturwissenschaft und Naturwissenschaft* [1926]. Stuttgart: Reclam.

Smith, L., Broad, S., and Weiler, B. (2008). A closer examination of the impact of zoo visits on visitor behaviour. *Journal of Sustainable Tourism* 16(5), pp. 544–562.

Steiner, E. (2011). Naturkunde im Landesmuseum Niederösterreich: Vom "heimatlichen Lehrmuseum" zum Erlebnismuseum und Zoo. *Museum Aktuell* 180, pp. 54–59.

Tapley, B., et al. (2014). Towards evidence-based husbandry for caecilian amphibians: Substrate preference in *Geotrypetes seraphini* (Amphibia: Gymnophiona: Dermophiidae). *Herpetological Bulletin* 129, pp. 15–18.

Tool, A. (2007). Wilhelm Dilthey on the objectivity of knowledge in human sciences. *TRAMES* 11(61/56), pp. 1, 3–14.

Zimmermann, M., Hatchwell, L., West, D., and West, C., eds. (2007). *Zoos in the 21st Century: Catalysts for Conservation?* Cambridge: Cambridge University Press.

10 The evolution of natural history museums and science centers

From cabinets to museums to...

Anna Omedes and Ernesto Páramo

Introduction

In 2007, the International Council of Museums (ICOM) defined a museum as a:

> non-profit, permanent institution in the service of society and its de-velopment, open to the public, which acquires, conserves, researches, communicates and exhibits the tangible and intangible heritage of hu-manity and its environment for the purposes of education, study and enjoyment.
>
> (ICOM Statutes, Article 3, Section 1, approved in Vienna, August 24, 2007)

This definition refers to heritage of any kind as safeguarded by a museum, and focuses on the fundamental role that this heritage plays in education, study, and enjoyment.

Museums with natural collections are known as "natural history" or "natural science museums." Nevertheless, Article 2 of the ICOM Code of Ethics for Museums states that, in addition to institutions designated as "museums," the following also qualify as natural history centers:

- Natural monuments and sites
- Institutions holding collections of and displaying live specimens of plants and animals, such as botanical and zoological gardens, aquaria, and vivaria
- Science centers and planetaria
- Nature reserves

Museums housing natural or technological science collections, most of which have a long history, have traditionally displayed their collections and communicated science in a static way.

By contrast, science centers focus mainly on science engagement, using a hands-on approach. They offer interactive exhibits that encourage visitors to experiment, explore, and discover. They are also sometimes referred to as "science museums" even if heritage conservation is not among their primary aims. Many institutions that are engaged in science communication are also considered science centers, such as:

- Science festivals
- Learned societies
- Environmental organizations
- University departments
- Specialist outreach organizations

All of these institutions endeavor to make science accessible in a dynamic way by enhancing the enjoyment of active discovery.

Natural history and science museums: origins and evolution

Since all cultural institutions evolve within the culture that envelops them, so, too, do natural history museums evolve to reflect the heritage they manage and how it is used. In turn, heritage as managed by museums is determined by the evolution of scientific knowledge and changes in the natural environment.

As described by Moldrzyk (2015), past concepts have a lot to teach us in this regard. What, if any, were the limitations of previous initiatives? By what means were changes introduced, and how did museums in the past deal with the same problems we are facing? Knowing where we come from helps pave the way for future development. Natural history and science museums, in the broadest sense, have a long and varied history, since they started out as cabinets of curiosities in the seventeenth and eighteenth centuries. Most natural history museums were formed in the nineteenth century, but have evolved to renew themselves and to adapt to the needs and realities of the twenty-first.

Nevertheless, the earliest collections of live animals date from as early as when animals first came to be domesticated, that is, around 10000 BCE (Kisling, 2001). Typically large and kept by powerful rulers, such collections were not documented until the emergence of the first urban civilizations. Excavations near Hierakonpolis in Egypt provide evidence of the earliest-known collection of live animals, dating to 3500 BCE. Evidence suggests the existence of zoos and botanical gardens in ancient Egypt and Mesopotamia from approximately 1000 BCE. Also around that time, the Chinese emperor Wen Wang maintained what he called the "Garden of Intelligence," consisting of a huge collection of animals, kept on 1,500 acres of land.

In 1520, Hernan Cortés discovered (and destroyed) a vast collection of animals in Tenochtitlán, the capital of the Aztec ruler Montezuma. One of the greatest royal menageries ever recorded, it consisted of two main houses, an aquarium and a botanical garden, and required three hundred people to care for the animals.

The sixteenth through the eighteenth centuries: curiosity cabinets, menageries, and physic gardens

Until the seventeenth century, science as we now understand it was known as "natural philosophy," that is, as a philosophical interpretation of nature. During the eighteenth century, this concept of natural philosophy came to be replaced by scientific interpretation based on the inductive method, marking the beginnings of the Scientific Revolution.

Curiosity cabinets held natural collections (*naturalia*) and interesting human-made objects (*artificialia*), whereas menageries and physic gardens kept collections of live animals and live plants, respectively. These collections largely resulted from explorers' and conquerors' acquisition of unknown, mysterious, and exotic specimens and objects. They were private symbols of wealth and power, not intended for public viewing but only shown to members of the elite. These collections formed the basis for modern day museums. The first botanical garden was founded by the University of Padova in 1545. The Muséum National d'Histoire Naturelle, established in Paris in 1635, is considered to be the first natural history museum.

Other well-known historical examples are the cabinet of Ferrante Imperato in Naples, dating from the sixteenth century; the Museum Wormianum in Copenhagen; the Uppsala University Botanical Gardens in Sweden; and the Versailles menagerie in Paris, the last three dating from the seventeenth century. The Royal Cabinet of Natural History, the precursor to today's

Figure 10.1 Detail of the original seventeenth-century furniture holding the Salvador Cabinet of Barcelona. © Jordi Vidal/MCNB.

National Museum of Natural Science in Madrid, was created in 1771 by the Spanish monarch Charles III.

Dating to the seventeenth to the eighteenth centuries is the Salvador Cabinet in Barcelona, which was established and managed by a dynasty of apothecaries. This cabinet is of special interest, as it is probably the only such example in Europe to have survived almost intact (Figure 10.1). It is preserved as a faithful reflection of pre-Linnaean knowledge of flora, fauna, mineralogy, paleontology, and the pharmacological applications of many natural products. Since the early twentieth century, it has been owned by the Barcelona City Council.

The eighteenth and nineteenth centuries: museums, menageries, and botanical gardens

During this period, the study of science gradually began to take hold among professionals and institutions, and the term "natural science" started to come into usage. Relatively small and scattered collections—many of them consisting of exotic specimens from colonial territories and the remotest corners of the planet—began to increase greatly in size. Institutions to house them were thus formed in enormous, imposing buildings in capital cities, becoming the first thematic museums to be opened to the public. The growing scale and availability of collections led to new studies and changes in scientific thinking. New subjects of interest emerged, such as diversity and adaptations by species, species husbandry, and propagation.

Figure 10.2 Façade of the Martorell Museum, which opened in Barcelona in 1887. The building was inspired by a gallery of the Muséum National d'Histoire Naturelle, which opened in Paris in 1841. © MCNB.

Menageries grew into zoos of caged animals, and botanical gardens began to exchange seeds worldwide. The early years of the nineteenth century saw the emergence of technology collections as a natural outcome of the Industrial Revolution. Rarely private and assembled to meet the practical needs of industry, these collections eventually developed into university technology museums.

Among the many large institutions founded in the eighteenth and nineteenth centuries are the Hungarian Natural History Museum in Budapest (1802), the Gardens of the Zoological Society and the Natural History Museum, both founded in London (1828 and 1881, respectively), and the Museum für Naturkunde in Berlin (1889). The precursor to today's Natural Science Museum of Barcelona, the Martorell Museum (Figure 10.2) opened in that city in 1887.

The twentieth century: museums, zoos, botanical gardens, interactive museums, and science centers

During the twentieth century, certain traditional disciplines came to be considered anachronistic and fell out of favor, for instance, taxonomy. The term "environmental science" was first used in 1923, and new disciplines gradually arose, including biology, ecology, ethology, and evolutionary ecology, just to name a few. The importance of the contributions of individuals as private collectors and as naturalists (bird-watchers among them) also came to be recognized.

In an effort to offer a more natural experience, institutions began to move beyond the concept of the diorama. This century saw the emergence of the temporary exhibition, which offered explanations of concepts and discoveries and was designed to attract a larger and more diverse public. Temporary exhibitions evolved into didactic tools that led to the employment of specific staff. New concerns also arose with twentieth-century museums, such as professionalization, the conservation role, the cooperative management of species, and the ethics of zoos. One major issue was the burden of maintaining large collections and the need to justify their cost. Rader and Kain (2008) state that much of the twentieth century should be viewed as a crucial turning point in the transformation of museums, with the gradual shift from specimen display to non-collection exhibits—from natural history to science.

In the closing years of the century, as longstanding natural history museums began to renew themselves, what are called interactive museums and science centers began to emerge, based on a modern approach to museography that excluded the display of collections as such. The Parque de las Ciencias of Granada, which opened in 1995, today covers a massive site encompassing seventy thousand square meters (Figure 10.3). At once practical and educational, the Science Park takes visitors on a journey through the body, the mind, and the world.

Figure 10.3 Main building of the Parque de las Ciencias, Granada © Parque de las Ciencias.

The twenty-first century: conservation centers?

Natural history museums in the twenty-first century are a constantly evolving entity, home to a heady mixture of sciences—evolution, biogeography, environmental biology, human biology, geology, and molecular biology—all in the context of growing public interest and a need for new modes of public access (Thomson, 2005). Global concern regarding environmental change has prompted interest in ecosystems and the survival of species. Science institutions today have a key role to play in the study of biodiversity, climate change, and environmental education. Natural history museums should be dynamic and interactive places that will incite curiosity and promote exploration and learning on the part of visitors of all ages. They should also stimulate, research, promote, document, and support activities that enhance knowledge of biodiversity and cultural pluralism, and promote sustainable development, respect, and protection of our environment (Omedes, 2005).

The way institutions function today reflects changes in response to global developments in society and technology. Institutions now organize themselves into broad-based networks and create alliances to develop research and education programs. In addition, the information available to institutions is now within reach of citizens: collections are open for consultation, and the Internet is used to make public as much information as possible. Thus, collections are being reassessed, and novel uses for existing and new collections are being developed. Citizens' participation and collaboration in the activities and management of institutions is increasingly frequent, so that at the present, the confluence of natural history museums and science centers is becoming a reality.

Currently, there are more than 6,500 such institutions worldwide, estimated to hold more than 3 billion specimens (Ariño, 2010). Each specimen is a carrier of valuable information and plays an important role in our understanding of the history of the Earth and the origins of life. This information needs to be made available to society to advance knowledge, raise awareness of the problems facing our planet, and respond with responsible stewardship of the environment.

When and how did science centers originate?

The science centers of today represent the outcome of a long and complex evolution inseparable from the history of traditional museums, not to mention numerous longtime initiatives marked, in one form or another, by the Enlightenment vision of education as a means to improve society. Any list of antecedents with a bearing on the creation and history of these successful institutions would be lengthy, but looking back in time, we can highlight certain key events that have shaped the tradition underlying science centers.

- In Paris in 1751, the monumental undertaking that was the *Encyclopédie, ou dictionnaire raisonné des sciences, des arts et des métiers* commenced under the guidance of Denis Diderot and Jean le Rond d'Alembert as a paradigmatic initiative to make the knowledge accumulated by humanity accessible to all (the Enlightenment ideal).
- In London in 1825, Michael Faraday offered the first of his famous demonstrations at the Royal Society. His initial cycle of six lectures on "The Chemical History of a Candle," part of the series of Royal Institution Christmas Lectures, was the inspiration for many other proposals for what we now call "the popularization of science."
- In Paris in 1844, the *Exposition National des Produits de l'Industrie Française* was held, clear evidence of how the Industrial Revolution was becoming entrenched and changing the world forever.
- In London in 1851, the first of the universal expositions—the *Great Exhibition of the Works of Industry of all Nations*—was held at the Crystal Palace in Hyde Park to respond to the public fascination with scientific progress and discoveries.
- In Berlin in 1888, the Urania Society was founded. A truly original project for its time, Urania was created to popularize science and technology by presenting them in a direct and understandable manner to the public; it included a theater where scientists and technologists demonstrated their inventions and discoveries. To further raise interest, the public could also participate in experiments using the original instruments.

The roots of science centers go both deep and wide, making it difficult to pinpoint a foundation date, but if we wanted to establish a benchmark year, it could well be 1969. This exciting year witnessed the big bang of science centers, with the opening of the Exploratorium in San Francisco by Frank Oppenheimer and of the Ontario Science Centre in Toronto.

The Exploratorium rapidly become the inspiration for many like-minded initiatives around the world, especially in Europe and North America (Oppenheimer, 1968). Projects with a similar philosophy of direct experimentation by the public include the Museum of Science and Technology in Detroit and the famous Evoluon in Eindhoven (Netherlands), fostered by the technology company Philips. Other key landmark institutions are the great historical museums such as the Deutsches Museum in Munich, the Science Museum in London, and the Palais de la Découverte in Paris, all of which were now exploring new ways of bringing the principles of science and technology to the public as a complement to the ordered exhibitions of the treasures in their collections.

Thanks to the creative energy of the first science centers and the ensuing public success, especially in schools, a domino effect reverberated to all corners of the planet, to the point that currently there are some three thousand centers worldwide and new ones being created all the time. The emergence of science centers was not an isolated phenomenon but the crystallization of a broad-based movement reacting to the growing awareness of the radically transformative power of science and technology. This movement, which sought to educate society through new methods for activating interest in science in schools and among the public in general, aimed to encourage interest and understanding through direct participation in purpose-built experiments and the development of innovative pedagogical initiatives.

In a characteristic collaborative momentum, the principles underpinning science centers soon led to their organization into various networks (Lipardi, 2012), which, in turn, stimulated the creation of new centers in other cities. These networks are highly active; along with promoting exchanges and the advancement of individual science centers, they hold annual conferences, including the Science Centre World Summit (SCWS), which acts as a major meeting point for science-center representatives and academics. The websites of these networks, with information on the geographical locales, activities, and profiles of the various centers, collectively comprise a faithful map of the current situation. Headquartered in Washington, DC, the first such consortium was the Association of Science and Technology Centers (ASTC), founded in 1973, consisting of some six hundred partners in fifty countries. Founded in 1989, the European Network of Science Centres and Museums (Ecsite) has some four hundred members in forty-five countries. Other major consortia are the Network for Popularization of Science and Technology in Latin America and the Caribbean (RedPop) and the North Africa and Middle East Science Centres Network (NAMES). National networks also exist in many countries, among them, the Association for Science and Discovery Centres (ASDC) in the United Kingdom, with sixty associated centers; the National Council of Science Museums in India; the Living Science network in Portugal; and similar networks in Spain, Germany, Japan, China, and Australia.

Natural history museums, science museums, and science centers (and much more) in today

According to Schubert (2008), the German historian Gebhard Friedrich August Wendeborn complained that, following a visit to the British Museum in London in 1785, before visitors could receive an admission ticket they had to present their credentials in the office and then wait for about fourteen days. This anecdote illustrates the long journey we have travelled, from the elitist museums of the past, to museum's explicitly educational aspirations and proactive attraction of visitors, the museums of 2017.

Science museums and science centers throughout the world have undergone a profound transformation in recent decades and, as a result, contemporary museums and centers are playing a new socio-educational role, seeing their social function transformed completely from the distant times when the first such institutions were created. This fascinating evolution of museums as cultural instruments has brought us to a new golden age. Such is especially the case for the institutions that have explored and exploited the opportunities offered by the new technologies and new ideas concerning the democratization of knowledge and, furthermore, that use the new communication technologies to promote critical participation in the scientific and technological revolution taking place in contemporary society. More and more, museums are utilizing participatory instruments and resources—often clearly educational and almost always motivational—drawing on the new knowledge and technological resources available: from infographics to film, from the theater to the laboratory or workshop, from manipulative interactivity to virtual reality, from the expert's explanation to the Internet, from the original historical object to the full multimedia experience—using the collections as an essential resource for the exhibition project, but not the only one. In short, the evolution has been radical, replacing the static exhibition with dynamic communication.

Traditional natural history museums and science centers are both constantly evolving to meet the needs of society, resulting in institutions that connect increasingly with their publics and users. Baratas Díaz and González Bueno (2013) describe how this evolution is closing the gap between these two types of institutions. Science centers use technology to offer a playful and comprehensible perspective on the scientific principles that underlie nature. Natural history collections are integrated into these centers as part of the expository language, with their heritage and scientific value subordinated to their educational mission. Science centers, especially popular with children and young people, have shown the way for a rapid evolution of the classical museum, fearful of losing its place in society. Traditional museums have gradually adapted to include educational programs, temporary exhibitions, interactive elements, and the like. They have, so to speak, removed the cabinet glass to allow better contact between the natural object and the visitor.

It is interesting to note that science centers have generally been closely associated with hard sciences like physics, most particularly, technology (experiments with mechanics, optics, and astronomy). However, they have gradually come to encompass activities associated with ecology and biology and to embrace a wide range of natural sciences and even social sciences, while including original and historical specimens in their exhibitions.

Natural history museums, science museums, and science centers today need to foster engagement with science and culture, to generate knowledge, and to become vehicles of cultural diffusion. They need to be places where service is rendered to the community as a means for introspection and the development of critical judgment.

Evolution, mutation, hybridization, and convergence

Today's world is characterized by a plethora of institutions, ranging from traditional museums with their formal collections to institutions marked by their constant mutation—genuine leading-edge laboratories of exper-imentation open to encounters with all the arts as seen, for instance, in the Science Gallery in Dublin. In between we have a wide range of centers reflecting varying mixes of ingredients. This is undoubtedly an interesting moment in the history of museums.

We are living in times of accelerated change, and cultural institutions can-not expect to remain immune to these developments. The new media and communication strategies combined with changing cultural profiles among the public are driving the development of new institutional models that are much more flexible than before (Páramo, 2005). Our institutions are leaving behind the immobility and inflexibility of the past to enter a period of constant mutations. In this context, we can speak of two characteristic phenomena of our time: the convergence of the natural history museum and the science center, and the emergence of what we might call the "hybrid museum."

A clear example of convergence is the recently created MUSE in Trento (Italy), which explicitly fuses the traditional museum and its important historical collections with the new science-center perspective. Two other examples are the Natural Science Museum of Barcelona and its new venue since 2011, the Museu Blau (Figure 10.4), with its exhibition *Planet Life* (Piqueras, Guerrero, and Omedes, 2012), and the new Gallery of Humankind of the Royal Belgian Institute of Natural Sciences in Brussels, both of which illustrate this new methodological approach based on a bal-anced use of collections and new media in the service of a better under-standing of exhibitions.

The Natural Science Museum of Barcelona generates and shares knowl-edge on the diversity and evolution of the natural world with the aim of helping conservation efforts and creating a society that is better informed, more closely connected, and more responsible where nature is concerned. It fulfills its aims by safeguarding natural collections, conducting research

Figure 10.4 Museu Blau, the new venue of the Natural Science Museum of Barcelona since 2011. © J. M. de Llobet/MCNB.

into biological and geological diversity, and creating experiences that encourage exploration, learning, appreciation, and enjoyment.

As for the hybrid museums or science centers, they take on functions that, to varying degrees, have historically corresponded to other institutions. And they do so very unequivocally. Hybrids incorporate zoological and botanical resources, technology and business-promotion platforms, universities' alliances with the media, and, increasingly, information dissemination regarding international research projects. Examples include the Universeum in Gothenburg and CosmoCaixa in Barcelona, with large spaces for live animals that re-create their original environments. Several museums have greatly enhanced their appeal by including tropical butterfly gardens or aquariums. City of Science in Naples includes a business incubator (a company that helps new and startup firms develop by providing services such as training or infrastructure), while the Copernicus Science Centre in Warsaw incorporates a technology platform.

Many centers have become culturally emblematic of their city, organizing events, conferences, and activities of all kinds outside the science realm, such as musical, poetry, and theater events that add credence to the slogan that "science is culture." The Parque de las Ciencias of Granada is a notable example of the hybrid model: it is a museum, interactive center, planetarium, botanical garden, aquarium, biopark, training center, debating forum, business incubator, cultural center, convention center, and research center all in one (Figure 10.5). It has created spaces suitable for multiple uses, as diverse and flexible as the world of the present, and reflecting continuous learning, creativity, culture, new technologies, intelligent entertainment, communication, the networked society, science, and innovation—in a nutshell, spaces where today's citizens can meet.

Figure 10.5 The *Biodomo*, pavilion on biodiversity at the Parque de las Ciencias in Granada, Spain, which opened in 2016. © Parque de las Ciencias.

Other examples include the Museum of Science in Boston, with a history dating back to 1830, and the Boston Society of Natural History with its classical Museum of Natural History, which evolved to the complex of 2017, a mixture of science and technology museum, science center, and host for the national platform for promoting science, technology, engineering, and mathematics education (STEM). Yet another notable example is the Universcience of Paris, an umbrella project for the Palais de la Découverteand the Cité des Sciences et de l'Industrie and a key catalyst for the promotion of science and technology culture in France. A final instance illustrating this interesting phenomenon of mutations, hybrids, and convergence is the remarkable re-creation of the Library of Alexandria in Egypt as a museum, interactive center, and planetarium, among other things.

Páramo drew an analogy between modern museums and science centers and platypuses, pointing to both as uncommon but not endangered:

> I like to joke that interactive science centers today are as rare as the platypus. These baffling creatures were first discovered in the 18th century and the first specimen, when sent to the UK, led British naturalists to think that this species was a gross falsification, the work of a mad taxidermist. An egg-laying mammal, with the bill of a duck and the tail of a beaver, which lives mostly in water, poisonous and with a remarkable system for electrolocating prey—how weird! But maybe the strangest thing about this curious animal endemic to Australia is that it is not endangered. In other words, despite being rare, evolution has not betrayed it but has enabled it to adapt to its world. Something similar is happening with modern museums and science centers. They have evolved into very different creatures from their ancestors

in their response to the demands of today's society and the enormous educational and cultural opportunities available today.

(2010, p. 163)

Museums of the twenty-first century are working to ensure that they play a more useful and relevant role in society and to fulfill the functions that, in fact, naturally correspond to them: advancing science and enhancing the stewardship of our planet (Omedes, 2015).

Today's museums are genuine vehicles for social communication (Páramo, 2009). They are also many other things and have other purposes, of course, but from the public's vantage point, that is their most visible mission. Another basic function of the museum is social responsibility. Museums need to understand inclusivity as a global concept that encompasses both the physical and the social dimensions and to express its commitment to this concept by developing initiatives inspired by the values of equality, accessibility, and participation, as the democratic expression of a public undertaking and a means of reaching all citizens and contributing toward social change by combatting exclusion (Omedes et al., 2015).

At the present moment, museums' social functions in conserving our environmental heritage and in research and education, as defined by International Council of Museums (ICOM), are widely acknowledged to be as important as ever. But there is an additional goal that should be considered: promoting the system of R&D&I (research and development and innovation), which furthers the public's understanding of the importance of investing in research (Páramo, 2016). In democratic societies, "public opinion" plays a determining role in the allocation of governmental resources. Due to the enormous competitiveness for public resources, in contemporary democracies, it is society that must support large investments. For this reason, it is a priority to increase the public's support for science and make more visible its link with general progress.

All things considered, if there is a single cultural institution that has changed significantly over time, it is the museum, which is no longer what it once was. We have seen how museums evolved throughout history, from curiosity cabinets and traditional collections to the enormously diverse and complex institutions they are in 2017. But what of their future? Since any prediction about the future in these complex times is difficult, we will simply make some proposals for reflection.

- **Diversity.** A greater diversity of institutions, as already exists, will respond better to available opportunities and the needs of different groups and societies. We will still have museums whose main role will be to preserve, study, and communicate their collections, but we will also see more interactive institutions with little or no collections that will complement the broad range of hybrid museums and public spaces already in existence.

- **Technology.** Technology is not likely to monopolize the lives of museums, but it will certainly play a vital role in relation to content. Users, however, in a society saturated with technological resources, may prefer the real experiences and direct contacts offered by museums as an alternative to digital reality.
- **Public spaces.** In an era marked by individualism, isolation, and even loneliness, it is becoming increasingly complicated to have public spaces where people can share culture. The social aspect of museum visits will thus be reinforced as museums become public spaces that, keeping human relationships at their center, will offer opportunities for sharing and exchange.
- **Social mediation.** Museums will strengthen their mediation role by developing other functions in demand in society, such as the provision of reliable information (necessary more than ever in the post-truth era), protection of the environment, ongoing learning, and social and cultural creativity.
- **New functions.** As long as they are open and flexible, museums themselves are likely to suggest many new uses that we cannot yet imagine. We could never have envisaged the evolution of the public museums that are so familiar to us today, which came into being when pioneers formed collections that were the province of a select few. Open and flexible cultural entities are likely to reveal opportunities for the institutions of the future.

Paradoxically, we may say that museums nowadays have more of a future than a past. With this, we will close with extracts from the Granada Statement, made at the Parque de las Ciencias, Granada, in 1999:

> It is no less important to determine the nature of scientific language or, better put, the nature of the language, which science must use in order to ensure effective and fluent communication between scientists and society. This is a challenge for everybody and must be constant food for thought....
>
> New spaces dedicated to the promulgation of science, science museums and planetariums, all serve a purpose as the places where many citizens come into contact with the world of science for the first time, and should therefore become consolidated and be given backing as exceptional tools for bringing scientific knowledge within reach.
>
> The scientific culture of the population must be nourished as a matter of urgency. Scientific information is the most fecund of seeds for the social, economic and political development of peoples from all countries. Complicity between scientists and the community at large is an exceptional celebration of democracy. But moreover, this new culture will play a part in putting the brakes on fake science, increasing citizens' capacity for critical thought, doing away with fears and

superstitions, and making human beings freer and bolder. The enemies that science must defeat are also the enemies of philosophy, art and literature: ignorance, obscurantism, barbarism, poverty and human exploitation.

(27 Mar. 1999)

References

Ariño, A. H. (2010). Approaches to estimating the universe of natural history collections data. *Biodiversity Informatics* 7, pp. 81–92.

Baratas Díaz, L. A., and González Bueno, A. (2013). De gabinete a "science center": 500 años de coleccionismo en historia natural. In: A. González Bueno and A. Baratas Díaz, eds., *Museos y colecciones de Historia Natural: Investigación, educación y difusión*. Madrid: Real Sociedad Española de Historia Natural.

Kisling, V. N., Jr., ed. (2001). *Zoo and Aquarium History: Ancient Animal Collections to Zoological Gardens*. London: CRC Press.

Lipardi, V. (2012). The evolution and worldwide expansion of science centres. In: A. M. Bruyas and M. Riccio, eds., *Science Centres and Science Events*. Milan: Springer–Verlag Italia.

Moldrzyk, U. (2015). New views on nature? Renewal of natural history museums by the Berlin example. *Mnemòsine: Revista Catalana de Museologia* 8, pp. 26–35. English translation available at: www.museologia.cat/wp-content/uploads/2014/03/Traduccions-dossier-Mnem%C3%B2sine-8-1.pdf.

Omedes, A. (2005). Los museos de ciencias naturales, piezas clave para la conservación de la biodiversidad. *Quark* 25, pp. 72–78.

Omedes, A., ed. (2015). Natural sciences museums: Monographic dossier. *Mnemòsine: Revista Catalana de Museologia* 8, pp. 9–90.

Omedes, A., Ballester, M., González, L., Ubero, L., and Viladot, P. (2015). The social dimension of the Museu de Ciències Naturals de Barcelona. *Mnemòsine: Revista Catalana de Museologia* 8, pp. 48–61. English translation available at: www.museologia.cat/wp-content/uploads/2014/03/Traduccions-dossier-Mnem%C3%B2sine-8-1.pdf.

Oppenheimer, F. (1968). Rationale for a science museum. *Curator: The Museum Journal* 1(3), pp. 206–209.

Páramo, E. (2005a). ¿Ciencia o espectáculo? Presentar la ciencia en una sociedad democrática. In: *Actas de las XXI Jornadas de la Sociedad Española de Paleontología*.

Páramo, E. (2005b). ¿Serían los museos interactivos muy diferentes si partieran de una gran colección? Hacer que los objetos hablen. *Quark* 35, pp. 37–41.

Páramo, E. (2009). Contar la ciencia desde los museos. In: A. Gonzalez Valverde, ed., *Contar la ciencia*. Murcia: Fundación Séneca.

Páramo, E. (2010). El museo "ornitorrinco": La ampliación del Parque de las Ciencias: Nuevos medios para nuevos tiempos." In: ICOM España, *5º Encuentro internacional actualidad en museografía*. Madrid: ICOM.

Páramo, E. (2016). Museos de ciencia hoy: Foro científico. *Investigación y Ciencia* 476, pp. 60–87.

Piqueras, M., Guerrero, R., and Omedes, A. (2012). The Museu Blau: A natural history museum for the 21st century. *Contributions to Science* 8(1), pp. 85–91.

Rader, K. A., and Kain, V. E. M. (2008). From natural history to science: Display and the transformation of American museums of science and nature. *Museum and Society* 6(2), pp. 152–171.

Schubert, K. (2008). *El museo: Historia de una idea*. Granada: Turpiana.

Thomson, K. S. (2005). Natural history museum collections in the 21st century. *ActionBioscience*. Available at: www.actionbioscience.org/evolution/thomson.html [Accessed 30 Apr. 2005].

11 National and international legislation

Lynda Knowles

Introduction

The future of natural history museums is tied to the global political climate. Whether it concerns the adequacy of laws and museum practices that protect cultural property in jeopardy, the rights of the indigenous, or the need for museums to demonstrate good governance to retain the public's respect, natural history museums will play pivotal roles in resolving the tensions these issues create.

The last fifty years have seen remarkable progress in international law pertaining to cultural (and biological) heritage, as reflected in a wide array of international treaties and conventions. While these legal vehicles have not been entirely successful and many challenges remain, they represent a significant undertaking on the part of the international community to develop codes and standards governing preservation. Natural history museums have been very involved in these efforts, establishing a consensus on how to protect and preserve artifacts and collections, secure cultural heritage, and care for artifacts.

The voices of the indigenous, so often silenced in the past, seek repatriation, compensation, and restorative justice for the taking of their cultures, both tangible and intangible. The law evolves slowly, and international law even more so, but cultural diplomacy through the museum sector has been instrumental in articulating the common values of the cultural heritage of humankind and in encouraging the development of universal rights within it. Natural history museums have played a valuable role in establishing new norms, particularly regarding the return of indigenous human remains. This work continues to prove indispensable as it refines and reconciles competing values to help clarify the law.

There can be no doubt that the current political situation in the United States has raised worldwide concerns regarding the direction of the nation and what that means for global security. While this situation may seem unique to the United States, the author hopes that a discussion of the legal structures of US museums, considered in light of the current assault on science by the US federal government, might prove instructive to other museums wishing to preserve and present science in politically challenging settings. This chapter will also discuss the effects and implications of a highly charged political atmosphere and how these might affect natural history museum practices.

Cultural heritage protection

International laws

The 1954 Hague Convention for the Protection of Cultural Property was the first international treaty specific to cultural property, addressing the need for nations to implement measures to protect cultural property from the effects of armed conflict (UNESCO, 1954, art. 4[1]). The convention requires parties to refrain from using cultural property, or its immediate surroundings, for purposes likely to expose it to destruction or damage, and to refrain from any act of hostility directed against cultural property. Cultural property is defined to include cultural facilities, art and scientific collections, as well as museums, libraries, and archives (art. 1).

The Hague Convention calls on member states to develop informational and educational programs that foster the appreciation of and respect for cultural property. An emblem, known as the "Blue Shield," was designed for use by the parties, whereby specific cultural structures display the Blue Shield, enabling them to be easily identified for preservation and protection in the event of an armed conflict (UNESCO, 1954, art. 6, 16). In 1999, the International Council of Museums (ICOM) helped found the International Committee of the Blue Shield, which works to meet Hague Convention goals and is the umbrella organization for all national Blue Shield committees (ICOM, 2010). Despite the shortcomings of existing international law in this area, a topic on which much ink has been spilled (Gerstenblith, 2016), the overwhelming international consensus to protect these cultural properties and their contents, is an evident global norm.

Approximately fifteen years after the Hague Convention, there appeared the first international instrument dedicated to the elimination of illicit trafficking of cultural property: the 1970 UNESCO Convention on the Means of Prohibiting and Preventing the Illicit Import, Export, and Transfer of Ownership of Cultural Property (UNESCO, 1970). The convention sets forth the notion that cultural institutions, museums, libraries, and archives must ensure that their collections are built in accordance with universally accepted moral principles (preamble, para. 6). It defines cultural property as property that is specifically designated by each member state as being of importance for archaeology, prehistory, history, literature, art, or science, and belonging to ethnological, archaeological, or other enumerated categories (art. 1).

The parties to the 1970 UNESCO Convention recognize that the illicit import, export, and transfer of cultural property are among the main causes of an impoverished cultural heritage in the origin countries (art. 2, para. 1). They further recognize that "international co-operation constitutes one of the most efficient means of protecting each country's cultural property" against the many dangers that result from illicit import, export, and transfer (art. 2, para. 1). The convention recommends that parties oppose practices with the means at their disposal, "by removing their causes, putting a stop to current practices, and by helping to make the necessary reparations" (art. 2, para. 2).

Another key international law concerning cultural heritage was passed in 1995: the Convention on Stolen or Illegally Exported Cultural Objects (UNIDROIT, 1995). The convention was enacted by the International Institute for the Unification of Private Law (UNIDROIT), an independent intergovernmental organization whose mission is to harmonize private and commercial laws between states. It requires the return of a stolen object by the possessor (art. 1[a]); claims may be barred by the passage of time in certain circumstances (UNIDROIT, 1995, art. 3, paras. 3–5). In addition, the return may require compensation to the possessor if the latter proves that they did not and should not have known that the object was stolen and exercised due diligence in acquiring the object (art. 4). This "innocent-purchaser" defense is absent from the 1970 UNESCO Convention, perhaps because UNIDROIT is focused on private property rights, whereas UNESCO is concerned more broadly with social and economic justice, including human rights. To date, the 1970 UNESCO Convention has been ratified by 131 member states (UNESCO, 2016a); there are 37 contracting parties to UNIDROIT (UNIDROIT, 2016).

The world's plant and animal species are the focus of the 1972 Convention on International Trade in Endangered Species of Wild Fauna, or CITES, which enumerates varying degrees of protection afforded to different species (CITES, 1973, arts. 3–4, apps. 1–3). The politics regarding the classification of species, combined with parties' efforts to weigh the economic benefits of some trade versus the need for conservation, have bedeviled much of this law's history. Unlike UNIDROIT, CITES lacks any such provision protecting innocent, good-faith purchasers. Possession of an endangered item is legal only with appropriate permits issued in accordance with CITES and the enacting laws of parties. Some members of the Native American community have observed that CITES offers more protection to fauna and flora than the UNESCO and UNIDROIT conventions do to the human remains of indigenous peoples.

An important successor to CITES is the Convention on Biodiversity (CBD). Opened for signature on 5 June 1992, and entered into force on 29 December 1993, the CBD is designed to conserve biological diversity, encourage sustainable use of the Earth's biological resources, and provide access to and equitable sharing of benefits arising from genetic resources (CBD, 1992, art. 1; CBD, 2017b). A supplementary agreement under the CBD is the Nagoya Protocol on Access to Genetic Resources and the Fair and Equitable Sharing of Benefits Arising from Their Utilization, which opened for signature in 2010 and was put into effect in October 2014 (CBD, 2017a).

The Nagoya Protocol provides the framework for implementation of the third objective of the CBD: the fair and equitable sharing of benefits stemming from the use of genetic resources (Nagoya Protocol, 2010, art. 1).

The CBD and the Nagoya Protocol represent a balancing of interests between countries with a rich supply of genetic or biological resources, and those with the technology and funding to develop them. The complexity of the economic resource allocations that the CBD seeks to redress, coupled with the urgency of the underlying scientific concerns, embodies unique challenges in establishing priorities between the needs of source countries and the expectations of those ready to harvest biological materials. This has nether impeded recognition of the legislation, nor the need for compliance. The CBD has 196 parties; the Nagoya Protocol, 9 (CBD, 2017c,d). Natural history museums continue to develop best practices in this area and must ensure that appropriate agreements are in place for field research in member states.

Natural history museums of the future will need to take these conventions into consideration when amassing collections and conducting field research. Even if a museum is located in a country that is not a party to one of these agreements (notably, the United States is a party neither to the CBD nor the Nagoya Protocol), it must still acknowledge the effect of the agreements in other countries from which artifacts and other cultural property may be coming.

Cultural heritage developments

The Al Mahdi case

In the summer of 2012, an Al Qaeda–affiliated group targeted the destruction of cultural property in the ancient city of Timbuktu (ICC, 2016a). Timbuktu is a designated World Heritage Site under the Convention Concerning the Protection of the World Cultural and Natural Heritage, whereby states designate cultural or heritage sites that warrant the utmost care and preservation due to certain criteria set forth in the convention (UNESCO, 1972, arts. 1–3). The Timbuktu site included a number of mosques and mausoleums—buildings that were chosen *precisely* because of their religious and historical nature (ICC, 2016b; UNESCO, 2016d). Al Mahdi, the group's leader, was the first individual ever charged with intentional cultural destruction as a war crime (ICC, 2016b, para. 13). In September 2016, he was tried by the International Criminal Court (ICC), where he was found guilty and sentenced to nine years in prison (ICC, 2016a). While the ICC is a global institution underfunded and often under attack, this successful prosecution marked a watershed moment in establishing a legal precedent for the destruction of cultural property as a war crime. It will provide a useful exemplar for future prosecutions, both national and international.

The ivory market

China is a significant source market for the ivory and rhino horn trades (Liljas, 2013; International Fund for Animal Welfare [IFAW], 2017). Public relations campaigns within China have been enacted to reduce demand for these items (Gabriel, 2014). On 30 December 2016, the official news agency Xinhua announced that by late 2017 China would gradually halt the processing and sale of ivory for commercial purposes (McRae, 2016). Hong Kong plans to do the same by 2021 (Dasgupta, 2016; Neme, 2016). China's recognition of the problem, and its efforts to address it, are welcome developments.

ICOM and UNESCO

The International Council of Museums (ICOM) was formed in 1946. A consortium of 35,000 museum professionals and experts from over 125 countries and territories, one that enjoys consultative status with UNESCO, ICOM is a unique forum that enables its members to engage in cultural diplomacy, working together on shared challenges and opportunities (ICOM, 2017a). It is a leading force in museum ethics and is often a leader in developing customs and practices that will eventually become law. ICOM is composed of 119 national committees and 30 international committees (ICOM, 2017a), including the International Committee for Museums and Collections of Natural History (ICOM NATHIST). Devoted to best practices in the natural sciences, ICOM NATHIST is a nimble subgroup that advises ICOM on matters pertaining to natural history collections, including the protection and preservation of unique archaeological and anthropological connections (ICOM, 2017b).

In October 2015, ICOM NATHIST held its annual conference in Taipei, Taiwan, where it issued the Taipei Declaration on Natural History Museums and Biodiversity Conservation (Cheng and Lin, 2015). The Taipei Declaration states that:

> human activities have created catastrophic declines in biodiversity. Both ethics and logic point to a mandate to conserve vulnerable habitats and species. To achieve best practice, natural history museums must take action to conserve natural habitats and populations.
> (ICOM NATHIST, 2015)

On 17 November 2015, UNESCO adopted the Recommendation on the Protection and Promotion of Museums and Collections, which was followed by the Shenzhen Declaration on Museums and Collections issued in November 2016 (UNESCO, 2016b, 2016c). Although nonbinding, both documents demonstrate the influence museums have in promoting international laws regarding cultural property protection.

International repatriation of indigenous human remains

The deep spiritual connection most indigenous communities have for their dead, including reverence for ancestors and the cultural necessity to return them home, is well-documented by anthropologists. To varying degrees, these profound religious beliefs have been acknowledged by cultural experts and the natural history museum sector. Many natural history museums house indigenous human remains as a consequence of historical collection activities based on colonization, or as anatomical or medical history museums. Laws and ethics on this topic are rapidly changing. Natural history museums will need to stay at the forefront of this issue in all its complexity and act as leaders in ensuring the moral integrity of their collections and, especially in the case of indigenous human remains, correcting historical wrongs.

Applicable international law

Perhaps nothing exemplifies twentieth-century jurisprudence more than the emergence of codified human rights. While norms and mores surrounding human rights existed long before the end of World War II, that conflict galvanized the global community to enshrine certain basic individual and societal rights as fundamentally human and universal. The United Nations Charter is the foundational treaty for the UN (UN, 1945). Under the charter, member states with territories "whose people have not yet attained a full measure of self-government" agree that "the interests of the inhabitants of these territories are paramount," and that a "sacred trust" exists to ensure due respect for "culture of the peoples concerned" (Ch. 11, Figure 73, in this volume).

Several years later, on 10 December 1948, the Universal Declaration of Human Rights (UDHR) took up these same themes. Issued in Paris, the UDHR asserts that every individual is entitled to all the rights and freedoms set forth in the declaration, without regard for the international status of a country or territory to which a person belongs, be it independent, trust, non-self-governing, or under any other limitation of sovereignty (UN, 1948, art. 2). While neither the UN Charter nor the UDHR address repatriation per se, the notion of respect for the rights of indigenous cultures as *cultures within cultures* is firmly entrenched in these documents.

On 13 September 2007, the UN adopted the United Nations Declaration on the Rights of Indigenous Peoples (UNDRIP) (UN, 2007). Although non-binding, it establishes international customary norms for indigenous rights. While the 1970 UNESCO and 1995 UNIDROIT conventions address Western norms of property rights, UNDRIP focuses on human rights. Some have argued that property rights are human rights and that any such distinction between the two is unhelpful (Hutt, 1998).

UNDRIP asserts that indigenous peoples are given the right to practice and revitalize their cultural conditions and customs, the right to the use and control of their ceremonial objects, and the right to the repatriation of their human remains (UN, 2007, art. 12, sec. 1). Under UNDRIP, states seek:

> to enable the access and/or repatriation of ceremonial objects and human remains in their possession through fair, transparent and effective mechanisms developed in conjunction with the indigenous peoples concerned.
>
> (Figure 12, sec. 2)

Repatriation of human remains to indigenous communities is, therefore, a growing legal issue that natural history museums cannot afford to ignore. States and museums alike have taken great strides in developing mechanisms for addressing the human rights concerns related to this issue, but there is a great deal of flux in this area, as is discussed below.

Specific national laws

United States

The Native American Graves Protection and Repatriation Act (NAGPRA) is a US law enacted in 1990 (NAGPRA 1990). It has no international application. In the words of Senator Daniel Inouye, NAGPRA is "not about the validity of museums or the value of scientific inquiry. Rather, it is about human rights" (Trope, 2013, quoting Inouye, para. 1). The law involves ongoing and consultative efforts between Native American tribes and museums. Much has been written about NAGPRA's track record in other publications. Its influence on the efforts of indigenous communities in other countries continues to evolve. The NAGPRA Program is operated through the US Department of the Interior (US DOI, 2017). While the Native American community has asked the US Department of Justice and the State Department for assistance with international repatriations, more could be done (National Congress of American Indians [NCAI], 2012).

New Zealand

New Zealand actively seeks the return of human remains taken from the country during its colonial period through the Protected Objects Act of 1975. The purpose of the Act is to regulate the export of protected New Zealand objects, provide for the return of unlawfully exported or stolen protected foreign items, and record the ownership and control the sales of *ngā taonga tūturu*, a term that refers to items relating to Māori culture, history, or society (Protected Objects Act, 1975, s. 1A, s. 2[1]). The Museum of New Zealand Te Papa Tongarewa Act of 1992 created a national institution to protect, preserve, and explore the heritage of New Zealand's cultures (Museum of New Zealand Te Papa Tongarewa Act of 1992, s. 4). The New Zealand government has invested the museum with authority and funding to implement a repatriation program for the Māori (Museum of New Zealand Te Papa Tongarewa Act). Through its Karanga Aotearoa Repatriation Programme, Te Papa has been able to recover Māori remains from over forty museums around the world (Museum of New Zealand Te Papa Tongarewa Act).

Australia

During the late nineteenth and early twentieth centuries, human remains and objects from Australia's indigenous communities were sent to natural history museums in other parts of the world. The Australian government and its museums have been developing agreements and programs with other countries to facilitate the return of human remains. These include the Indigenous Repatriation Program, a program administered by the Australian Ministry of Arts, whereby funds are provided to Aboriginal and Torres Strait Islander organizations and major Australian museums to facilitate the return of ancestral remains. The cost of international repatriations is met directly by the Australian government. Making reference to UNDRIP, the official policy statement on the indigenous repatriation asserts that repatriation:

> acknowledges the wrong done... and allows the ancestors to finally rest in peace in their homelands. It recognises the unbreakable bond, customary obligations and traditional practices between the living, the land and the dead.

The United Kingdom and Europe

Opposition to repatriation is notable in Britain and Europe, where institutional and legal impediments have been formidable. The British Museum's Human Remains Policy states as an overarching principle that human remains collections should remain intact (British Museum, 2013, s. 5.1). Human remains less than one thousand years old may be transferred out of the collections, but the museum will *strongly* favor retention where the human remains are over three hundred years old (s. 4.1, s. 5.16.1). Moreover, it will *very strongly* favor retention where the human remains are over five hundred years old (s. 5.16.2, emphasis in the original). If human remains are more than one hundred years old, the:

> significance of the *cultural continuity* and the *cultural importance* of the human remains demonstrated by the community making the request must outweigh the public benefit to the world community of retaining the human remains in the Collection.
>
> (s. 5.17.2, emphasis in the original)

The Recommendations for the Care of Human Remains in Museums and Collections, published by the German Museum Association in April 2013, acknowledge that in repatriation:

> questions of ethics and human dignity are omnipresent. At the same time, man's interest in mankind is also the starting point for the great importance of research.
>
> (Deutscher Museumsbund, 2013, p. 7)

The recommendations claim that UNDRIP does not, in itself, or as a matter of customary international law, require the return of human remains (pp. 38–40). They address the sensitivities of indigenous peoples but give them no standing to make repatriation claims, as they are not nation-parties to the 1970 UNESCO Convention (p. 40).

The Human Remains in Collection Policy issued by National Museums Scotland in 2016 refers to Scottish law that allows transfer of human remains to other appropriate entities, subject to a recommendation by the organization's board of trustees and approval by the relevant Scottish ministers (NMS, 2016, s. 4.2). However, permanent transfers out of National Museums Scotland's (NMS) collection must be considered on a case-by-case basis, with each request assessed on its own merits by the board of trustees (s. 4.2). It requires that the request is made by a national government with a clear endorsement from the community claiming the return of ancestral remains. Scottish museums have been noted for their responsiveness to repatriation issues (Curtis, 2010; NMS, 2016, s. 6.2).

In France, national legislation must be passed for every repatriation, as items in French collections are deemed inalienable as a matter of national law (Cornu and Renold, 2010, p. 9). Such legislation has been successfully passed for the return of human remains to New Zealand, but the process remains cumbersome, and fears of the depletion of museum collections persist (Sciolino, 2012).

ICOM ethics guidance

As noted earlier, ICOM is a global museum community, founded on its Code of Ethics for Museums (ICOM, 2013a). The Code of Ethics applies to any human remains in any institution, and offers a broader view of professional practices regarding the treatment, display, and use of human remains in, for instance, anatomical collections (ICOM, 2013a). Under the Ethics Code, collections of human remains, and material of sacred significance should be acquired only if they can be housed securely and cared for respectfully (s. 2.7). This must be accomplished in a manner consistent with professional standards *and* the interests and beliefs of members of the community, ethnic, or religious groups from which the objects originated, where these are known (s. 2.7). Moreover, research on human remains and materials of sacred significance must be consonant with professional standards and consider the interests and beliefs of the community, ethnic, or religious groups from whom the objects originated, where these are known (s. 3.7). Finally, human remains and materials of sacred significance must be displayed in a manner befitting professional standards and, where known, take into account the interests and beliefs of members of the community, ethnic, or religious groups from whom the objects originated (s. 4). Human remains must be presented with great tact and respect for the feelings of human dignity held by all peoples (s. 4.3).

The ICOM Ethics Code also provides that "[t]he possibility of developing partnerships with museums in countries or areas that have lost a significant part of their heritage should be explored" (s. 6.1); museums are also encouraged to initiate the dialogue for the return of cultural property. The latter:

> should be undertaken in an impartial manner, based on scientific, professional and humanitarian principles as well as applicable local, national and international legislation, in preference to action at a governmental or political level.
>
> (s. 6.2)

Prompt restitution is appropriate if a specimen was transferred in violation of the principles of international and national conventions and shown to be part of that country's or people's heritage (s. 6.3). Taking these provisions as a whole, this forward-looking document calls for respectful dialogue with communities of origin within a context that recognizes humanitarian principles and international legislation.

The ICOM Code of Ethics for Natural History Museums is specific to natural history museums and supplements the ICOM Ethics Code of Ethics for Natural History Museums (ICOM, 2013b). It, too, states that human remains can only be displayed with dignity and in accordance with the highest professional standards (s. 1[c]). The origin of human remains, including the wishes of descendants or stakeholders, must be observed (s. 1[b]). Where extant representatives of the cultural group exist, any display, representation, research, and/or deaccession must be done "in full consultation with the groups involved" (s. 1[d]). If an object confers a spiritual and/or cultural significance, it may be repatriated only with the full knowledge and agreement of all parties and in compliance with applicable laws (s. 1[g]). The Code of Ethics also requires thoughtful consideration of the wishes of cultural groups and the opportunity for full consultation in matters of spiritual and/or cultural significance (s. 1[e]).

Given these recent legal and cultural developments, the repatriation of indigenous humans will most likely be considered a question of legal, human rights. The ethical obligations of museums, along with their own developing guidelines, mirror this development. Relationship building and continued dialogue with indigenous groups on issues of repatriation will be the norm for museums of natural history in the future.

Museums in the United States: governance and challenges

The vast majority of museums in the United States are founded as non-profit corporations under state law, or as state or municipal entities. When a museum is established, one of its first duties is to create certain governing documents. These are the articles of incorporation, its bylaws, and a set of policies recommended under the US tax code and suggested by accreditation authorities.

The articles of incorporation set forth a museum's mission, or reason for being. This document is filed with the secretary of state's office for the state in which the museum is formed, and is a public record. Since the mission establishes the basis for the museum's standing as a non-profit, the museum will need to ensure that it does not stray from it. For instance, a wildlife museum may not morph into an animal rescue center without amending its articles of incorporation (if not its name). A museum's mission can be changed by filing amended articles of incorporation, but caution should be exercised to ensure amendments do not compromise the museum's charitable status.

A museum's bylaws further refine the mission and articulate operational guidelines. Bylaws establish the number, tenure, and removal process for the museum's board of trustees (or directors, as they are sometimes called). They indicate how, when, and where meetings of the board are held and often include descriptions of the functions of its officers (typically, president, vice-president, secretary, and treasurer). They also establish standing committees, such as an executive committee for larger museums, a finance committee, an audit committee, and nominating/governance committees, the last of which generally encourage ethical policies and assess potential candidates for board membership. The bylaws are usually not public documents but comprise a museum's internal guide on how to function.

Most natural history museums have a collections policy in place to govern acquisitions and deaccessioning. The US Internal Revenue Service expects to see a conflict of interest/ethics policy, among others (National Council of Non-profits, 2017b). The American Alliance of Museums (AAM) suggests a number of other policies, including a gift acceptance policy. If wisely stewarded, these policies serve to empower an ethical and principled culture (American Alliance of Museums, 2017).

Museums established under state law are governed by a board of trustees. Fiduciary responsibilities flow from the trustees to the institution under state statutes. These are typical duties of loyalty and care. Museums are also formed with specific status under the federal tax laws generated by the Internal Revenue Service (IRS). These entities are informally known as 501(c)(3) non-profit or charitable organizations, a reference to the section of the IRS Code under which they are created. US jurisprudence pertaining to charitable organizations is deep and broad, and reflects a social contract that, in exchange for providing charitable services, a 501(c)(3) corporation need not pay any state or income tax on its earnings. The IRS Code formalizes this arrangement with the following caveat: in order for a 501(c)(3) to keep its tax-exempt status, it must refrain from engaging in politics (IRS, 2016b). The rationale is that the more political an organization becomes, by definition, the less devoted it is to charitable pursuits and should, therefore, pay into the public coffers the same as any other for-profit company.

Over time, a distinction has been made between permissible lobbying activity (within certain statutorily defined amounts) and impermissible campaign activity (National Council of Non-profits, 2017b). Thus, a museum is in no danger if it lobbies for bond funds to renovate a museum, but it may not endorse or oppose a specific candidate for any political election (IRS, 2016b). The IRS offers a litany of scenarios to explain what is and is not permissible, as the topic tends to come up every four years (IRS, 2006).

There is nothing in federal law that precludes a museum from taking stands on the science of evolution or climate change; many US museums are careful in crafting position statements on potentially controversial science. But this reticence is the result of the dynamics between a museum, its board, and the source of its funds—not federal law.

While a museum's financial health enjoys an advantage when it is released from any obligation to pay taxes, it must still have funds to keep the doors open. These funds are traditionally derived from a range of sources, and the more varied, the better. Some state or municipalities have established "cultural taxes" on the sale of goods that go toward providing funding to the cultural institutions within their territories (for an example, see Missouri Revised Statutes, 2016, s. 184.845.1). Museums also derive (tax-free) income from public exhibitions, child and adult programs, and the like. Some may accept grants from federal, state, or private foundations that fund a particular activity or research, although these sources may be withdrawn or curtailed, depending on a government's appetite for certain kinds of research.

A long-cherished source of income for most American museums is private donations. Donations to charity are nontaxable, providing a great incentive to those with extra income to minimize their tax liability by making charitable donations (IRS, 2016a). Any attempts to change this longstanding law are typically met with fierce resistance from the non-profit community. Private donations, which come from members of the public and members of a board, are heavily solicited, and relationships carefully nurtured, over years of effort and outreach. The fear is that without the tax advantages of making donations, donors will cease making contributions to a museum.

One of the challenges facing natural history museums is whether, and under what circumstances, natural history museums accept funds from donors that may not share or support the science presented by the museum itself. There is no clear legal answer to this. Most museums rely on their own gift acceptance policies, and one of the most commonly found provisions is that no donation can be accepted if it compromises the scientific autonomy of the institution. Museums are also wise to include similar language in the donation agreement itself. Non-profit corporations prefer unrestricted gifts, that is, gifts that are not tied to conditions. This gives a museum the greatest latitude in determining where funds are most needed, and such was the norm for many years. Recently, donor advocates have argued for the use of restrictions, so that a donor can ensure their money is spent appropriately (Cohen, 2013). A conditional gift always creates internal discussion on how and whether the gift can be accepted in a way that does not adversely impact the museum's autonomy or scientific standing. This is usually an easy problem to resolve, as most restrictions can be as innocuous as creating a specific children's program or endowing a chair in a specific science. But the more control over content sought, the more problematic the gift.

If a donor is also a member of the museum's board, the degree of influence sought may be even greater. For a board member, however, the legal fiduciary duty to the institution is paramount. If a board member disagrees with the museum's position on any given science-related issue or makes donations conditioned on the museum's presentation of science, there is a danger that the fiduciary obligation the trustee owes to the organization will be compromised. This situation also undermines the museum's ability to meet its fiduciary obligation to the public, if it shies away from taking a scientifically accurate public position because its board members might be offended.

Grappling with governance issues like this is no easy task. Natural history museums need policies and practices in place to provide an *objective* frame of reference. Indeed, both ICOM and the American Alliance of Museums (AAM) have created governance practices and policies so that when these difficult issues arise, there is an ethical framework in place to guide decision-making (ICOM, 2013; AAM, 2017a). Even if these policies have not been adopted by a museum, these sources provide a useful resource for consideration. A natural history museum's mission and purpose may indeed need to be refined based on varying conditions discussed by other authors in this book. The winds of change come and go, but a solid legal foundation and ethical policies will help a museum weather the storm, be it political, economic, or social. Good governance allows a natural history museum to do what it does best—science.

References

AAM (2017a). *Ethics, Standards, and Best Practices.* Available at: http://aam-us.org/resources/ethics-standards-and-best-practices [Accessed 1 Mar. 2017].

AAM (2017b). American alliance of museums. *Financial Stability.* Available at: www.aam-us.org/resources/ethics-standards-and-best-practices/financial-stability [Accessed 1 Mar. 2017].

British Museum (2013). British Museum's Human Remains Policy. Available at: www.britishmuseum.org/about_us/management/human_remains.aspx [Accessed 30 Apr. 2017].

CBD (1992). Convention on Biological Diversity. Rio de Janeiro, 5 June 1992.

CBD (2017a). *About the Nagoya Protocol.* Available at: www.cbd.int/abs/about/default.shtml [Accessed 24 Feb. 2017].

CBD (2017b). *History of the Convention.* Available at: www.cbd.int/history/default.shtml [Accessed 24 Feb. 2017].

CBD (2017c). *List of Parties.* Available at: www.cbd.int/information/parties.shtml [Accessed 24 Feb. 2017].

CBD (2017d). *Parties to the Nagoya Protocol.* Available at: www.cbd.int/abs/nagoya-protocol/signatories/ [Accessed 24 Feb. 2017].

Cheng, C. W., and Lin, L. (2015). ICOM-NATHIST declaration stresses need for biodiversity conservation. *Focus Taiwan News Channel,* 21 Oct. Available at: http://m.focustaiwan.tw/news/aedu/201510210042.aspx [Accessed 24 Feb. 2017].

CITES (1973). *Convention on International Trade in Endangered Species of Wild Fauna and Flora.* Washington, DC: United Nations, 3 Mar. 1973.

Cohen, P. (2013). Museums grapple with the strings attached to gifts. *New York Times,* 4 Feb. Available at: www.nytimes.com/2013/02/05/arts/design/museums-grapple-with-onerous-restrictions-on-donations.html [Accessed 1 Mar. 2017].

Cornu, M., and Renold, M.-A. (2010). Available at: www.art-law.org/centre/recherches/fns/jdiCornu-Renold-en.pdf [Accessed 25 Apr. 2017].

Curtis, G. W. (2010). Repatriation from Scottish museums: Learning from NAGPRA. *Museum Anthropology* 33(2)

Dasgupta, S. (2016). Hong Kong to ban ivory trade by 2021. *Mongabay,* 22 Dec. Available at: https://news.mongabay.com/2016/12/hong-kong-to-ban-ivory-trade-by-2021/ [Accessed 24 Feb. 2017].

Deutscher Museumsbund (2013). Available at: www.museumsbund.de/wp-content/uploads/2017/04/2013-recommendations-for-the-care-of-human-remains.pdf [Accessed 24 Apr. 2017].

Gabriel, G. G. (2014). With a New Year in China comes a new campaign. *IFAW.org,* 30 Jan. Available at: www.ifaw.org/united-states/news/new-year-china-comes-new-campaign [Accessed 24 Feb. 2017].

Gerstenblith, P. (2016). The destruction of cultural heritage: A crime against property or a crime against people? *John Marshall Review of Intellectual Property Law* 15(3), pp. 336–393.

ICC (2016a). *Case Information Sheet: Situation in the Republic of Mali; The Prosecutor v. Ahmad Al Faqi Al Mahdi ICC-01/12–01/15.* Available at: www.icc-cpi.int/mali/al-mahdi/documents/almahdieng.pdf [Accessed 24 Feb. 2017].

ICC (2016b). *In the Case of the Prosecutor v. Ahmad Al Faqi Al Mahdi ICC-01/12–01/15.* Available at: www.icc-cpi.int/CourtRecords/CR2016_07244.PDF [Accessed 24 Feb. 2017].

ICOM (2010). *ICOM and the International Committee of the Blue Shield.* Available at: http://archives.icom.museum/emergency.html#organisations [Accessed 24 Feb. 2017].

ICOM (2017a). *ICOM in Brief.* Available at: http://icom.museum/the-organisation/icom-in-brief/ [Accessed 24 Feb. 2017].

ICOM (2017b). *NATHIST—Natural History.* Available at: http://icom.museum/the-committees/international-committees/international-committee/international-committee-for-museums-and-collections-of-natural-history/ [Accessed 24 Feb. 2017].

ICOM NATHIST (2015). *Taipei Declaration on Natural History Museums and Bi-odiversity Conservation.* Available at: https://icomnathist.wordpress.com/taipei-declaration-on-nhms-and-biodiversity-conservation/ [Accessed 24 Feb. 2017].

IFAW (2017). *Ivory Market in China: China Ivory Trade Survey Report.* Available at: www.ifaw.org/united-states/node/6352 [Accessed 24 Feb. 2017].

IRS (2006). *Election-Year Activities and the Prohibition on Political Campaign Intervention for Section 501(c)(3) Organizations.* Available at: www.irs.gov/uac/election-year-activities-and-the-prohibition-on-political-campaign-intervention-for-section-501-c-3-organizations [Accessed 1 Mar. 2017].

IRS (2016a). *Charitable Contribution Deductions.* Available at: www.irs.gov/charities-non-profits/charitable-organizations/charitable-contribution-deductions [Accessed 1 Mar. 2017].

IRS (2016b). *The Restriction of Political Campaign Intervention by Section 501(c)(3) Tax-Exempt Organizations.* Available at: www.irs.gov/charities-non-profits/charitable-organizations/the-restriction-of-political-campaign-intervention-by-section-501-c-3-tax-exempt-organizations [Accessed 1 Mar. 2017].

Liljas, P. (2013) China: The ivory trade is out of control, and China needs to do more to stop it. *Time,* 1 Nov. Available at: http://world.time.com/2013/11/01/the-ivory-trade-is-out-of-control-and-china-needs-to-do-more-to-stop-it/ [Accessed 24 Feb. 2017].

McRae, M. (2016). China just announced it will ban all ivory trade by the end of 2017. *Science Alert,* 31 Dec. Available at: www.sciencealert.com/china-just-announced-it-will-ban-all-ivory-trade-by-the-end-of-2017 [Accessed 24 Feb. 2017].

Missouri Revised Statutes (2016). Chapter 184: Museums—Metropolitan park districts and memorials section 184.845.1. Available at: www.moga.mo.gov/mostatutes/stathtml/18400008451.HTML [Accessed 1 Mar. 2017].

Museum of New Zealand Te Papa Tongarewa Act (1992). 1992 N.Z. Stat. No. 19); 1992 N.Z. Stat. No. 19, as amended. Available at: www.legislation.govt.nz/act/public/1992/0019/latest/whole.html?search=ts_act_museum_resel&p=1#dlm 260204 [Accessed 27 Feb. 2017].

Nagoya Protocol (2010). *Nagoya Protocol on Access to Genetic Resources and the Fair and Equitable Sharing of Benefits Arising from Their Utilization to the Convention on Biological Diversity.* Nagoya, 29 Oct. 2010.

NAGPRA (1990). 25 U.S.C. 3001 et seq., 16 Nov. 1990.

National Council of Nonprofits (2017a). *Good Governance Policies for Nonprofits.* Available at: www.councilofnonprofits.org/tools-resources/good-governance-policies-nonprofits [Accessed 1 Mar. 2017].

National Council of Nonprofits (2017b). *Taking the 501(h) Election.* Available at: www.councilofnonprofits.org/taking-the-501h-election [Accessed 1 Mar. 2017].

NCAI (2012). Available at: www.ncai.org/resources/ncai-publications/ncai-annual-reports/2012_ncaiannualreport_final.pdf [Accessed 25 Apr. 2017].

Neme, L. (2016). Wildlife watch: Elephants win as Hong Kong's leader says it will ban ivory trade. *National Geographic,* 14 Jan. Available at: http://news.nationalgeographic.com/2016/01/160114-Hong-Kong-ivory-ban/ [Accessed 24 Feb. 2017].

NMS (2016). Available at: www.nms.ac.uk/media/1151584/nms-2016-human-remains-in-collections-policy.pdf [Accessed 25 Apr. 2017].

Protected Objects Act (1975). N.Z. Stat. No. 4; 1975 N.Z. Stat. No. 4, as amended. Available at: www.legislation.govt.nz/act/public/1975/0041/latest/DLM432116. html?search=ts_act_protected+objects_resel&p=1&sr=1 [Accessed 27 Feb. 2017].

Sciolino, E. (2012). Artsbeat: Mummified Maori heads returned to New Zealand. *New York Times*, 24 Jan. Available at: https://query.nytimes.com/gst/fullpage. html?res=9401E3DD1039F937A15752C0A9649D8B63&rref=collection% 2Fbyline%2Felaine-sciolino&action=click&contentCollection=undefined& region=stream&module=stream_unit&version=latest&contentPlacement= 138&pgtype=collection [Accessed 24 Apr. 2017].

Trope, J. (2013) *Native American Graves Protection and Repatriation Act.* Association on American Indian Affairs. Available at: http://saige.org/words/wp-content/ uploads/2013/06/NATIVE-AMERICAN-GRAVES-PROTECTION-AND-REPATRIATION-ACT-saige-2013.pdf [Accessed 27 Feb. 2017].

US DOI (2017). *National NAGPRA.* Available at: www.nps.gov/nagpra/. [Accessed 27 Feb. 2017].

UN (1945). Charter of the United Nations, 1 UNTS XVI. San Francisco, 24 Oct. 1945. Available at: www.refworld.org/docid/3ae6b3930.html [Accessed 27 Feb. 2017].

UN (1948). The Universal Declaration of Human Rights. Paris, 10 Dec. 1948.

UN (2007). United Nations Declaration on the Rights of Indigenous Peoples. 13 Sept. 2007.

UNESCO (1954). Convention for the Protection of Cultural Property in the Event of Armed Conflict with Regulations for the Execution of the Convention. The Hague, 14 May 1954.

UNESCO (1970). Convention on the Means of Prohibiting and Preventing the Illicit Import, Export, and Transfer of Ownership of Cultural Property. Paris, 14 Nov. 1970.

UNESCO (1972), Convention Concerning the Protection of the World Cultural and Natural Heritage. Paris, 16 Nov. 1972.

UNESCO (2016a). *Illicit Trafficking of Cultural Property.* Available at: www. unesco.org/new/en/culture/themes/illicit-trafficking-of-cultural-property/ 1970-convention/states-parties/ [Accessed 24 Feb. 2017].

UNESCO (2016b). *Recommendation on the Protection and Promotion of Museums and Collections.* 17 Nov. 2015.

UNESCO (2016c). Shenzhen Declaration on Museums and Collections. Shenzhen, 12 Nov. 2016. Available at: www.unesco.org/fileadmin/MULTIMEDIA/HQ/ BPI/EPA/images/media_services/Director-General/Shenzhen-DeclarationENG. pdf [Accessed 24 Feb. 2017].

UNESCO (2016d). *World Heritage List: Timbuktu.* Available at: http://whc.unesco. org/en/list/119 [Accessed 24 Feb. 2017].

UNIDROIT (1995). Convention on Stolen or Illegally Exported Cultural Objects. Rome, 24 June 1995.

UNIDROIT (2016). *UNIDROIT Convention on Stolen or Illegally Exported Cultural Objects (Rome, 1995)—Status.* Available at: www.unidroit.org/status-cp [Accessed: 24 Feb. 2017].

12 Natural history museums as enterprises of the future

Eric Dorfman

My dear, here we must run as fast as we can, just to stay in place. And if you wish to go anywhere you must run twice as fast as that.
—Lewis Carroll, *Through the Looking Glass* (1871)

Introduction

The last few years have been difficult ones for cultural institutions. In the United States, between 2000 and 2015, more than fifty museums shut their doors (Dickman, 2016), while in the United Kingdom in 2015, one in five regional museums closed either a part or a branch of their operations (Museums Association, 2015). In the same year, the African Association of Museums (AFRICOM) underwent a significant downscaling, an indication of how little sector support exists there. In 2016, the trend continued. The Walter P. Chrysler Museum in Auburn Hills, Michigan, closed permanently, as did the Morbid Anatomy Museum in New York City, along with three French museums: the Pinacothek of Paris, the Paris Museum of Eroticism, and the Normandy Tank Museum in Catz, to name but a few.

While regional differences are important—China, for instance, opens about two hundred new museums each year, for a total of almost five thousand museums nationally (China Daily, 2016)—the global context over the last decade has been one of the successively diminishing resources. Natural history museums bear additional costs, maintaining often vast collections, frequently garnered through expensive, research-based fieldwork. This, coupled with growing pressure to help address increasingly pressing environmental problems, means that in the coming decades, natural history museums will find it necessary to balance higher priorities and greater risks with ever more complex "real-world" questions and precarious political circumstances. Those that will thrive in this atmosphere are either so large and well-funded as to be relatively invulnerable or extraordinarily good at doing business, or both.

At the same time, opportunities abound for those museums ready to embrace them. In the next two decades, new technology will continue to generate breakthroughs in medicine, manufacturing, transportation, and many other fields, which means there will be a sizable demand for workers schooled in biology, chemistry, math, and engineering. For institutions such as natural history museums, which deliver effective education programming in science, technology, engineering, and mathematics (STEM), as well as arts (STEAM), this trend has considerable promise. Using advances in 3-D scanning and printing, drone technology and robotics can be of direct benefit to the scientific questions we pose. Dealing with global climate change may require new technology not yet even on the drawing board. Environmental and conservation science will also rise in importance, as the planet's biodiversity and fragile ecosystems are steadily degraded. Opportunities for museums to leverage in-house knowledge exist in the form of environmental consultants and professional trainers. Attendance at the world's top twelve natural history museums in 2015 was just shy of thirty-five million visits (Cheu, Chang, and Papamichael, 2015), giving impetus to fresh thinking surrounding the monetizing of collections, for example, through sales of imagery, merchandising, and knowledge-based products and services.

This chapter is devoted to grappling with these challenges and opportunities in the years ahead. Much of the literature available on the topic comes from the late 1990s and early 2000s. The fact that it rings true in 2017 is testament both to the universality of these ideas and the fact that so few natural history museums (with important exceptions) have embraced best practice.

Crutchfield and Grant (2002) describe best practice for non-profits wanting to make a high impact as forces for good. In their view, true success has more to do with how non-profits work outside the boundaries of their organizations than with the management of their internal operations. The organizations they studied were equally concerned with external relationships as they were with developing internal systems. While arguably one cannot have the former without the latter, the writers came up with six general practices that resonate especially well with natural history museums contemplating their impact:

1   *Serve and Advocate*: High-impact non-profit organizations develop expertise in policy advocacy to influence legislation, bridging the gap between delivery and advocacy.
2   *Make Markets Work*: Moving past traditional notions of charity, successful non-profits find ways to work with markets and help companies "do good while doing well." Some non-profits run their own small businesses, generating income that helps fund their programs.
3   *Inspire Evangelists*: Successful non-profits value volunteers, donors, and advisers not only for their time, money, and guidance, but also as passionate ambassadors.
4   *Nurture Non-profit Networks*: High-impact organizations help their peers succeed, building networks of non-profit allies and devoting remarkable time and energy to advancing their fields.

5   *Master the Art of Adaptation*: Exceptionally adaptive, high-impact non-profits use external cues to modify their tactics to increase success amid changing conditions. In a "cycle of adaptation," these organizations listen to external feedback and seek opportunities for improvement.

6   *Share Leadership*: The leaders of the organizations alluded to by Crutchfield and Grant all exhibit charisma, but without oversized egos, realizing they must share power to be stronger forces for good.

Responding to change

It is an almost universal truism that natural history museums are slow to change. It many circumstances, this is a good thing, keeping as they do a collective three billion specimens in the public trust (Wheeler et al., 2012). However, notwithstanding what the future will hold, we know it will, inexorably, arrive and bring with it change. The concept of adaptability is particularly relevant for natural history museums, awaiting the multitude of circumstances that will collectively make up the future that will be imposed on our institutions. How uncertain is it, and what should we do to prepare? Predictability of a future for any business has been graded from "sufficiently clear to allow predictive confidence" to "true ambiguity" (Courtney, Kirkland, and Viguerie, 1997). Where on this continuum our future lies should influence our strategies for planning change and responses to unplanned events.

While planned change, such as implementing a new strategic plan, restructuring an organization to facilitate collaboration across program areas, or launching a new reporting method, is not without challenges, many well-established systematic approaches have been created to assist with this type of change (Suchy, 2004). At the other end of the spectrum outlined by Courtney, Kirkland, and Viguerie (1997) are situations in which practitioners are confronted with unplanned or unanticipated change. While planned change is typically expected to initiate some type of improvement, unplanned change can be chaotic and lead to unknown results. It is characteristically something that happens to people, whether they want it or not; whereas planned change is often a way to avoid unplanned change, there are times when it arrives anyway. In these cases, some general strategies assist in navigating precarious situations.

For instance, basing decisions on statistical models that don't rely on a high degree of accuracy can be more useful when trying to predict the future than more detailed and complex techniques, which are better saved for analyzing past data. Preparing for multiple outcomes can provide hypothetical data for these simple models, especially if it is possible to identify at least some of the high-influence parameters accurately.

Remaining aware and response-ready facilitates the ability to take appropriate action as soon as events occur. Part of this strategy is empowering personnel to act quickly and decisively, for instance, with a social media policy that is strong on principle but general enough to be flexible. Regularly refreshed media training is a good way to keep best practice at the forefront. Whatever the exigencies of the situation, institutions that cultivate their reputation and focus on doing the right thing maximize a broad base of trust that helps maintain loyalty in their community.

Trends

Understanding trends in risks and opportunities is key to preparing for the future. Here, I present a list of the trends that I have observed as having the potential to affect the future of how business is conducted in natural history museums. These will, no doubt, be different from the lists amassed by others looking at the future of the sector. Mine is the result of close observation while working in the field, searching the literature, as well as communicating with colleagues.

Development

In the United States, where philanthropy is a critical component of museums' annual budgets, fundraising budgets at natural history museums will continue to be chronically underfunded (in keeping with non-profits in general). While this might cause dismay to those engaged professionally in development, institutional leaders must balance ongoing operational needs with long-term growth. This means that for museum fundraising to succeed, better and more efficient strategies will be developed to use what resources are put to development. As the old school of philanthropists fades into distant memory, to be replaced by billionaires who want to decide the detail of where their money goes, and the young, newly wealthy who expect more consideration for less outlay, museums that understand and can work within this environment will thrive, and those that do not will suffer.

Best practice thinking in this area can be summarized as "customer focus," "donor loyalty," "donor retention," "donor centricity," or any of the other myriad phrasings that encapsulate the notion of doing right by the people who provide the funds to keep a business afloat. Much like the Golden Rule, a basic tenet of working with donors is (or should be) grounded in authentic behavior: thinking about them as people with needs and motivations, rather than stopping short at their giving capacity. This is why three of Emily Post's grandchildren begin their book *The Etiquette Advantage in Business* (Post et al., 2014) with a chapter on "Etiquette and Ethics." For the Posts, both etiquette and ethics are grounded in genuineness:

> Your actions need to be grounded in sincerity because when they are, people develop confidence in you, and confidence begets trust, and relationships are built on trust. Try to fool someone, be someone you are not, use flattery to get what you want, and that person will soon see

through you and consequently have little if any trust in your motives—
at which point regaining that person's trust will be very difficult.

(Post et al., 2014, p. 6)

Joyaux (2011) also ascribes to this philosophy, writing, "Effective organizations understand that fund development goals and strategies focus on things
other than money," a concept articulated by Burk in *Donor-Centered Fundraising* (2003):

> Being conscious of how donors feel when they give makes it easy to
> respond in kind. A gift given eagerly in the anticipation of achieving
> something worthwhile should be matched by an equally enthusiastic
> response from the solicitor or the charity. However, in the rush to deal
> quickly and fairly with large numbers of donors, organizations produce
> generalized communications, the tenor and content of which leave
> donors cold. A not for profit's first post-gift contact with a donor can
> either be reassuring or it can be the beginning of a nagging doubt in the
> donor's mind about whether he has done the right thing.
>
> (Burk, 2003, p. 15)

How fundraising will play out in the future will also be different. New technology gives us new dialects and new audiences for fundraising. Crowdfunding is currently the new frontier and, arguably, produces more failures than
successes (despite some spectacular triumphs such as the more than US $1.7
million raised in 2012 by Matthew Inman through Indiegogo to build a Tesla
museum), as museums grapple with what projects to promote, what to offer,
and how to communicate effectively in this forum. This is a skill we must develop. New financing alternatives, such as microfinance, crowdfunding, and
peer-to-peer lending are expanding rapidly (see Bruton et al., 2014), and present either an opportunity or a risk if we are the only ones not embracing them.

These changing times mean less access to unrestricted fundraising and
greater accountability. Many donors worry about integrity, waste, and how an
organization is planning to use their money, and wonder how museums measure up against organizations that, for instance, are curing blindness or saving
children's lives in the developing world (for example, Singer, 2009). "Impact
investing," "venture philanthropy," and "social enterprise" are all descriptors
of our future. We are moving into a period where specific projects are being
valued above general funding and donors have high expectations regarding our
demonstrating the impact of these projects, as well as how accessible we are
(both technologically and personally) and how authentically they are treated.

Accountability, impact, and relevance

If those who have donated money to us want proof that we are using their
gift to its greatest benefit, how are the impact and reach of our initiatives

measured and verified? Have we yet developed indicators to characterize it appropriately, in a way that allows philanthropists to compare our activities with those of another type of organization that might compete with us for funding?

And yet, as Joyaux (2011) writes, relationships with donors are about more than money, philanthropy, or fundraising. At the same time, our relationships are broader than just with donors. In the future, natural history museums will think more about partnering with our stakeholders and apply a more holistic approach to who those stakeholders are: museum visitors, academic colleagues, indigenous peoples, even customers at our retail outlets can all interact with as partners. These relationships take us a long way toward attaining the utopian state of relevance (see Weil, 2002).

One important and useful step is to involve stakeholders in citizen science. The proliferation of research employing members of the public to assist in gathering ecological data (Dickinson, Zuckerberg, and Bonter, 2010), combined with its evident potential for success (Cooper, Shirk, and Zuckerberg, 2014), points to its persistence and growth going forward. The value of these projects lies at least as strongly in their public engagement potential as the data that are collected, and communicating this benefit will figure more consistently in the vocabulary of natural history museums when describing the impact.

Engagement is critical for us. While most people who work in and around natural history museums would agree that their achievements are important and address pressing social and environmental issues, whether the general public concurs depends on how much they understand regarding the activities museums undertake, and the implications of those activities. Certainly, effective marketing can help raise awareness, but for some time there has been a growing expectation of deeper engagement and participants' ability to help curate their own educational trajectory (Falk and Dierking, 2000). There is, now, a sense of prerogative that visitors are gaining—being entitled, through the cost of admission or simply the time devoted to being at a museum, that they should have a say in what happens there.

This prerogative plays out especially visibly on social media, on which users scrutinize everything from the font size of labels to the greeting they receive at the front desk. Visitors enjoy exhibitions in which they can make choices, filter their experiences, and effect change. Combining this experience with citizen science becomes a powerful recipe for engaging the public emotionally and intellectually while demonstrating genuine impact. Over the next decades, natural history museums that do this, and can measure it, will thrive.

Authentic partnering between museums and indigenous people has often been more elusive, particularly since a preponderance of artifacts held in anthropology collections were not acquired, or interpreted, with permission (Simons, 2000). A notable exception may be found in New Zealand, which, because of the 1840 Treaty of Waitangi, is one of the most progressive countries with respect to indigenous partnerships. Indeed, bicultural museums there may be seen as a model for natural history institutions in many other regions:

> Māori and non-Māori alike, agree with the general direction of museums towards partnership with *iwi* [tribes] but are also positive about current developments and signs of greater Māori autonomy and independence. The years 1980 to 2010 have seen a museum-centered concern with responding to Māori switch to a Māori-centric use of museums for their own ends. One of the main findings of this research has been the shift from museum-based programmes to community outreach, and from servicing Māori to developing relationships with *iwi* so they can manage their own cultural resources.
>
> (McCarthy, 2011, p. 246)

Despite some progress in this direction, these relationships—even in New Zealand—are not thoroughly resolved. Within the sector, there is not even agreement as to whether, and in what circumstances, to display human remains—a subject of great importance in many traditional cultures (Alberti, Blenkowski, and Chapman, 2009). A developing spirit of partnership will help provide answers to some of these questions and allow us to ground our impact in social justice.

We must not, as Reach Advisors (2014) said, cede "ownership of the public perception of museums by not being able to demonstrate, clearly and accurately, their impact." The successful future of natural history museums will lie, in part, in engaging in purposefully impactful activities and finding appropriate measures to demonstrate that impact, our reach and, by extension, our relevance. While indicators still need to be developed and will differ from place to place, some topics present themselves as strong possibilities:

- Demonstrate that the organization is well-run (that its activities align with its mission)
- Conserve biodiversity in situ
- Engage underserved groups in ways (like training) that benefits them in a lasting way
- Use museum collections to tackle real-world problems like wildlife trafficking
- Create opportunities to involve the public in the activities of the museum, for example, through digitization and citizen science
- Mount exhibitions that explore the research being done at a museum, not merely in a corner of the institution that appears to give lip service
- Turn annual reports into "impact reports" that describe tangible benefits

Disruptive innovation

A disruptive innovation is one that creates a new market and value network and eventually disrupts an existing market and value network, displacing established, leading market firms, products, and alliances (Christensen, 1997). Every new technology disrupts the one that came before, and "however carefully you plan for the future, someone else's actions will inevitably modify the way your plans turn out" (Burke, 1978). A commonly cited example is how Hewlett-Packard overtook Kodak with its home printers, allowing users greater independence in a famous battle for relevance that in the mid-1990s cost each company $50 million in research and development (Courtney, Kirkland, and Viguerie, 1997).

What are the likely disruptive innovations for natural history museums? One important possibility is the "average" person who uses social media to become a curator. A compelling example of this is Chris Wild, curator of the website www.retronaut.com. A former museum curator, Wild is a blogger and creator of Retronaut, a virtual "time machine" that allows visitors to the site to access millions of pieces of historical content, including videos, pictures, music, and text from public and private archives. In it, visitors can pick their own entry point (be it people, places, or objects) and are free to view and assemble images as they wish. It is essentially an ever-expanding virtual exhibition that, if you sign up for it, will send images to your inbox on a weekly basis. At the time of writing, thirty-five thousand people have done exactly that. By using the Internet, Wild is bypassing the need for his curatorial expertise to be mediated by a museum and providing an experience, for free, once thought to be the sole purview of collecting institutions. The books they publish (for example, Wild, 2014) are also curating historical archives, even those of National Geographic, independent from the context of a museum.

The maker movement is another form of disruptive innovation that puts into the hands of the public the ability to create, or even re-create, museum objects, using their own 3D printers and dedicated maker spaces (see Anderson, 2013). Technology outpaces intellectual property laws, ethics, and museum operations. Now that a home version of a 3-D printer is available, and it is easily possible using current technology to create a 3-D model from a 2D photograph, anyone with a modicum of skill and interest can enter a museum, take a picture, and, by the next day, end up with a 3D rendering—albeit likely a relatively poor one—of anything they wish.

How does all this impact museums' intellectual property rights? Moving information from physical to digital and back to physical has superseded the intentions of the drafters of most intellectual law. From the perspective of someone working in the reality-capture space, it is probably not worth the time or money required to deploy intellectual property laws to protect scan data. Instead, some progressive institutions are giving away their data freely. For instance, in 2013 the National Museum of Natural History of the Smithsonian released a 3-D modelling tool, complete with free scans of some of its most famous objects, such as the Wright brothers' plane, a whale fossil, a bee, Abraham Lincoln's life mask, a complete woolly mammoth skeleton, and the Cassiopeia A remnant, with plans to do many more.

Open source is the way of the future. The National Museum of Ethiopia in Addis Ababa has allowed the arm, shoulder, and knee bones of Lucy, the 3.18-million-year-old hominin *Australopithecus afarensis* to be 3-D scanned, and the data to be given away as open source in association with a paper in *Nature* (Kappelman et al., 2016), to help confirm her suspected cause of death. Images and content on their associated website, www.eSkeletons.org, are created by faculty, staff, and students at the University of Texas, and, while the product is freely available for download, it is still regulated. Photographs, images, and text are licensed by Creative Commons, and reproduction and re-creation are restricted to non-profit enterprises with appropriate attribution (Liberal Arts Instructional Technology Services, 2016). While this licensing specifically prohibits commercial production, those limitations are only as effective as the organization's ability to monitor production.

Home film editing, blogging, self-publishing, Wikipedia, even crafting in its way, all comprise disruptions to museums' traditional way of doing things, competing more nimbly and pervasively than museums for people's attention because of the low cost of entry and the vast numbers of individuals engaged in doing them. One thing museums do retain in this environment is the depth of knowledge that comes from professional experience and training. Natural history museums are improving their ability to leverage this knowledge and will continue to do so. It's difficult to find one that doesn't have a Facebook page, public programs, and outreach.

However, much like the quote from the Red Queen that begins this chapter, many of the improvements we as a sector have so far developed, serve to streamline the business in which we are already engaged, but only give us a reprieve: better outreach, more clever Facebook pictures. It is time for revolutionary thinking.

Monetizing collections

An opportunity that has been embraced only patchily across the natural history museum field is the leveraging of collections, and collection expertise, for commercial gain. Admittedly, larger natural history museums create traveling blockbuster exhibitions, some of which, like *Chocolate* (Field Museum) and *Whales/Tōhora* (Museum of New Zealand Te Papa Tongarewa), can tour for a decade without a break. These producing museums do compete in a commercial space with consultants who create exhibitions as a service. Principally, however, that commercial space belongs to museums, because, even if a consulting firm makes an excellent exhibition, the firm still needs, with rare exception, a museum in which to show it. That notwithstanding, typically only the largest and most capacitized museums can create touring products and only the most successful of these stand a chance of making money.

Returning briefly to the topic of scanning hominins, a company—Bone Clones—has taken a place in the market that could have been filled by a natural history museum. On the company's website, they describe their process of producing a hominin replica:

> The Bone Clones® Hominid line is composed of discoveries from anatomically modern humans, archaic humans, early Homo, early hominins, and other hominids. The majority of the casts in this line have been recreated by our team of anatomical sculptors in conjunction with our anthropology consultants, using published osteological data... We continue to produce new finds as they occur, leaving time for original papers to be published and enough scientific data to be obtained so we may produce our casts as precisely as possible... The hominins offered in this series are high quality recreations that are intended for exploration of anthropological and evolutionary concepts. These are not recommended for advanced research purposes.
>
> (Bone Clones, 2016)

This is an important service for anyone wishing to interpret human evolution. It is, however, only possible for Bone Clones to provide it if they leverage the work of physical anthropologists who have published their findings in the scientific literature before considering the commercial implications. This would not happen in cancer research.

Where, then, might additional leveraging occur? One obvious source is consultancy. There are many examples of this, for instance, the National Ecological Observatory Network (NEON), a vehicle to advance scientists' ability to examine and understand the interactions between life and the environment at the scale of an entire continent. In it, hundreds of scientists and engineers have contributed their expertise to plan, design, and operate a grand instrument that could harness the power of networked technology to gather and provide high-quality information on interactions between land, life, water, and climate across a continent and over the course of a human generation. The NEON project is constructed with National Science Foundation (NSF) Major Research Equipment and Facilities Construction (MREFC) funding and is currently in its construction phase, whereby eighty-one field sites will be developed, along with the information infrastructure needed to amass data and metadata from sensors and field sampling, ensure data quality, process the information into data products, and deliver those products to users via an online portal. NEON is scheduled to enter full operation in 2018. As part of this undertaking, institutions with expertise are being contracted to accession, store, and identify material, making it available for future research. The project's ground beetles, for instance, are housed at the Carnegie Museum of Natural History, the Denver Museum of Nature and Science, and the Essig Museum at the University of California, Berkeley.

Consulting can be more formalized than this, whereby institutions offer specific services in line with their expertise. For example, research scientists at the San Diego Natural History Museum offer a broad range of consulting services through their PaleoServices (resource assessment of property, full mitigation, professional fossil curation, and storage) and BioServices (providing specialized, comprehensive assessment surveys) departments. These services include rare plant and animal surveys, voucher specimen collection and documentation, habitat assessment, species inventories, and environmental impact surveys.

Similarly, the Australian Museum's Australian Centre for Wildlife Genomics, comprising accredited deoxyribonucleic acid (DNA) laboratories and a biological tissue collection, offers DNA-based molecular diagnostic services to a wide variety of external partners, with a primary focus on ecological applications such as species identification, individualization, conservation, and small population management. Their services include wildlife forensics, aviation airstrike and bird strike, provision of frozen tissue, and management of captive and wild populations.

Natural history museums can offer training and public speakers, they can rent space (and many do), and fabricate exhibition furniture. The key is formalizing the offer. If we do this across the field, it will create a situation in which clients will become accustomed to receiving an array of goods and services from our sector. While potentially leading to some interinstitutional competition, this situation would put all our organizations in a better place, collectively.

Products and services must not, however, necessarily be so literally connected to collections to provide an authentic and compelling relationship to a museum's mission. Merchandising offers an important, and often overlooked, potential for many museums. Families of products featuring a museum's iconic symbols, books (if strategically designed and priced), whiteware, and paper products are frequently overlooked as revenue streams, despite the potential not only for direct revenue but their utility in long-term marketing. For instance, the high-quality, scientifically accurate dinosaur models of the Carnegie Museum of Natural History have been sold for decades in many museum shops worldwide, which enhances the museum's reputation as an authority and provides a sustainable revenue stream. Once again, the largest natural history museums, which can afford large production runs, do this regularly. However, smaller institutions can still create their own greeting cards, T-shirts, and the like, providing a small but steady source of revenue that is generally preferred by customers over generic products that may be purchased at any toy store.

In the end, success for natural history museums, as with any type of provider organization, resides in our ability to understand how our activities benefit the lives and well-being of those willing to pay to engage with us. Most natural history museums are non-profits. Even though this designation is nothing more than a tax status, the implications with which it is usually associated have become part of our identity. However, there are other models. In parts of the United States, at least, there exists the structure of a "benefit corporation," a type of for-profit corporate entity that includes a positive impact on society, workers, the community, and the environment in addition to profit as its legally defined goals. While not possible here to evaluate the implications for a museum exploring this model, suffice it to say that it does present an alternative.

Rethinking museums

Are natural history museums ready to rethink radically their business models? I do not believe so. Yet, given the political and economic climate of the planet, coupled with the prevalence of fake news, government cutbacks, and the unprecedented spread of social change, pressure on us as businesses is set to increase. This might be in our future, whether we like it or not.

How can natural history museums continue to exist and advance their missions during these changing times? The hard truth is that only a major shift in the political discourse over what we owe the most vulnerable members of our society, along with a reversal of our nation's fiscal fortunes, can turn the tide—and both appear unlikely in the foreseeable future. The sobering reality is that natural history museums, and non-profits in general, will have to become even more entrepreneurial in their funding templates, efficient in deploying their resources, response-ready, and vigilant in serving their mission to make headway.

Do non-profits have any hope of agency—of exerting influence or power? Natural history museums that are poised for success in the future are pursuing strategies that enable them to seek and secure public funding while advancing their mission, sustaining their organization, and retaining some room to maneuver in the process.

Strategic clarity

In 2005, Stephen Weil wrote, "What makes a museum well run is that its efforts are channeled exclusively into the pursuit of its purpose and not scattered elsewhere." The first step in attaining this strategic clarity is to set priorities for where the impact should be. Establishing an organization's mission-critical priorities can be difficult, however. For natural history museums, which must balance collection stewardship and research with public engagement and education, making comparative judgments and setting priorities across different kinds of programs and beneficiaries may be challenging. It is accomplished by clarifying priorities, articulating the impact for which a museum wants to be held accountable, and articulating how they will go about it.

It is also necessary to understand the "true" cost of each program or set of services: both the *direct costs* (the program's frontline staff, rent for service, and delivery sites) and the *indirect costs* (the program's share of management, and information technology, along with other agency-wide expenditures). Even many well-managed organizations must work hard to understand the true costs of a program—especially how to allocate indirect costs, which are often difficult to attribute directly to a given program or service.

In making better decisions about whether or how to pursue a given opportunity, it is key for an institution to consider both the potential mission and the financial impact. Program contribution analysis helps non-profits with multiple programs to understand the contribution each program makes to both the mission and the financial health of the organization. A useful way to display the results is to plot all programs on a 2 × 2 matrix (Figure 12.1; after Mayne, 2008), with mission contribution on one axis and financial contribution on the other. Simultaneously considering both dimensions can be a powerful tool in making portfolio management decisions.

In the matrix, the horizontal axis shows programs' relative impact on the mission, while the vertical axis indicates programs' net fiscal contribution (return on investment). Programs in the upper right—with a strong mission and strong financial contributors—are clear winners, and could be good candidates for expansion. Those in the lower left, "potential distractions," are relatively weak, and might be candidates to retire, contract, or modify to improve their mission fit and/or financial performance. Programs in the lower right, "investments in the mission," require the financial subsidy from unrestricted funding but contribute strongly to the institution's core purpose. In practice, much of what natural history museums do in terms of collection stewardship falls into this category. Those in the upper left, "income opportunities," while not always mission-critical, are financial contributors that provide the institution with resources needed to fulfill its core obligations. Museum parking fees are a good example of this.

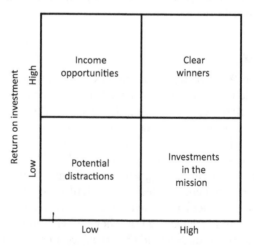

Figure 12.1 Program Contribution Analysis, after Mayne, 2008.

In an ideal world, all programs would lie in the upper-right quadrant—strongly aligned with the mission, covering their full costs, and generating revenue for infrastructure. Natural history museums do not, however, operate in an ideal world, and initiatives in this quadrant must often be supplemented with other activities. Thus, finding opportunities to increase the financial contribution of their mission investments as well as develop and optimize revenue from other sources is critical.

Systems

The program portfolio matrix is just one among a suite of structures that together enable museums to act with purpose in realizing their mission (see Weil, 2002). Any chance of achieving this mammoth task requires robust systems that allow the institution to run smoothly while focusing on the creation of the innovations that take it to the next level. The most efficient business in the world, however, will fail if it is headed in the wrong direction.

> For an organization to attract and maintain its support, it must not merely do things right (maintain good procedures) but also do the right things (achieve its intended results, make its intended impact). More than ever before, performance counts.
>
> (Weil, 2005, p. 40)

Although these words were written over twelve years ago, they resonate as much for the next decades as they did for the last one.

References

Alberti, S. J. M. M., Blenkowski, P., Chapman, M. J. (2009). Should we display the dead? *Museums and Society* 7(3), pp. 133–149.

Bone Clones (2016). Available at https://boneclones.com/category/all-fossil-hominids/fossil-hominids#view=grid&category=94&page=1&pageSize=30 [Accessed 7 Jan. 2017].

Bruton, G., Khavul, S., Siegel, D., and Wright, M. (2014). New financial alternatives in seeding entrepreneurship: Microfinance, crowdfunding, and peer-to-peer innovations. *Entrepreneurship Theory and Practice* 39(1), pp. 9–26.

Burk, P. (2003). *Donor Centered Fundraising*. Chicago: Cygnus Applied Research.

Burke, J. (1978). *Connections*. New York: Little, Brown.

Carroll, L. (1971). *Through the Looking-Glass, and What Alice Found There*. New York: Macmillan.

China Daily (2016). China to build more museums. *China Daily*. Available at: www.chinadaily.com.cn/china/2016-11/11/content_27341793.htm [Accessed 2 Jan. 2017].

Christensen, C. M. (1997). *The Innovator's Dilemma: When New Technologies Cause Great Firms to Fail*. Boston, MA: Harvard Business School Press.

Cooper, C. B., Shirk, J., Zuckerberg, B. (2014). The invisible prevalence of citizen science in global research: Migratory birds and climate change. *Plos One* 9(9), pp. 1–5. Available at: http://dx.doi.org/10.1371/journal.pone.0106508 [Accessed 4 Jan. 2017].

Courtney, H., Kirkland, J., and Viguerie, P. (1997). Strategy under uncertainty. *Harvard Business Review* (Jan./Feb.), pp. 2–15.

Crutchfield, L. R., and Grant, H. M. (2002). *Forces for Good: The Six Practices of High-Impact Nonprofits*. San Francisco, CA: Jossey-Bass.

Dickinson, J. L., Zuckerberg, B., and Bonter, D. N. (2010). Citizen science as an ecological research tool: Challenges and benefits. *Annual Review of Ecology, Evolution, and Systematics* 41, pp. 149–172.

Dickman, R. E. (2016). What we can learn from closed museums. *ILR* (Mar./Apr.), pp. 14–19.

Falk, J. H., and Dierking, L. (2000). *Learning from Museums*. Walnut Creek, CA: AltaMira Press.

Joyaux, S. P. (2011). *Strategic Fund Development: Building Profitable Relationships That Last*. 3rd ed. Hoboken, NJ: John Wiley & Sons.

Kappelman, J. R., et al. (2016). Perimortem fractures in Lucy suggest mortality from fall out of tall tree. *Nature* 537, pp. 503–507.

Liberal Arts Instructional Technology Services (2016). Available at http://eskeletons.org/ [Accessed 6 Jan. 2017].

Mayne, J. (2008). Contribution analysis: An approach to exploring cause and effect. *ILAC Brief* 16, p. 4.

McCarthy, C. (2011). *Museums and Māori*. Wellington: Te Papa Press.

Museums Association (2015). *Cuts Survey, 2015*. London: Museums Association.

Post, P., Post, A., Post, L., and Post Senning, D. (2014). *The Etiquette Advantage in Business*. New York: HarperCollins.

Reach Advisors (2014). *Impact-Based Philanthropy*. Monthly Memo 1:1. Boston: Reach Advisors/Museum R+D.

Simons, M. S. (2000). Aboriginal heritage art and moral rights. *Annals of Tourism Research* 27(2), pp. 412–431.

Singer, P. (2009). *The Life You Can Save*. New York: Random House.

Suchy, S. (2004). *Leading with Passion: Change Management in the Twenty-First Century Museum*. Plymouth: AltaMira Press.

Weil, S. E. (2002). *Making Museums Matter*. Washington DC: Smithsonian Books.

Weil, S. E. (2005). A success/failure matrix for museums. *Museum News* (Jan./Feb.), pp. 36–40.

Wheeler, Q. D., et al. (2012). Mapping the biosphere: Exploring species to understand the origin, organization, and sustainability of biodiversity. *Systematic Biodiversity* 10, pp. 1–20.

Wild, C. (2014). *Retronaut*. Washington, DC: National Geographic.

Part 4
Commentary and synthesis

13 The future of natural history museums

Commentary

Conal McCarthy

It is my pleasure to write a commentary on this fascinating new book. This comprehensive, far-reaching, and thought-provoking volume is full of insights and useful ideas on the future of natural history museums (NHMs), expressed with passion and candor by experienced professionals. Before discussing the contents of the book, and then responding to them, I need to spell out where I am coming from so that readers will understand my perspective on the topic.

I am an academic in a museum and heritage studies program at a New Zealand university, having spent several years working in museums and art galleries in a variety of roles, including collections, exhibition, education, public programming, and interpretation. Although, my background is in the humanities and social sciences, in the 1990s I worked at New Zealand's national museum, Museum of New Zealand Te Papa Tongarewa, dealing with a range of subject matter including science and the natural environment. My comments on this book take the form of an afterword that summarizes, reviews, and critically analyzes its key arguments. In the process, I am addressing research and teaching within the field of museum studies, and the often-neglected place of NHMs within it and the museum sector, where professional practice is often overlooked in the academic literature (McCarthy, 2015a), as well as ways in which to bring these two domains more closely together. This book is a good step in that direction. If the future of NHMs sketched out in this collection is to be realized, our ways of thinking about them must also find new methods, theories, and approaches, and it is hoped that the ideas offered here may help in this quest.

First, what does this book say, and how does it contribute to the literature on the subject? I want to congratulate the editor and all the authors for producing a much needed analysis of where NHMs have come from, where they are right now, and, importantly, where they might go in the future. In the concise introduction, Dorfman gives an overview of the aims of the book and an outline of its contents, mentioning various aspects of what he regards as "best practice": active stewardship of the natural world, including wildlife conservation and biodiversity, ethics, and museums' relationship with indigenous peoples. He immediately states outright that his vision is not the stereotypical "dead zoo" of the popular imagination (think Hollywood movie *Night at the Museum*), but:

> a new breed of institution ... responsible and responsive to its community, employing newly developed methods to unravel the mysteries of the world and weave them into engaging stories for an eager and engaged public.

What an appealing picture of the twenty-first century natural history museum (NHM), captured in a single sentence! He points out, in a striking phrase, that the future of NHMs, is, in a sense, the "future of the planet" we all inhabit. That is a serious and onerous task and responsibility, but Dorfman faces it squarely and reminds readers that those working in NHMs have to respond to this challenge or risk irrelevance. "If we do not decide our fate, it will be decided for us," he declares. "That is what this book is about."

In Chapter 1, on the future of natural history collections, Chris Norris from the Yale Peabody Museum provides a thorough analysis of the past, present, and future of natural history collections, including topical issues such as access and digitization. He makes a strong case for the continued value of these collections in a present troubled by species extinction, climate change, and other major threats to the planet's survival and its life, while also being realistic about having to make a case for collections, quoting the old adage: "Collections that are not used are useless collections." He also notes the increasing scrutiny of traditional museum collecting practices that appear paradoxical to non-scientists, such as killing animals in order to collect them, and the fact that museums have to consider these public concerns more carefully in the future (especially, I might add, if they are to depend on public support and be measured by their service to them).

Some similar issues are picked up by the authors in Chapter 5, which looks at wildlife conservation at the American Museum of Natural History in New York. The authors point out that NHMs have a crucial broader role: "to promote the informed engagement and stewardship of our biological and cultural heritage through research, collaboration, institutional programming, and on-the-ground collaborations." Other chapters discuss a range of diverse issues facing NHMs today: ethical, security, and legal/policy issues; visitors, education, and learning; exhibitions; and the relationship with science centers and zoos. In the general discussion that follows this commentary, Eric Dorfman, Isabel Landim, and Osamu Kamei discuss the key themes that permeate the book, the critical points that the NHM of the present needs to face if it is to have a future: social and political change and particularly the age of "post-truth" politics, new technology, ethics, new business models, and partnerships with the public.

In my comments, I am going to focus on two or three chapters that respond directly to the challenges to NHMs posed in the book, as deftly summarized by Krishtalka and Humphrey (2000, p. 4) and cited in Chapter 8 of this volume. Krishtalka and Humphrey argue that there are four main challenges facing NHMs: deploying information to face the looming biodiversity crises, using collections and science education to tackle complex topics, actively engaging visitors in conservation action, and fostering an evolving management culture. Chapters 1 and 5, mentioned above, respond to the first three challenges very well, offering many pertinent examples from around the world.

Of these challenges, the last, and one often overlooked in studies of museums generally is covered effectively by Eric Dorfman in the final chapter, which points to the importance of being aware and response-ready, as that facilitates the ability to take appropriate action as soon as events occur. In Dorfman's view, few NHMs have embraced best practice—they are slow to change. He then goes on to survey the emerging trends apparent in other fields from which NHMs need to learn: the effective development of funds, through monetizing and consultancy, among other things; greater accountability; the clear demonstration of public value; and what he calls "disruptive innovation," as manifested in new concepts of the digital age like open-source information and the maker movement. I found this discussion refreshing and compelling, and thought the examples showed great promise. Overall, I enjoyed the tone of this chapter, which urged us to rethink museums (in rethinking business models), as called for by Krishtalka and Humphrey. I agree with Dorfman that strategic clarity, and a systematic approach to a commercially positive organizational culture, which he calls for here, are critical if NHMs are going to survive into the future. My only concern with this, a concern recently identified by Robert Janes, is that we need to be cautious about conventional capitalist business models that encourage growth that the planet cannot sustain (Janes, 2016a). As Janes has forcefully argued, museums need to be bold and responsible, to come out of their innate lethargy and become activists when it comes to issues like climate change—we don't need one-year business plans, he says, we need one-thousand-year business plans!

Another author who responds with imagination and verve to the challenges facing NHMs in the future is Garthe in Chapter 8. Like Dorfman (and Janes, whom Garthe cites), he thinks museums are naturally conservative and need to embrace change. Garthe refers to the California Academy of Sciences, which has conservation as its core mission, and says that more NHMs should do this. He also points out that the workforce of NHMs is too exclusive and narrow, and that greater diversity of the professional sector will create more inclusive outcomes. Furthermore, he argues that an all-of-systems approach, which is holistic and integrated in terms of how the museum works internally and relates to the world externally, works against the decoupling of nature and culture, which is one of the fundamental philosophical problems of the modern Western world (see Latour, 2005, and comments below).

In reading this book, I found Garthe's model of the "natural futures museum" the most exciting and positive new vision for museums with natural science collections. I liked the fact that his model of NHMs was "problem centered" rather than "object focused." I feel that all museums struggle with the legacy of collections and collecting, which means that they think their modus operandi are the objects themselves, when it is actually the *uses* to which those objects are put [on this point, see the indispensable book by Simon Knell (2004) on museums and the future of collecting; see also James Gardiner (in McCarthy, 2015b) on strategic planning for collections]. Moreover, Garthe's model is integrated and holistic, and advocates the use not just of the natural sciences but also the social sciences, an impressively networked and relational approach that, as I argue below, are features of recent thinking in social theory. He talks about the audience as the "participative scientific society," seeing visitors and the general public as co-creators (and co-curators) of content; see Figure 1 of his essay, which draws on Nina Simon's ideas on the participatory museum (2010). This refreshing sense of a transparent, two-way, and even playful, relationship with the visitors who come to museum exhibits will do much to address what Field and Powell (2001) discuss vis-à-vis the public understanding of science.

This is a far cry from most professionals in the museum sector more broadly, who still think of themselves as experts communicating to people outside museums, seeing those visitors as empty vessels to be filled with knowledge. Garthe is also good on exhibitions, writing of the "public understanding of collections," which facilitate visitor's understanding through "object-related research" as well as digital collections/open access. This focus on the power of material objects is fascinating, and contrary to the fashion of the digital and its occasional tendency to dematerialize real objects. It resonates with much good work underway in the fields of science communication and interpretation using everyday objects to construct collective understandings of the natural world; see, for example, the remarkable PhD dissertation by Italian science interpreter Michele Fontana (2015) on the "Science Museum in a Pizza Box."

Overall, I found Garthe's model of the natural futures museum most persuasive, and strongly linked to similar concepts regarding other kinds of ideal models for museums, such as Eilean Hooper-Greenhill's "postmuseum" (2007), Elizabeth Crooke's "active museum" (in McCarthy, 2015b), Simon's "participatory museum" (2010), Janes's "mindful museum" (2016b), and others. Figure 2 in Garthe's conclusion captures his main ideas regarding interaction and participation in the museums of the future, and the way that these practices suffuse an entire institution from the bottom up, through the layers of governance, management, curating, and exhibitions. This whole-of-institution notion is very attractive. In addition, I appreciated his comment that NHMs must develop from institutions presenting "dead" nature to "making connections with living nature," and do so by emphasizing the *local*. I found illuminating his comment that NHMs should be like visitor centers in national parks, which have a clear sense of attachment to a specific place, and ground the visitor experience in it. A good follow-up to this chapter, I suggest, would be an investigation of the new breed of *cultural* science centers that have sprung up in Europe, such as the Wellcome Collection in London, and others in Dublin and Copenhagen. Lively, experimental, and interdisciplinary spaces, these facilities successfully engage the public in the big questions related to health, the body, and the natural world through innovative exhibitions and public programs (see Arnold in McCarthy, 2015b).

Another topic that I would like to address in my commentary is the issue of museum research, which is broached very well by Frank Howarth in Chapter 4. Drawing on his experience as director of the Australian Museum in Sydney, and a survey of new and emerging trends in science around the world, as well as wider influences on museum research, Howarth provides an illuminating overview of what is going on in museums and laboratories and where this work does, and does not, intersect.

I found this very informative from the perspective of a university academic, even one such as me who works in the humanities. In particular, I was fascinated by his observation that traditional taxonomy is a thing of the past and that the use of whole specimens has arguably been superseded by developments in bioinformatics and genetics. In a similar fashion, Howarth points out that the geosciences have been profoundly affected by technological advances in the mining industry, such as mineralogy in relation to new analytic techniques, and paleontology in relation to the latest imaging wizardry. I wondered, reading this, whether NHMs are guilty of clinging to outmoded and unsustainable practices when it comes to research, as with many museums of anthropology, art, and history that arguably do not respond to comparable new developments. I, too, have observed that "research," and usually a relatively old-fashioned style of collection-based research at that, is often the excuse for *not* adopting more progressive aspects of the new museology; the recent outward emphasis on the visitor experience is often pitted against the "old" internal stewardship of collections, as a kind of default response.

As I read Howarth's account of how research has changed radically due to new, particularly digital, technologies and wider shifts in education and learning, it became clear to me that museums could adopt the same approach to research that universities have been forced to do in recent decades—to be collaborative, strategic, and mindful of both the old, such as historical collections and the value they hold, and the new, such as powerful, innovative ways of conducting research. In the case of universities, this necessity to adapt was forced upon them by a funding crisis, a predicament not unlike that which faces museums, while the changes the tertiary sector underwent were attended by the same, somewhat anxious, debates over their meaning and purpose in society. Indeed, Howarth's conclusion that NHMs need to work *with* universities and adapt and change is in line with the argument I made in a recent book on contemporary museum practice, which was and is bedeviled by a separation of theory and practice, academics and professionals, and museums and the academy (McCarthy, 2015a). This false dichotomy of abstract ideas in the ácademy and the real work in the museum is harmful to both university reseárch and professional work, as museum educator Hilde Hein has pointed out.

> The challenge that museums face in a time of transition is obscured on the one hand by theoretical rhetoric that interprets museums from a distance and ignores their concrete vulnerabilities, and, on the other, by too close a focus on the immediate exigencies of circumstance, which then discourages speculative contemplation.
>
> (2000, p. ix)

In response, I have argued that there is great potential for synergies between academia and museums that can fill the apparent gap; university courses and industry training, academic theory and professional practice, can come together in partnership to provide a continuous, integrated, and coordinated framework. If museums are the ideal site for analysis and forum for debate, the place where all disciplines and methods are bought to bear on the problems and issues facing the public today, and if the findings of this research are fed back into university teaching and professional development working in partnership with them, then practice will become a more important aspect of museum studies, grounding and consolidating it to better serve academics, students, professionals, and, indeed, museums themselves (see introduction in McCarthy, 2015b).

A related and more particular problem, it seems to me, is that the discipline of museum and heritage studies does not engage enough with the natural history found in museums, or the natural heritage outside them encountered in parks, landscapes, and other sites, or the sciences more generally. Most university courses are dominated by the arts and humanities and barely consider the sciences, dealing mainly with art galleries and museums of history, anthropology, and related fields. The majority of professionals working in NHMs, naturally, are science graduates, who have not done museum studies. We can do more to bridge this divide, and integrate not only our qualifications but also training and professional development on the job, to try and encourage a cross-sector perspective that cuts across the gulf between NHMs and other museums. It seems to me that zoos, aquaria, science museums and centers, and NHMs operate in quite a separate professional sphere and can be isolated from developments taking place in the broader sector, as well as from new thinking in museum studies. Many of the issues raised in this book could be usefully discussed, extended, and refined by reference to the latest thinking in the wider museums sector or academic museum studies and related fields (see, for example, Fleming on mission and purpose; Merriman on collecting; Scott on museum value;

Woollard and Reeve on education; Davidson on visitor studies; Arnold on curating; and Spock on exhibition design; all in McCarthy, 2015b).

This long-held division between the sciences and the arts is unfortunate and debilitating, but, as it is itself the product of history, it can be overcome. For a wonderful example of how this can be accomplished through a creative synergy of science and theater, see Thorpe (2012), and for the new interdisciplinary cultural science centers, see Arnold (in McCarthy, 2015b). The longtime split between the "two cultures" of the sciences and the humanities has to be healed, and the two sides integrated, so that students in courses and professionals in museums benefit from a more holistic and interdisciplinary nexus of training, practice, theory, and research. One way to do this, which is discussed here by Howarth and other authors, is through citizen science, which decenters, distributes, and collectivizes the practice of science. The idea of reaching out beyond the walls of the museum to the community, which is included in the acts of collecting, exhibiting, and research, has great potential and is already being pursued with success in a number of NHMs, as demonstrated on the pages of this book.

Aside from this collaborative integration of the management of research, which other themes in this book stuck out for me? I received the strong impression that NHMs are preoccupied with a sense of crisis. In the introduction, Dorfman states: "Much like the wildlife they represent, natural history museums have had to adapt or die." Other authors use the word "crisis." Yet despite this sense of being at a crossroads, and the need to respond to it, NHMs appear to be somewhat overwhelmed by the enormity of their predicament, and tend to justify their existence and traditional raison d'être. What seems to be needed are commentators who can analyze the situation acutely, look ahead clearly, and articulate future paths with passion and conviction, exactly as this collection seeks to do. In the wider museum world, people like Elaine Heumann-Gurian, Robert Janes, Stephen Weil, and others perform this task. Janes's recent book (2016b), for example, is a thrilling but sobering call to arms for museums to overcome their essential conservatism and become activist institutions, particularly in response to the challenge of climate change.

On a related matter, that of the past, there is much talk in this book of the historical record, and of the present as a natural and somehow inevitable progression from the past. However, I would like to know more about the future, and see a more critical and historicized analysis of museum history and the history of science. NHMs tend to talk about the "history" of their institutions in a chronological and teleological manner, articulating a Whiggish sense of progress that leads up to the present. In the humanities, this chronological approach has been challenged by cultural and social theory, which emphasizes the constructedness of human meaning and the way historical accounts function to justify power relations by projecting backward the present onto the past (Karp and Lavine, 1991). The literature includes penetrating studies of the history of science and/in museums by Paula Findlen (1994), Carla Yanni (1999), Ken Arnold (2006), Sharon MacDonald (1998), Sharon MacDonald and Paul Basu (2007), and Tony Bennett (1995, 2004). The work of Steven Conn, among the most interesting scholars of museum history (1998), and a perceptive critic of contemporary trends in science museums (2006), has much to offer those who study museums and those who work in them by putting contemporary practice in a wider and deeper social context.

Both in this sense, the looking backward and forward, and in other regards, it seems that much of the professional commentary on NHMs is distanced from the larger scholarship and debate on museums, and museum studies, perhaps as a result of the split between sciences and humanities I mentioned above; because professionals working in NHMs typically have degrees in science and not museum studies; or because scholars of museum and heritage studies overlook NHMs. Quite naturally, the literature on NHMs tends to focus on the field of science of which professionals are a part, but much could be learned from the research and writing that emerged from the new museology, which shifted from *what* museums did, to *how* and *why* they did it, in other words, the philosophy, history, theory, and practice of what museums do in their social context (Vergo, 1989; Stam, 2005). What can NHMs learn from other museums? Many of the challenges they face are being addressed by other institutions in the sector. The lessons are there—in anthologies and readers, in journal and conference papers—albeit with a humanities bias and uninformed by the technical specifics of natural history. But, I would argue, technical expertise is not what is required at this juncture. What NHMs need are politics and ethics of professional practice, of the kind energetically pursued in recent years by the International Council of Museums' Committee for Museums and Collections of Natural History (ICOM NATHIST).

Another fruitful avenue that NHMs can explore is the exciting new theory that has emerged in recent years addressing the history and culture of science, Science and Technology Studies (STS), and related theories such as Actor Network Theory (ANT) and Indigenous Ontological Perspectivism (IOP). This literature has had a profound impact on disciplines such as history, literature, philosophy, sociology, anthropology, and cultural studies, and my own field of museum and heritage studies (Bennett and Healy, 2011), but ironically it has yet to exert a major influence on the sciences or institutions of public science such as NHMs.

This is not the place to rehearse the arguments of STS, which can be readily digested elsewhere (Pickering, 1995, 2010; Latour, 2005; Law, 2010). Crudely put, STS explores the ways in which science and technology, as socially imbedded practices, shape and are shaped by their cultural and historical contexts. Unsurprisingly, the critique of scientific authority, and its social construction makes it difficult to swallow in scientific circles—and this is a pity, as there is much to learn that would serve to open NHMs to questioning, debate, and productive experimentation. STS's stress on complexity, integrated social relations, and the symmetry of ontologies and worldviews, all helps break down the problematic dualisms of nature and culture, human and nonhuman, which mark the Western way of looking at the natural world as set apart from people. Courses in STS have become popular in universities and have the potential to produce the kind of graduates that NHMs, and the planet, need: engaged, sharp, able to see things from different perspectives. The Program of Science, Technology, and Society at Harvard, for example, sets out to "promote cross-disciplinary integration, civic engagement, and critical thinking." The program goes on to describe the subject in the following terms, showing how it can address the problems confronting society as a whole (and NHMs in particular):

> The rise of STS as a teaching field reflects a dawning recognition that specialization in today's research universities does not fully prepare future citizens to respond knowledgeably and reflectively to the most important challenges of the contemporary world. Increasingly, the dilemmas that confront people, whether in government, industry, politics or daily life, cut across the conventional lines of academic training and thought. STS seeks to overcome the divisions, particularly between the two cultures of humanities (interpretive inquiry) and natural sciences (rational analysis).
>
> ("What is STS?," 2017)

I want to end now by discussing one more issue that comes up for me in reading this book, and which points a way forward for NHMs in addressing its historical legacy and speaking to the future. Several chapters (Dorfman; Koster, Dorfman, and Nyambe; Norris) mention parallels between NHMs and anthropology museums. This history, and its links to colonization and environmental destruction, are both complex and contested (Karp and Lavine, 1991; MacKenzie, 1998; Bennett et al., 2017). Of course, the "sciences" of anthropology and ethnology have been included in the category of natural history, and colonized peoples collected and displayed alongside flora and fauna in NHMs, a practice debated in the last few decades as indigenous peoples have challenged their representation as seemingly "frozen" in an ethnographic past (Peers and Brown, 2003). The specter of Indiana Jones mentioned by Norris has not entirely been dispelled, I fear, at least in the popular imagination.

As Dorfman quite rightly points out, however, the ways in which anthropology and anthropology museums have, since decolonization and the crises of ethnographic authority, responded to this situation and transformed themselves, establishing new relationships with native and tribal peoples by working in collaboration with them, offers hope to NHMs. They, like anthropology museums, can reinvent themselves and reposition both their academic discipline and their collecting and exhibiting practices, in relation to the "objects" of their study, learning to speak *with* the people and not *for* them. Indeed, as Dorfman perceptively points out, there are many lessons for NHMs in the reinvention of museums in postcolonial countries like Aotearoa New Zealand. As I argue in the book on this topic that he cites, the dramatic changes in local museums and the way they have engaged with the Māori people remind us that, if history is made, then it can be unmade and remade (McCarthy, 2011). That is an encouraging, and, I would hope, enabling lesson for NHMs.

References

Alberti, S. (2009). *Nature and Culture: Objects, Disciplines, and the Manchester Museum.* Manchester: Manchester University Press.

Arnold, K. (2006). *Cabinets for the Curious: Looking Back at Early English Museums.* Aldershot: Ashgate.

Bennett, T. (1995). *The Birth of the Museum: History, Theory, Politics.* London and New York: Routledge.

Bennett, T. (2004). *Pasts Beyond Memory: Evolution, Museums, Colonialism.* London and New York: Routledge.

Bennett, T. (2015). Thinking (with) museums: From exhibitionary complex to governmental assemblage. In: A. Witcomb and K. Message, eds., *Museum Theory.* Oxford and Malden: Wiley-Blackwell.

Bennett, T., and Healy, C., eds. (2011). *Assembling Culture.* London and New York: Routledge.

Conn, S. (1998). *Museums and American Intellectual Life, 1876–1926.* Chicago, IL: University of Chicago Press.

Conn, S. (2006). Science museums and the culture wars. In: S. Macdonald, ed., *A Companion to Museum Studies.* Oxford and New York: Wiley-Blackwell.

Field, H., and Powell, P. (2001). Public understanding of science versus public understanding of research. *Public Understanding of Science* 10(4), pp. 421–426.

Findlen, P. (1994). *Possessing Nature: Museums, Collecting, and Scientific Culture in Early Modern Italy.* Berkeley, CA: University of California Press.

Fontana, M. (2005). "Science Museum in a Pizza Box: Performance, Museum Tour Guiding, and Science Communication." PhD dissertation, Victoria University of Wellington.

Hein, H. S. (2000). *The Museum in Transition: A Philosophical Perspective.* Washington, DC: Smithsonian Institution Press.

Hooper-Greenhill, E. (2007). Education, postmodernity, and the museum. In: S. Knell, S. Watson, and S. Macleod, eds., *Museum Revolutions: How Museums Change and Are Changed.* London and New York: Routledge.

Janes, R. R. (2016a). "Museums without borders: A Manifesto." The Michael Volkerling Memorial Lecture, Museum of New Zealand Te Papa Tongarewa, 27 Sept. Available at: www.youtube.com/watch?v=zci2AQlV0l8 [Accessed 30 Jan. 2017].

Janes, R. R. (2016b). *Museums without Borders: Selected Writings of Robert R. Janes.* London and New York: Routledge.

Karp, I., and Lavine, I. (1991). *Exhibiting Cultures: The Poetics and Politics of Museum Display.* Washington, DC: Smithsonian Institution.

Knell, S. J., ed. (2004). *Museums and the Future of Collecting.* Aldershot: Ashgate.

Knell, S. J. (2007). Museums, fossils, and the cultural revolution of science: Mapping change in the politics of knowledge in early nineteenth-century Britain. In: S. J. Knell, S. Macleod, and S. Watson, eds., *Museum Revolutions: How Museums Change and Are Changed.* London and New York: Routledge.

Kreps, C. F. (2006). Non-Western models of museums and curation in cross-cultural perspective. In: S. MacDonald, ed., *A Companion to Museum Studies.* Oxford and Malden: Wiley-Blackwell.

Latour, B. (1987). *Science in Action: How to Follow Scientists and Engineers through Society.* Cambridge: Harvard University Press.

Latour, B. (2005). *Reassembling the Social: An Introduction to Actor-Network-Theory.* Oxford: Oxford University Press.

Law, J. (2010). The materials of STS. In: D. Hicks and M. Beaudry, eds., *The Oxford Handbook of Material Culture Studies.* Oxford: Oxford University Press.

MacDonald, S., ed. (1998). *The Politics of Display: Museums, Science, Culture.* London and New York: Routledge.

MacDonald, S., and Basu, P., eds. (2007). *Exhibition Experiments.* Oxford and Malden: Wiley-Blackwell.

MacKenzie, J. M. (1998). *The Empire of Nature.* Manchester: Manchester University Press.

MacKenzie, J. M. (2009). *Museums and Empire: Natural History, Human Cultures, and Colonial Identities.* Manchester: Manchester University Press.

McCarthy, C. (2011). *Museums and Māori: Heritage Professionals, Indigenous Collections, Current Practice.* Wellington: Te Papa Press.

McCarthy, C. (2015a). Grounding museum studies: Introducing practice. In: C. McCarthy, ed., *Museum Practice.* Oxford and Malden: Wiley-Blackwell.

McCarthy, C., ed. (2015b). *Museum Practice.* Oxford and Malden: Wiley-Blackwell.

McCarthy, C., Bennett, T., Harrison, R., Jacknis, I., Cameron, F., Dibley, B., and Dias, N. (2017). *Collecting, Ordering, Governing: Anthropology, Museums, and Liberal Government.* Durham: Duke University Press.

Peers, L., and Brown, A. K., eds. (2003). *Museums and Source Communities: A Routledge Reader.* London and New York: Routledge.

Pickering, A. (1995). *The Mangle of Practice: Time, Agency, and Science.* Chicago: University of Chicago Press.

Pickering, A. (2010). Material culture and the dance of agency. In: D. Hicks and M. Beaudry, eds., *The Oxford Handbook of Material Culture Studies.* Oxford: Oxford University Press.

Shelton, A. (2013). Critical museology: A manifesto. *Museum Worlds*, pp. 7–23.

Sherman, D. J., ed. (2008). *Museums and Difference.* Bloomington: Indiana University Press.

Simon, N. (2010). The Participatory Museum. Available at: www.participatorymuseum. org/ [Accessed 30 Jan. 2017].

Sissons, J. (2005). *First Peoples: Indigenous Cultures and Their Futures.* London: Reaktion Books.

Stam, D. (2005). The informed muse: The implications of "the new museology" for museum practice. In: Gerard Corsane, ed., *Heritage, Museums, and Galleries: An Introductory Reader.* London and New York: Routledge, pp. 54–70.

Thorpe, V. (2012). A new discovery for science and art: The cultural divide is all in the mind. *Observer*, 24 Nov. Available at: www.theguardian.com/culture/2012/nov/24/science-art-two-cultures [Accessed 1 Mar. 2017].

Vergo, P., ed. (1989). *The New Museology*. London: Reaktion Books.

"What is STS?" (2017). Programme on Science, Technology and Society, Harvard Kennedy School, Harvard University. Available at: http://sts.hks.harvard.edu/about/whatissts.html [Accessed 1 Mar. 2017].

Yanni, C. (1999). *Nature's Museums: Victorian Science and the Architecture of Display*. London: Athlone Press.

14 The future of natural history museums

General discussion

Eric Dorfman, Isabel Landim, and Osamu Kamei

> Change is the only constant.
>
> —Heraclitus (535–475 BCE)

Natural history in a world after truth

The authors of this volume have provided a glimpse, so far as is possible, of the direction that natural history museums may be heading and the challenges they face as they continue to build on their potential in the context of the planet's environmentally uncertain future. Natural history museums comprise an extremely diverse institutional lineage, and their approaches reflect this diversity. Thus, while the range of operating environments favors a wide selection of social, entrepreneurial, and even curatorial strategies, they share common internal structures developed around collections stewardship, research, and public engagement. More recently, they have added to this brief by engaging in conservation activities that also protect biodiversity in situ (Miller et al., 2004).

Certainly, the dissemination of "facts" and "truth" is generally perceived as a responsibility within the province of natural history museums. It is an often-quoted maxim, cited, for instance, by Arengo et al. (Chapter 5) and Novacek (2008), that museums enjoy a level of credibility largely unmatched by other types of institutions. Whether this phenomenon is a purely historical artifact or not (for example, Alberti, 2011), the concept informs museums' self-identity and, therefore, standards and patterns of self-regulated behavior. The grounding of natural history museum practice in the study of physical specimens means that these institutions have at least a goal of objectivity, however influenced by curatorial subjectivity the framing of questions can sometimes be (see Dorfman, 2016). The articulation of evidential knowledge, the concern over changing political environments, even the quality of governments themselves, is neither new nor restricted to the museum field. In the opening to her 1984 book, *The March of Folly*, Barbara Tuchman explores governments' lack of trustworthiness throughout the course of history, even to the extent of undermining policies that are demonstrably beneficial to them:

> A phenomenon noticeable throughout history regardless of place or period is the pursuit by governments of policies contrary to their own self-interests. Mankind, it seems, makes a poorer performance of government than almost any other human activity. In this sphere, wisdom, which many be defined as the exercise of judgement acting on experience, common sense and available information, is less operative and more frustrated than it should be. Why do holders of high office so often act contrary to the way reason points and enlightened self-interest suggests? Why does intelligent mental process seem so often not to function?
>
> (Tuchman, 1984, p. 5)

This is, for example, evidenced in a phenomenon called the "green paradox," in which "well-meaning but imperfectly designed environmental policies to mitigate carbon emissions do in fact increase them" Castellucci (2014). This point is also made by Wood (2000) when he considers that land-use policies that ignore biodiversity are "unjust" (and, by extension, counter to the notion of good governance).

How will museums respond to the mélange of environmental, socio-political, and technological changes that will define the context in which they operate? Despite the diversity of backgrounds, specializations, and institutions the authors in this volume represent, common themes may be discerned in the perspectives they embody. These themes offer us at least some predictive power, which we can use to construct something of a road map for our field.

Shared themes

Authentic partnerships between museums and the public

One of the overarching themes, touched on by nearly every author, is the notion of forming an authentic partnership, based on mutual understanding and, in some cases, direct engagement between those versed in science and those, such as visitors, donors, indigenous communities, and politicians, with other life experiences and other perspectives. In Chapter 1, Christopher A. Norris addresses this with respect to collecting practices by arguing that:

> as we seek to engage a wider range of stakeholders in the work of the museum, we need to modify our long-held work practices to address the concerns of the public. We can no longer rely on distance, be it physical or intellectual, to protect us from criticism.

This perspective must, and is beginning to, shape the way we frame our work.

Museum research is on a trajectory of being more engaged with, and informed by, our communities, which is articulated by Frank Howarth (Chapter 4) and Felicity Arengo et al. (Chapter 5), and represents a major theme of Christopher J. Garthe's essay (Chapter 8), when they consider citizen science as a way not only to gather data but to make those data more relevant to an invested public. This investment is also inherent in the concept of students and other visitors producing their own meaning from the content on display (Dufresene-Tassé and Pénicaud, Chapter 7; Falk and Dierking, 2000).

Norris makes the point, too, that relationships with the public also leave us open for uncomfortable conversations, but ones in which we must be ready to engage. In his book *The Art of the Focused Conversation*, Brian Stanfield describes best practice for internal business meetings:

> Organizations today need meetings that help people move from a reactive into a proactive focus on solutions. They need meetings that give people as much say as possible over the issues that affect their lives and work. Such meetings are needed at every level in the organization, so it is clear that everyone's input and involvement is important and that tested methods will accomplish the agenda, maximize participation, and get the job one.
>
> (Stanfield, 2000, p. 15)

Stanfield's view, while certainly useful in the daily business of running a museum, has far broader implications, resonating with the way many of the authors in this book approach the issue of connecting to stakeholders of all kinds. Customer focus and the use of people's own languages, both culturally and linguistically, to communicate, informs every aspect of activities at natural history museums, including exhibitions, marketing, strategic planning, science, cleaning regimes, and providing sufficient seating at events. Conflating individuals' perspectives into stereotyped offers based on age, gender, race, socioeconomic background, and sexual orientation undermines the relevance and, to some degree, the credibility on which natural history museums pride themselves (Weil, 2002; Brown, 2004; Falk, 2009). Every institution has the opportunity to provide leadership in the sense identified by Covey (2005): "leadership is communicating to people their worth and potential so clearly that they come to see it in themselves."

Indigenous rights and human remains

One sense of partnership that is addressed frequently throughout the book pertains to the rights of indigenous peoples surrounding their tangible and intangible heritage, the arcane information that is shared in a museum context, storage and display of artifacts, research, and repatriation. Lynda Knowles (Chapter 10) reviews landmark national and international regulations regarding human remains. Dorfman (Chapter 12) highlights the importance of coauthoring indigenous history in natural history museums, by predicting that:

> In the future, natural history museums will think more about partnering with our stakeholders and apply a more holistic approach to who those stakeholders are: museum visitors, academic colleagues, indigenous peoples, even customers at our retail outlets can all interact with as partners.

Pennock's (Chapter 3) consideration of the "Decolonize This Place Tour" 2016 demonstration in response to the equestrian statue of Theodore Roosevelt is a salutary lesson regarding what can happen when that sense of partnership is not achieved.

Discussing intangible natural heritage, Dorfman and Carding (2012) explore indigenous knowledge with respect to biodiversity, around which acknowledgment is increasingly finding its way into collecting institutions:

> Indigenous peoples with a long-term continuity of extracting resources from their local environment often have a deep understanding of the complex behavior of ecosystems, garnered from the slow accumulation of observations, passed down as oral history from generation to generation. Their understanding of the relationship between biodiversity and the provision of environmental goods and services, as well as a longitudinal, heuristic approach to acquiring knowledge about the environment, has led to suggestions that this approach has much to offer the synchronic methodology of Western science and, indeed, is vital to effective management of natural resources.
>
> (p. 163)

This topic will continue to remain at the forefront of our sector, influencing codes of ethics and research programs, repatriation of human remains, grave goods, and other culturally important objects (Fletcher, Antoine, and Hill, 2014). Conal McCarthy (Chapter 13) points out that new thinking around indigeneity and museums is currently being developed. This work also bears directly on anthropological depictions in natural history museums, a mainstay of museums of many types and sizes. The framing and recounting of arcane knowledge (Bennett et al., 2017), and even deciding whether it is even appropriate to display this knowledge in a natural history context, are all decidedly in the future of natural history institutions.

Ethics

While relationships with indigenous peoples form a key ethical issue for natural history museums (International Council of Museums [ICOM], 2013), the issue is only one of myriad considerations for institutions that deal with accessioning material from the outside world into a collection in perpetuity. As noted earlier, museum practice standards are tightly linked to a deep-seated belief that what museums do is of value and that institutions are invested with a fundamental trust from society.

> Ethics is about who we are as persons and professionals. Endorsing an ethical attitude is in the interest of every museum professional and every person working in or with a museum. The world is neither ethical or unethical; only people and actions may be unethical. Therefore, museum ethics considers the theoretical and practical elements of the philosophy of conduct in relation to critical contemporary issues... All persons active in museum matters—whether as custodians, curators, trustees or in other roles—have an ethical obligation to the museum professionals and the public.
>
> (Edson, 2016, pp. 131–132)

Ethical standards for natural history museums are multifaceted and, in some cases, magnified by the fact that since most museums are public institutions, caring for tangible heritage in perpetuity is, by design, for the public good. This point is mentioned by Pennock (Chapter 3), who reviews issues of security in collections and argues that keeping objects safe from theft and physical damage is an ethical consideration.

As the public scrutiny of museums' activities continues to grow, the ethics associated with collecting wild animals to add to museum collections will receive increasing attention. Animals collected by museums should, arguably, be subject to the same ethical considerations as animals being used for experimentation. Guhad (2005) reviews the "3Rs" of research on laboratory animals used in biomedical research: refinement, reduction, and replacement. These are echoed in the ICOM Code of Ethics for Natural History Museums (ICOM, 2013), especially in regard to the numbers of specimens taken (for example, for a specific research project with a robust methodology grounded in statistical sampling). Applying restrictions on collection practices is not, at least currently, favored by some museums (Dorfman, pers. obs.), despite the fact that museum collection has contributed demonstrably to the extinction of a number of species (Minteer et al., 2014). However, we believe that, as the world's species continue to decline precipitously (see Kolbert, 2014), this is the direction the sector is heading, and the coming decades will see a continued shift in thinking about collections animals, not least levied by an increasingly concerned public.

Technology

Another topic that recurs in this volume is the steadily rising incorporation of technology into every aspect of museum practice. Advances bring us the ability to communicate, collaborate, and exchange ideas in an environment

234 E. Dorfman, I. Landim, and O. Kamei

to some degree free from the constraints of geography, mobility, socioeconomic background, race, and even language. While it can be argued that many of these advances have not helped the most financially challenged segments of society, they have substantially improved the quality of life for the world's middle class. Before the Internet, information was rare and expensive. Learning something new or garnering important facts required visiting a library or a museum, purchasing proprietary research, or consulting directories for service providers. News came exclusively from a small number of profit-driven television networks and newspapers, provided by one or two news wire services. Today, one can simply search Google or any of a million websites devoted to a specific niche.

Computer technology, in general, affords us an opportunity to digitize collections and, correspondingly, to provide public access and participation (Norris, Chapter 1). Howarth (Chapter 4) characterizes the Digital Revolution as one of the most significant changes for natural history museum research, citing genetic techniques, growth in bioinformatics, remote sensing, and high-resolution imaging. This is echoed by Janet Carding, director of the Tasmanian Museum and Art Gallery, in Australia (pers. comm.):

> In Australia, platforms such as the Atlas of Living Australia are proving a huge success and discoverability of our collections, backed up of course by vouchered specimens is ensuring we are relevant in the 21st century to the research community looking at, for instance, climate change, threatened species and invasive weeds. The usage of our collections grows as we make it more available, and as the world increasingly accesses information online.

Arengo et al. (Chapter 5) concur with Howarth's perspective on digitization, adding CT-scan tomography, stable isotope analysis, massively parallel sequencing, and proteomics to the list of laboratory skills that contribute to the future of wildlife conservation in museums. Major advances in the quality and accessibility of 3-D printing, and the proliferation of the worldwide maker movement (Anderson, 2012) also help paint a picture of how natural history museums will be able to leverage emerging technologies, receiving an opportunity to augment their brief.

How might artificial intelligence (AI), geographical information systems (GIS), drones, and other branches of robotics enhance, or disrupt, the process at natural history museums? In some cases, such as automating labor-intensive tasks (microphotography, online ticket sales, visitor counting) makes considerable sense. In others (automated phone reception), the artificial distance placed between the visitor and the museum can undermine the sense of partnership and engagement that is the hallmark of best practice in museums.

Numerous authors, including Arengo et al. (Chapter 5), Garthe (Chapter 8), and Omedes and Páramo (Chapter 10), point out that museums are more and more using the design of interactives and games to enhance visitors' experience and understanding of collections, augmenting the spectacle of their displays in unpacking the deeper stories of the objects. This has resulted in various efforts to integrate an interactive, game-based dimension into the museum experience, as opposed to relying solely on more passive observation of collections. When done well, multiple platforms such as augmented reality, tabletop games, or digital displays allow curators and designers to immerse visitors more deeply in the experience, extending the boundaries of the visit deeper into the museum context. Museums must offer something to people that entice them want to leave their home, and their computer screens, to come to the museum and experience something, going beyond virtual appreciation to connect with the objects themselves.

That said, best practice suggests that museum interpretation should be led by the story rather than the medium and that not every narrative is best explained through the medium of an interactive. Garthe echoes this sentiment in Chapter 8 when he writes, "it is important to realize that mobile devices are only useful in this context when they can offer place-specific content and services." The concept of "intrinsic motivation" (performing an action or behavior for the enjoyment of the activity itself, as opposed to "extrinsic motivation," which is undertaken for the sake of an external outcome) lies at the heart of the user engagement created by digital games. All too often, educational software and, by extension, museum multimedia, have traditionally attempted to harness games as extrinsic motivation by using them to sugarcoat the learning of content (Dufresne-Tassé and Pénicaud, Chapter 7; Habgood and Ainsworth, 2011). The astounding pace of software development, coupled with long exhibit development lead times and relatively poor nonprofit resourcing, suggest that most institutions will always lag behind the industry in their digital offer. As this inequity is only likely to increase, forming alliances with IT companies seems a viable model for most museums in the foreseeable future.

In some cases, new technology may add further public scrutiny to natural history museums' research and other operations. For instance, using camera traps to photograph wildlife in situ (see O'Connell et al., 2011) may often abrogate the need to collect specimens from the wild. Norris (Chapter 1) recounts the public outrage leveled at the American Museum of Natural History for acquiring an extremely rare specimen of the moustached kingfisher (*Actenoides bouganvillea*). As mentioned in the *Ethics* section of this commentary, above, natural history museums are following zoos (see Dick, Chapter 9) in needing to meet a public expectation to justify their activities in terms of the habitats and biodiversity they protect.

Although natural history museums may benefit in many ways from the increased capacity offered by digital technology, a counterargument is that while society benefits from easier access to information, it is also becoming increasingly difficult to distinguish fact from fantasy, as they are frequently packaged identically. Oxford Dictionaries chose the word "post-truth" to

characterize the year 2016. The definition is "relating to or denoting circumstances in which objective facts are less influential in shaping public
opinion than appeals to emotion and personal belief" (Oxford Dictionaries,
2016). When interacting with a generation that consumes information
from social media and other unreliable sources and has little patience with
nuanced messaging, imparting scientific information and encouraging
critical thought takes on a new and challenging perspective. Even as, at
least in some circumstances, the value of science as a paradigm is being
questioned, the need for evidence-based practice has never been greater.

There are additional risks. For instance, as Pennock (Chapter 3) points out,
while advances in technology give more options for increased security for
collections, this comes with the risk that new technology like cloning will render more types of specimens useful to bioprospectors. The omnipresent danger
of database hacking has the potential to affect not only museums directly, but
also visitors who pay for museum goods and services by credit card. The fact
that major corporations are being hacked makes it necessary for our field to
consider what assurances we can provide our patrons and stakeholders.

Yet new technology brings with it an additional challenge (or an opportunity) that is arguably more significant than hacking or the haphazard,
or even intentional, dissemination of misinformation across the web. Real
and potential museum audiences who have ready access to the Internet
are able to tap into alternative sources of first-rate information, high-
resolution photos of objects, and recordings of lectures by distinguished
knowledge holders, both from within and outside the museum sphere.
The best of the digital sphere is well researched, nuanced, and engaging. This disruptive innovation can, for museums—or any business—
represent the difference between thriving, survival, and oblivion (O'Reilly
and Tushman, 2016). This challenge is one to which the natural history
museums can, and must, rise.

New business models

Today's museum practitioners are faced with shepherding heritage efforts amid
ever-changing technological and political landscapes, organizational structures,
resources, funding streams, and partners. Whether change involves establishing a relationship with new government officials, reorganizing or integrating
program areas, shifting gears to take advantage of a new grant opportunity,
or sustaining efforts when there is a gap in funding, natural history museums
are increasingly juggling the responsibility of piloting community change on
one hand while having to manage internal and external change on the other.
Although dealing with change and transition are not novel issues, the impact
of these common scenarios, if not managed effectively, can have a significant
impact on an institution's ability to achieve its mission.

As mentioned previously in this volume, change is not something that
comes easily to museums (Dorfman, Chapter 12), which are frequently large,

unwieldy, and entrenched in decades or even centuries of tradition. However, natural history museums cannot afford to let inertia hamper their preparedness to respond to changes in the legislative and intellectual environments, public expectations, and funding possibilities. We are approaching a crossroad of planned change on the one hand and unplanned change on the other.

As natural history museums move into their future, practitioners will need to work to manage the many change agents coming at them in their working environment, many of which are out of their control. They are, and will continue to be, charged with acting as transformational leaders with their respective communities. To manage these challenges and lead effectively, natural history museums must become more adept at recognizing change, and more aware of the issues that come with creating it.

This is alluded to by Conal McCarthy (Chapter 13, in this volume) when he points out that natural history museums will not succeed simply by adopting traditional capitalist growth models. Aside from being antithetical to their ethical perspectives and missions, natural history museums' large collections are likely to prevent them from adopting a purely entrepreneurial trajectory. That notwithstanding, the future of natural history museums must include robust business thinking that can, and should, include a strong ethical compass, re-enlivening the place of credibility in which natural history institutions have traditionally been held; ensuring relevance is understood in all its nuances; and thinking about how collections can be leveraged creatively to provide for their care, improve access, and create a positive revenue stream.

When these models are adopted, there are important tools to assist in implementing them. One of the most compelling of these is described by Rogers (2003) in his book *Diffusion of Innovations*, in which he writes that dissemination of ideas is achieved through two-way conversations and mutual compatibility.

A heightened sense of purpose

Many authors in this book (Norris, Chapter 1; Koster, Dorfman, and Nyambe, Chapter 2; Howarth, Chapter 4) envision a positive future for natural history museums. All authors, in one way or another, cite change as both inevitable and necessary. In toto, their thinking bespeaks a new and heightened sense of purpose for our sector. While this commitment to some degree touches on concerns related to the global political situation and its ramifications for science, education, and the environment, considerable momentum is being initiated from within the sector. We believe that this trajectory is, and will continue to be, influenced by several key big-picture concepts:

• **Biodiversity Conservation**
  In the face of skyrocketing biodiversity loss and rising global temperatures, deeper concern over the future of the planet will come

from both within the museum and from the public. This will encourage natural history museums to continue to take a proactive role in in situ conservation, increasingly becoming one of natural history museums' core functions.

- **The Anthropocene**
  The proposed new epoch (expected to be announced officially in 2017) acknowledges that human impact on the Earth's geosphere has been sufficient to form a distinct chemical and fossil signature in the crust being currently laid down. While the concept of the Anthropocene includes issues of biodiversity, because of changing fossil records to include animals such as domestic chickens, it also encompasses many other substances including anthropogenic chemicals and the buildup of carbon. At least as interesting, however, is the response by the art world to this concept. Whether directly or indirectly, it has informed an exciting and slightly dystopic blend of science and art in the works of artists such as Joann Brennan, Mark Dion, and Laurel Roth Hope. These activities will, we predict, have an increasing impact on museum programming.

- **Wildlife and Heritage Crime**
  Black market activities like trafficking of cultural artifacts, fossils, live animals, and rare natural commodities (rosewood and rhinoceros horn) are growing rapidly, despite international efforts to curb them. As these practices are linked to, and probably fund, other criminal activities, this is a global problem that should logically involve many types of agencies, including the International Police organization (INTERPOL), United Nations Environment Programme (UNEP), and United Nations Educational, Scientific and Cultural Organization (UNESCO). With notable exceptions (for example, the Australian Museum), natural history museums are not actively involved in supporting efforts to stop these crimes. However, this will undoubtedly change as environmental issues continue to intensify and the sector becomes more attuned to them.

- **The Place of Art and Nature in Shaping Society**
  As far back as 1907, Henri Poincaré stated, "It is only through science and art that civilization is of value." Since then, this topic has been explored in a variety of contexts. Dutton (2009) considers that love of art and the urge to represent it, has its basis in evolution. We are comfortable with, and even drawn to, imagery with features that resonate with the landscapes in which our distant ancestors evolved. Louv (2011) describes the "nature-deficit disorder," which is "an atrophied awareness, a diminished ability to find meaning in the life that surrounds us, whatever form it takes," and which has an impact on the health of our bodies, minds, and society. Latour (2015), goes further, rejecting the notion of a separation between human and nature "that has paralyzed science and politics since the dawn of modernism." Natural history museums, sitting at the crux of nature and its artistic representations,

have an important role in facilitating exploration of personal identity. Inasmuch as enhancing self-perception can have a positive influence on behavior (see Falk, 2009), natural history museums' capacity to contribute to society will grow, as their activities in this sphere become more purposeful.

A case for natural history museology in tertiary education

Conal McCarthy (Chapter 13) eloquently observes that much of the literature that inspires the broader field of museology does not appear to be translating into practice within natural history institutions. We argue that one reason for this is that the path through which personnel enters a curatorial position at natural history museums is rarely through the auspices of a university museum studies program. Typically, natural history curators hold PhDs from university biology departments in fields like taxonomy or ecology. Conversely, those museum staff responsible for exhibition design, marketing, education, and program development normally have little if any formal understanding of the life sciences or science practice. Mismatched perspectives from the different subgenres of experiences comprise one of the major hurdles in staff cohesion at natural history museums.

To be completely sustainable, the field of natural history museology would do well to bring in its leaders from an early age. What might a natural history course at a university look like? For starters, a course in natural history museology should be cross-listed with museum studies and natural sciences, giving students from both fields an opportunity and incentive to participate. A good program would include social history, ethics, philosophy, business theory, as well as practical skills such as taxidermy, visual communication, writing, taxonomy, and natural history collections management. Interns would be placed within museums to attain a firsthand understanding of museum operations. We are unaware of any course like this that exists at present, although there are tertiary institutions considering this sort of development.

A future for natural history museums

When faced with danger, the vampire squid (*Vampyroteuthis infernalis*) adopts a defensive posture, in which it spreads its arms and web over its head and mantle. In this "pineapple posture," the cephalopod (not a true squid) is essentially turning itself inside out (Seibel, Thuesen, and Childress, 1998). Although it might seem out of place to introduce this behavior in the context of the future of natural history museums, the idea that institutions must turn themselves inside out resonates in certain ways. Being donor-centric, visitor-centric, and responsive to our communities requires us to take data and science process, once the province of the backrooms and basements, and make them front-facing, responsive to the reactions of the public. We believe this is a trajectory that has already begun and is where natural history museums are headed in the future. It is at the core of relevance and public engagement that, to a degree, buffers our sector from the boom and bust cycles of public funding.

In the most recent edition of *TrendsWatch*, published by the American Alliance of Museums, author Elizabeth Merritt discusses the importance of a general decline in empathy over recent decades, and museums' potential role in closing the gap:

> As museums strive to document the tangible benefits they provide to society, some evidence is emerging that the immersive storytelling that takes place in museums can engender empathy... And since socioemotional skills, in general, including empathy, influence long-term outcomes in education and life, museums have the opportunity to make the case that by cultivating empathy, they are increasing the emotional, educational and economic success of their communities.
>
> (Merritt, 2017, p. 13)

This perspective resonates with the concept of emotional intelligence (Goleman, 1995), relating emotional skill, self-awareness, self-management, empathy, and effective relationships. While natural history museums are busy innovating, stewarding natural heritage collections, and being at the forefront of addressing some of the world's major issues, our greatest opportunity to achieve and maintain relevance lies in authentically connecting our future to the needs and drivers of our community.

References

Alberti, S. J. M. M. (2011). Authority, identity, and material culture. In: D. N. Livingstone and C. W. J. Withers, eds., *Geographies of Nineteenth-Century Science*. Chicago: University of Chicago Press.

Anderson, C. (2012). *Makers: The New Industrial Revolution*. London: Random House.

Bennett, T., et al. (2017). *Collecting, Ordering, Governing: Anthropology, Museums and Liberal Government*. Durham: Duke University Press.

Brown, C. K. (2004). The museum's role in a multicultural society. In: G. Anderson, ed., *Reinventing the Museum: Historical and Contemporary Perspectives on the Paradigm Shift*. Walnut Creek: Rowman & Littlefield Publishers.

Castellucci, L. (2014). Environmental protection and the green paradox. In: L. Castellucci, ed., *Government and the Environment: The Role of the Modern State in the Face of Global Challenges*. London and New York: Routledge.

Covey, S. R. (2005). *The Eighth Habit: From Effectiveness to Greatness*. New York: Free Press.

Dorfman, E. J. (2016). Who owns history? Diverse perspectives on curating an ancient Egyptian kestrel. In: *Proceedings of the International Biennial*

Conference of Museum Studies Commemorating the 80th Birthday of Professor Pao-teh Han 30th and 31th October 2014. Taipei: Taiwan National University.

Dorfman, E. J., and Carding, J. (2012). Toward a unified concept of intangible natural heritage. In: E. J. Dorfman, ed., *Intangible Natural Heritage: New Perspectives on Natural Objects*. New York: Routledge.

Dutton, D. (2009). *The Art Instinct: Beauty Pleasure and Human Evolution*. New York: Bloomsbury Press.

Edson, G. (2016). Unchanging ethics in a changing world. In: B. L. Murphy, *Museums, Ethics and Cultural Heritage*. London and New York: Routledge.

Falk, J. H. (2009). *Identity and the Museum Visitor Experience*. New York: Routledge.

Falk, J. H., and Dierking, L. (2000). *Learning from Museums: Visitor Experience and Visitor Experiences and the Making of Meaning*. Walnut Creek: AltaMira Press.

Fletcher, A., Antoine, D., and Hill, J. D. (2014). *Regarding the Dead: Human Remains in the British Museum*. London: British Museum Press.

Goleman, D. (1995). *Emotional Intelligence: Why It Can Matter More Than IQ*. New York: Bantam Books.

Guhad, F. (2005). Introduction to the 3Rs (refinement, reduction, and replacement). *Journal of the American Association for Laboratory Animal Science* 44(2), pp. 58–59.

Habgood, M. P. J., and Ainsworth, S. E. (2011). Motivating children to learn effectively: Exploring the value of intrinsic integration in educational games. *Journal of the Learning Sciences* 20(2), pp. 169–206.

ICOM (2013). *Code of Ethics for Natural History Museums*. Paris: International Council of Museums.

Kolbert, E. (2014). *The Sixth Extinction: An Unnatural History*. New York: Henry Holt.

Latour, B. (2015). Telling friends from foes in the time of the Anthropocene. In: Hamilton, C., Bonneuil, C. and Gemenne, F., eds., *The Anthropocene and the Global Environmental Crisis: Rethinking Modernity in a New Epoch*. London and New York: Routledge.

Louv, R. (2011). *The Nature Principle: Reconnecting with Life in a Virtual Age*. Chapel Hill, NC: Algonquin Books.

Merritt, E. (2017). *A Mile in My Shoes: Closing the Empathy Gap. TrendsWatch 2017*. Washington, DC: American Alliance of Museums.

Miller, B., et al. (2004). Evaluating the conservation mission of zoos, aquariums, botanical gardens, and natural history museums. *Conservation Biology* 18(1), pp. 86–93.

Minteer, B. A., Collins, J. P., Love, K. E., and Puschendorf, R. (2014). Avoiding (re)extinction. *Science* 344(6181), pp. 260–261.

Novacek, M. J. (2008). Engaging the public in biodiversity issues. *Proceedings of the National Academy of Sciences of the USA* 105, pp. 11571–11578.

O'Connell, A. F., Nichols, J. D., and Karanth, K. U. (2011). *Camera Traps in Animal Ecology: Methods and Analysis*. New York: Springer.

O'Reilly, C. A., and Tushman, M. L. (2016). *Lead and Disrupt: How to Solve the Innovator's Dilemma*. Stanford, CA: Stanford University Press.

Oxford Dictionaries (2016). *Word of the Year 2016 Is...* Available at: https://en.oxforddictionaries.com/word-of-the-year/word-of-the-year-2016 [Accessed 23 Feb. 2017].

Poincaré, H. (1907). *The Value of Science.* Authorized translation with an introduction. New York: Science Press.

Rogers, E. M. (2003). *Diffusion of Innovations.* 5th ed. New York: Free Press.

Stanfield, R. B. (2000). *The Art of the Focused Conversation.* Gabriola Island: New Society Publishers.

Seibel, B., Thuesen, E., and Childress, J. (1998). Flight of the vampire: Ontogenetic gait-transition in *Vampyroteuthis infernalis* (Cephalopoda: Vampyromorpha). *Journal of Experimental Biology* 201(16), pp. 2314–2324.

Tuchman, B. (1984). *The March of Folly: From Troy to Vietnam.* New York: Random House.

Weil, S. E. (2002). *Making News Matter.* Washington, DC: Smithsonian Books.

Wood, P. M. (2000). *Biodiversity and Democracy: Rethinking Society and Nature.* Vancouver, BC: UBC Press.

Index

246 *Index*

National Science Foundation (NSF) 84,
  94, 117, 209
National Taiwan Museum 3, 33
Native American Graves Protection
  and Repatriation Act (NAGPRA),
  1990 190
natural disasters 49, 62, 111
natural futures museum 6–7,
  140–52, 220
Natural History Museum, London 84,
  94; Darwin Centre 106, 143
Natural History Museum, Los Angeles:
  Nature Lab 112, 113
Natural History Museum, Vienna 162
natural history museums (NHMs):
  accountability in 8, 30, 204–6, 219;
  best practice in 4–5, 8, 32, 82, 158,
  187, 188, 201–2, 203, 217–18,
  219, 235; exhibition development
  in 103, 107, 114, 115–16, 235;
  funding for 5, 21, 23, 24, 33, 34,
  44, 49, 56–7, 59, 67–8, 70, 74, 75,
  78, 105, 116–17, 191, 195, 204–5,
  211, 212, 236, 237, 240; fundraising
  at/for 103, 203–4, 205; legislation
  pertaining to 7, 54, 60–1, 184–96,
  201; security and 49–62, 233, 236;
  see *also* collections
Natural History Museum (website)
  71, 74
Naturalis 51, 52, 61–2
naturalists 94, 120, 172, 179
Natural Science Museum, Barcelona 93,
  172, 177–8; Museu Blau 177, *178*
Netherlands 49, 50, 51, 52, 54, 55, 175
New York City 94, 200
New York Times 36, 65
New Zealand 33, 75, 76, 190–1, 192,
  205–6, 217, 226
North America 143, 175
North Carolina Museum of Natural
  Sciences 41–3, 93
Notes from Nature 21

Oceanographic Museum 157, 160
online/virtual exhibitions 93, 148, 207
open research labs 142, 149–50
Osborn, Henry Fairfield 14, 26

paleontology 65, 73, 74, 75, 88, 107,
  109, 122, 123, 171, 221
Paris: Cité des Sciences et de l'Industrie
  123, 179; Jardin du Roi 119–20,

126; Muséum National d'Histoire
  Naturelle, Paris 119–20, 123–4, *124*,
  170, 171; Palais de la Découverte
  123, 175, 179
Parque de las Ciencias, Granada 172,
  173, 178, 181–2; *Biodomo 179*
Pavlov, Ivan 13
Peabody Museum of Natural History
  13–14, 19–20, 23
pesticides 2, 19, 61, 68; dichloro
  diphenyl trichlorethane (DDT) 72, 83
phylogeny 69, 124, 164
pollution xix, 1, 36, 61, 163
Postman, Neil 36–7
post-truth 181, 218, 235–6
Protected Objects Act, 1975 190
Protocol to the Committee on
  Biological Diversity, Nagoya, 2010
  15–16, 54, 60, 186–7

repatriation: of cultural property 5, 78,
  193; of human remains 75, 184, 186,
  189–92, 232
replicas 60, 106, 145; Bone Clones 209
rhinoceros horns, theft of/trafficking in
  5, 55, 162, 188, 238
Rijksmuseum 50, 51, 148
Rikuzentaka City Museum 56
robotics 59, 201, 234
Roosevelt, Theodore 58, 83, 232
Royal Alberta Museum 104–5

Salvador Cabinet of Barcelona *170*, 171
San Diego Natural History Museum 210
Science 17
science, technology, engineering, and
  mathematics (STEM) 7, 37, 179, 201
Science and Technology Studies
  (STS) 224–5
science centers 30, 31, 40, 93, 116–17,
  168–9, 221, 223; emergence/
  evolution of xviii, 7, 112, 172,
  174–80; natural history museums
  and 7, 35, 39, 112, 116–17, 168–9,
  173, 176–7, 218, 221; Parque de las
  Ciencias 172, *173*, 178, *179*, 181–2;
  at Peabody Museum 19–20
Science Museum Exhibit Collaborative
  116–17
Serrurier, Lindor 49
Simon, Nina 220
Skorton, David 37–8
Skramstad, Harold 34